THE CAMBRIDGE ANTHOLOGIES

AN ANTHOLOGY OF THE POETRY

OF THE

AGE OF SHAKESPEARE

To

M. G.

AN ANTHOLOGY OF THE POETRY

OF THE

AGE OF SHAKESPEARE

CHOSEN AND ARRANGED

BY

W. T. YOUNG, M.A.

LECTURER IN ENGLISH LANGUAGE AND LITERATURE AT THE
UNIVERSITY OF LONDON, GOLDSMITHS' COLLEGE

Cambridge :
at the University Press
1910

CAMBRIDGE UNIVERSITY PRESS
Cambridge, New York, Melbourne, Madrid, Cape Town,
Singapore, São Paulo, Delhi, Mexico City

Cambridge University Press
The Edinburgh Building, Cambridge CB2 8RU, UK

Published in the United States of America by Cambridge University Press, New York

www.cambridge.org
Information on this title: www.cambridge.org/9781107673199

First published 1910
First paperback edition 2013

A catalogue record for this publication is available from the British Library

ISBN 978-1-107-67319-9 Paperback

THE CAMBRIDGE ANTHOLOGIES *are intended for the general reader, who, whilst he is familiar with the greater masters, has little leisure, and, it may be, little inclination, to become a professed student of literature. They seek to provide such a reader with first-hand knowledge of the literary atmosphere and social conditions in which these masterpieces were created. At present, this need is satisfied only by reference to histories of literature, which have too many pre-occupations to deal justly with it, or to authorities even less accessible.*

It is the object of this series to let each age speak for itself, and to give coherence and prominence to what seem to be its significant features. Thus, the thought, temper, manners and activities of the period of Shakespeare, which is the theme of the first two volumes, are exemplified in selections from contemporary poetry and prose. The former illustrates the literary interests, models and aspirations, as well as the lyrical and rhetorical quality of the time ; the latter gives a picture of the Elizabethan Englishman, painted by himself, in pursuit of his business, sport or roguery.

Volumes dealing in like manner with other periods will follow, and the series will include a history of English literature for general readers.

W. T. YOUNG.

J. DOVER WILSON.

10 *August* 1910

PREFACE

THIS series of books aims at an adjustment of the claims of literature and literary history. Only the instructor in literature knows how prone the student is to sacrifice his right to first-hand knowledge and private judgment, and to rely upon the critic and historian. In this book, some selections are presented with no more of history or criticism than is implicit in an arrangement of the poems according to subject and chronological succession. This should suffice to set in clear view the kinds of poetry practised by the Elizabethans, and the process of development through which each has passed; and it should help to disentangle the study of poetry from the encumbrance of formulas, epigrams and generalisations, which are sometimes substituted for it; poetry may very well stand without them.

The bulk of the book consists of lyric; three arrangements of this section were considered before the present one was adopted. The basis of it is chronological, the criterion being the date of birth of the author; this has the advantage of facility of reference, though it does not exemplify so clearly as one previously attempted the varied themes touched upon by these poets. The book lies open to the charge of offering rather meagre selections of the other kinds ; the defence is that it does not pretend to do anything more than illustrate Elizabethan poetry. It is hoped at the same time that the student who has read what is here given of *Rosamond*, or *Nimphidia*, or *The Induction*, or whatever may have drawn his interest, will be induced to turn to the complete poem and make his approach to the author through his work.

The source of the text is specified in all cases in a head-note ; the dates are those of publication, except in the case of Shakespeare's plays, where a conjectural date of performance is accepted. When two dates are given (as, for example, *Astrophel and Stella*, 1591—1598) they, in general, indicate that the poem was first published at the earlier date, whilst the text is derived from the edition of the later date. The text is modernised except in the case of Spenser, whose archaisms are deliberate and must not suffer violence.

In the matter of punctuation, as little alteration is admitted as is consistent with the production of a comprehensible text. Emendations are adopted only where the printed copy is obviously corrupt ; instances are :—*Faction* for *affection*, page 24 ; *guards* for *guides*, page 62 ; *Melpomene* for *Melponie*, page 65 ; *struck* for *stuck*, page 85 ; and some few others. Every poem is taken directly from the original, excepting only those rare cases in which the British Museum contains no early copy. When titles accompany lyrical poems, they are taken from the source named ; for poems in other sections, titles have been invented. There are one or two cases in which the attribution to certain authors may appear dogmatic ; ' Silence augmenteth grief' is fathered upon Fulke Greville, though this is not an established conclusion ; similarly, 'Underneath this sable hearse' is accredited to Ben Jonson, albeit the MS. in T.C.D. is signed William Browne.

PREFACE

The responsibility for the selection falls upon the editor alone ; it may be premised that the design of the book does not admit the pursuit of novelty to any large extent, and, furthermore, that the ground of choice is not always supreme excellence, but often rather representative or illustrative quality.

To Mr A. H. Bullen every student in this province is a debtor ; the student who follows Mr Bullen through his sources will find, first, that there are still many gleanings in a wide field ; and, secondly, that the harvest garnered into his selections from the dramatists, song-books and romances, includes all the richest produce. To Mr E. K. Chambers, and to Messrs Routledge (the present publishers of the *Muses' Library*), the writer is beholden for permission, readily granted, to use the text of the poems of John Donne ; and to Messrs Macmillan for the same indulgence in regard to extracts from Spenser. To the interest and suggestions of Mr A. R. Waller the book owes the pruning of some faults, and the addition of some features which should increase its usefulness. Thanks are due also to those in charge at the Museum, and to the skilful and exact readers of the Cambridge University Press.

W. T. Y.

10 *August* 1910

CONTENTS

If all the pens that ever poets held
Had fed the feeling of their masters' thoughts,
And every sweetness that inspired their hearts
Their minds and muses on admired themes;
If all the heavenly quintessence they 'still
From their immortal flowers of poesy,
Wherein as in a mirror we perceive
The highest reaches of a human wit;
If these had made one poem's period,
And all combined in beauty's worthiness,
Yet should there hover in their restless heads
One thought, one grace, one wonder at the least
Which into words no virtue can digest.

MARLOWE

LYRIC POEMS

From Tottel's Songs and Sonnets, 1557

Complaint for true love unrequited

What 'vaileth truth, or by it to take pain?
To strive by steadfastness for to attain
How to be just, and flee from doubleness?
Since all alike, where ruleth craftiness,
Rewarded is, both crafty, false, and plain.
  Soonest he speeds that most can lie and feign;
True meaning heart is had in high disdain.
Against deceit, and cloaked doubleness,
What 'vaileth truth, or perfect steadfastness?
  Deceived is he, by false and crafty train,
That means no guile, and faithful doth remain
Within the trap, without help or redress;
But for to love, lo, such a stern mistress,
Where cruelty dwells, alas, it were in vain.

Sir T. Wyatt

From Tottel's Songs and Sonnets, 1557

The lover complaineth the unkindness of his love

My lute, awake! perform the last
Labour, that thou and I shall waste,
  And end that I have now begun;
And when this song is sung and past,
  My lute be still! for I have done.

SIR THOMAS WYATT

As to be heard where ear is none,
As lead to grave in marble stone,
  My song may pierce her heart as soon.
Should we then sigh, or sing, or moan?
  No, no, my lute! for I have done.

The rocks do not so cruelly
Repulse the waves continually,
  As she my suit and affection;
So that I am past remedy,
  Whereby my lute and I have done.

Proud of the spoil that thou hast got
Of simple hearts through love's shot,
  By whom unkind thou hast them won;
Think not he hath his bow forgot,
  Although my lute and I have done.

Vengeance shall fall on thy disdain,
That makest but game on earnest pain.
  Think not alone under the sun
Unquit to cause thy lover's plain;
  Although my lute and I have done.

May chance thee lie withered and old
In winter nights, that are so cold,
  Plaining in vain unto the moon;
Thy wishes then dare not be told;
  Care then who list, for I have done.

And then may chance thee to repent
The time that thou hast lost and spent
  To cause thy lovers sigh and swoon;
Then shalt thou know beauty but lent,
  And wish and want as I have done.

Now cease, my lute! this is the last
Labour that thou and I shall waste,
  And ended is that we begun:
Now is this song both sung and past;
  My lute be still! for I have done.

Sir T. Wyatt

SIR THOMAS WYATT

From Tottel's Songs and Sonnets, 1557

The lover sheweth how he is forsaken of such as he sometime enjoyed

They flee from me, that sometime did me seek,
  With naked foot stalking within my chamber.
Once have I seen them gentle, tame, and meek,
  That now are wild, and do not once remember,
  That sometime they have put themselves in danger
To take bread at my hand ; and now they range
Busily seeking in continual change.

Thanked be fortune, it hath been otherwise
  Twenty times better ; but once especial,
In thin array, after a pleasant guise,
  When her loose gown did from her shoulders fall,
  And she me caught in her arms long and small,
And therewithal so sweetly did me kiss,
And softly said, Dear heart, how like you this ?

It was no dream, for I lay broad awaking ;
  But all is turn'd now, through my gentleness,
Into a bitter fashion of forsaking ;
  And I have leave to go of her goodness ;
  And she also to use newfangleness.
But, since that I unkindly so am served,
How like you this, what hath she now deserved ?
                                        SIR T. WYATT

From Tottel's Songs and Sonnets, 1557

*He ruleth not, though he reign over realms,
that is subject to his own lusts*

If thou wilt mighty be, flee from the rage
  Of cruel will ; and see thou keep thee free
From the foul yoke of sensual bondage.
  For though thy empire stretch to Indian sea,
  And for thy fear trembleth the farthest Thule,
If thy desire have over thee the power,
Subject then art thou, and no governor.

SIR THOMAS WYATT

If to be noble and high thy mind be moved,
  Consider well thy ground and thy beginning;
For he that hath each star in heaven fixed,
  And gives the moon her horns, and her eclipsing,
  Alike hath made thee noble in his working;
So that wretched no way may thou be,
Except foul lust and vice do conquer thee.

All were it so thou had a flood of gold,
  Unto thy thirst yet should it not suffice;
And though with Indian stones, a thousand fold
  More precious than can thyself devise,
  Ycharged were thy back; thy covetise
And busy biting yet should never let
Thy wretched life, ne do thy death profet.

Sir T. Wyatt

From **Devonshire MS (Nott)**

*The lover's lute cannot be blamed though it sing
of his lady's unkindness*

Blame not my Lute ! for he must sound
  Of this or that as liketh me;
For lack of wit the Lute is bound
  To give such tunes as pleaseth me;
Though my songs be somewhat strange,
And speak such words as touch thy change,
            Blame not my Lute !

My Lute, alas ! doth not offend,
  Though that perforce he must agree
To sound such tunes as I intend
  To sing to them that heareth me;
Then though my songs be somewhat plain,
And toucheth some that use to feign,
            Blame not my Lute!

4

SIR THOMAS WYATT

My Lute and strings may not deny,
　But as I strike they must obey;
Break not them then so wrongfully,
　But wreak thyself some other way;
And though the songs which I indite
Do quit thy change with rightful spite,
　　　　　　Blame not my Lute!

Spite asketh spite, and changing change,
　And falsed faith must needs be known;
The faults so great, the case so strange,
　Of right it must abroad be blown;
Then since that by thine own desert
My songs do tell how true thou art,
　　　　　　Blame not my Lute!

Blame but thyself that hast misdone,
　And well deserved to have blame;
Change thou thy way, so evil begun,
　And then my Lute shall sound that same;
But if till then my fingers play
By thy desert their wonted way,
　　　　　　Blame not my Lute!

Farewell! unknown; for though thou break
　My strings in spite with great disdain,
Yet have I found out, for thy sake,
　Strings for to string my Lute again:
And if, perchance, this sely rhyme
Do make thee blush, at any time,
　　　　　　Blame not my Lute!

SIR T. WYATT

From **Devonshire MS**

An earnest suit to his unkind mistress not to forsake him

And wilt thou leave me thus?
　Say Nay! say Nay! for shame!
To save thee from the blame
Of all my grief and grame.
And wilt thou leave me thus?
　Say Nay! say Nay!

5

SIR THOMAS WYATT

And wilt thou leave me thus,
  That hath loved thee so long,
  In wealth and woe among?
  And is thy heart so strong
As for to leave me thus?
  Say Nay! say Nay!

And wilt thou leave me thus,
  That hath given thee my heart
  Never for to depart,
  Neither for pain nor smart?
And wilt thou leave me thus?
  Say Nay! say Nay!

And wilt thou leave me thus,
  And have no more pity
  Of him that loveth thee?
  Helas! thy cruelty!
And wilt thou leave me thus?
  Say Nay! say Nay!

SIR T. WYATT

From Devonshire MS

The lover beseecheth his mistress not to forget his steadfast faith and true intent

Forget not yet the tried intent
Of such a truth as I have meant;
My great travail so gladly spent;
          Forget not yet!

Forget not yet when first began
The weary life ye know, since when
The suit, the service none tell can;
          Forget not yet!

Forget not yet the great assays,
The cruel wrong, the scornful ways,
The painful patience in denays;
          Forget not yet!

6

SIR T WYATT *and* LORD VAUX

Forget not yet, forget not this,
How long ago hath been, and is
The mind that never meant amiss;
    Forget not yet!

Forget not then thine own approved,
The which so long hath thee so loved,
Whose steadfast faith yet never moved;
    Forget not this!

SIR T. WYATT

From The Paradise of Dainty Devices, 1576—1578

No pleasure without some pain

How can the tree but waste, and wither away,
That hath not sometime comfort of the Sun:
How can that flower but fade, and soon decay,
That always is with dark clouds run.
Is this a life? nay death you may it call,
That feels each pain, and knoweth no joy at all.

What foodless beast can live long in good plight?
Or is it life where senses there be none?
Or what availeth eyes without their light?
Or else a tongue to him that is alone?
Is this a life? nay death you may it call,
That feels each pain, and knows no joy at all.

Whereto serve ears, if that there be no sound,
Or such a head, where no devise doth grow,
But all of plaints, since sorrow is the ground
Whereby the heart doth pine in deadly woe.
Is this a life? nay death you may it call,
That feels each pain, and knows no joy at all.

THOMAS LORD VAUX

THOMAS LORD VAUX

From The Paradise of Dainty Devices, 1576—1578

Of a contented mind

When all is done and said,
In the end thus shall you find,
He most of all doth bathe in bliss
That hath a quiet mind:
And, clear from worldly cares,
To deem can be content
The sweetest time in all this life
In thinking to be spent.

The body subject is
To fickle Fortune's power,
And to a million of mishaps
Is casual every hour:
And death in time doth change
It to a clod of clay;
When as the mind, which is divine,
Runs never to decay.

Companion none is like
Unto the mind alone;
For many have been harm'd by speech,
Through thinking few or none.
Fear oftentimes restraineth words,
But makes not thoughts to cease;
And he speaks best, that hath the skill
When for to hold his peace.

Our wealth leaves us at death;
Our kinsmen at the grave;
But virtues of the mind unto
The heavens with us have.
Wherefore, for virtue's sake,
I can be well content
The sweetest time of all my life
To deem in thinking spent.

THOMAS LORD VAUX

8

HENRY HOWARD EARL OF SURREY

From Tottel's Songs and Sonnets, 1557

A praise of his love

Give place, ye lovers, here before
That spent your boasts and brags in vain;
My Lady's beauty passeth more
The best of yours, I dare well sayen,
Than doth the sun the candle light,
Or brightest day the darkest night.

And thereto hath a troth as just,
As had Penelope the fair;
For what she saith, ye may it trust,
As it by writing sealed were.
And virtues hath she many moe
Than I with pen have skill to show.

I could rehearse, if that I would,
The whole effect of Nature's plaint,
When she had lost the perfect mould,
The like to whom she could not paint;
With wringing hands how she did cry,
And what she said, I know it, I.

I know she swore with raging mind,
Her kingdom only set apart,
There was no loss, by law of kind,
That could have gone so near her heart;
And this was chiefly all her pain,
She could not make the like again.

Sith Nature thus gave her the praise,
To be the chiefest work she wrought;
In faith, methink! some better ways
On your behalf might well be sought,
Than to compare, as ye have done,
To match the candle with the sun.

HENRY HOWARD EARL OF SURREY

9

EARL OF SURREY *and* RICHARD EDWARDES

From Tottel's Songs and Sonnets, 1557

The means to attain happy life

Martial, the things that do attain
The happy life, be these, I find:
The riches left, not got with pain;
The fruitful ground, the quiet mind;

The equal friend; no grudge, no strife;
No charge of rule, nor governance;
Without disease, the healthful life;
The household of continuance;

The mean diet, no delicate fare;
True wisdom joined with simpleness;
The night discharged of all care,
Where wine the wit may not oppress:

The faithful wife, without debate;
Such sleeps as may beguile the night.
Contented with thine own estate,
Ne wish for death, ne fear his might.

HENRY HOWARD EARL OF SURREY

From The Paradise of Dainty Devices, 1576—1578

Amantium Iræ

In going to my naked bed, as one that would have slept,
I heard a wife sing to her child that long before had wept:
She sighed sore, and sang full sweet, to bring the babe to rest,
That would not cease, but cried still, in sucking at her breast.
She was full weary of her watch, and grieved with her child;
She rocked it and rated it, till that on her it smiled:
Then did she say, Now have I found this proverb true to
    prove,
The falling out of faithful friends, renewing is of love.

Then took I paper, pen, and ink, this proverb for to write,
In register for to remain of such a worthy wight;
As she proceeded thus in song, unto her little brat,
Much matter utter'd she of weight, in place whereas she sat;

10

RICHARD EDWARDES

And proved plain there was no beast nor creature bearing life,
Could well be known to live in love without discord and
    strife :
Then kissed she her little babe, and swore by God above,
The falling out of faithful friends, renewing is of love.

She said that neither king, ne prince, ne lord could live aright,
Until their puissance they did prove, their manhood and
    their might ;
When manhood shall be matched so that fear can take no
    place,
Then weary works make warriors each other to embrace,
And leave their force that failed them, which did consume
    the rout,
That might before have lived their time and nature out :
Then did she sing as one that thought no man could her
    reprove,
The falling out of faithful friends, renewing is of love.

She said she saw no fish, ne fowl, nor beast within her haunt,
That met a stranger in their kind, but could give it a taunt ;
Since flesh might not endure, but rest must wrath succeed,
And force the fight to fall to play, in pasture where they feed ;
So noble nature can well end the work she hath begun,
And bridle well that will not cease, her tragedy in some :
Thus in her song she oft rehearsed, as did her well behove,
The falling out of faithful friends, is the renewing of love.

I marvel much, pardie, quoth she, for to behold the rout,
To see man, woman, boy, and beast, to toss the world about ;
Some kneel, some crouch, some beck, some check, and some
    can smoothly smile,
And some embrace others in arm, and there think many a
    wile ;
Some stand aloof at cap and knee, some humble and some
    stout,
Yet are they never friends indeed until they once fall out.
Thus ended she her song, and said, before she did remove,
The falling out of faithful friends, is the renewing of love.

RICHARD EDWARDES

GEORGE TURBERVILLE

From Epitaphs, 1570

To a Gentlewoman

That always willed him to wear rosemary (a tree that is always green) for her sake, and in token of his goodwill to her

The green that you did wish me wear
            Aye for your love,
And on my helm a branch to bear,
            Not to remove;
Was ever you to have in mind,
Whom Cupid hath my Feer assigned.

As I, in this, have done your will,
            And mind to do,
So I request you to fulfil
            My fancy too.
A green and loving heart to have,
And this is all that I do crave.

For if your flowering heart should change
            His colour green,
Or you at length a Lady strange
            Of me be seen;
Then will my branch, against his use,
His colour change for your refuse.

As Winter's force cannot deface
            This branch his hue;
So let no change of love disgrace
            Your friendship true.
You were mine own, and so be still;
So shall we live and love our fill.

Then may I think myself to be
            Well recompensed,
For wearing of the Tree that is
            So well defenced
Against all weather that doth fall,
When wayward Winter spits his gall.

TURBERVILLE *and* QUEEN ELIZABETH

And when we meet, to try me true
        Look on my head;
And I will crave an oath of you,
        Where faith be fled?
So shall we both assured be;
Both I of you, and you of me.

                                G. TURBERVILLE

From Puttenham's Art of English Poesy, 1589

The doubt of future foes exiles my present joy,
And wit me warns to shun such snares as threaten mine annoy.
For falsehood now doth flow, and subject faith doth ebb,
Which would not be if reason ruled or wisdom weaved the
    web.
But clouds of toys untried do cloak aspiring minds
Which turn to rain of late repent, by course of changed
    winds.
The top of hope supposed, the root of ruth will be,
And fruitless all their graffed guiles, as shortly ye shall see.
Then dazzled eyes with pride, which great ambition blinds,
Shall be unseeled by worthy wights, whose foresight falsehood
    finds.
The daughter of debate, that eke discord doth sow,
Shall reap no gain where former rule hath taught still peace
    to grow.
No foreign banished wight shall anchor in this port,
Our realm it brooks no stranger's force, let them elsewhere
    resort.
Our rusty sword with rest shall first his edge employ
To poll their tops that seek such change and gape for joy.

                                QUEEN ELIZABETH

13

GEORGE GASCOIGNE

From Flowers, 1575

The Lullaby of a Lover

Sing lullaby, as women do,
  Wherewith they bring their babes to rest;
And lullaby can I sing too,
  As womanly as can the best.
With lullaby they still the child:
And, if I be not much beguil'd,
Full many wanton babes have I,
Which must be still'd with lullaby.

First lullaby my youthful years!
  It is now time to go to bed:
For crooked age and hoary hairs
  Have won the haven within my head.
With lullaby, then, youth be still,
With lullaby content thy will;
Since courage quails and comes behind,
Go sleep, and so beguile thy mind.

Next, lullaby my gazing eyes,
  Which wonted were to glance apace;
For every glass may now suffice
  To shew the furrows in my face.
With lullaby, then, wink a while;
With lullaby your looks beguile;
Let no fair face, nor beauty bright,
Entice you eft with vain delight.

And lullaby, my wanton will!
  Let reason's rule now reign thy thought,
Since all too late I find by skill
  How dear I have thy fancies bought.
With lullaby now take thine ease,
With lullaby thy doubts appease.
For, trust to this, if thou be still,
My body shall obey thy will.

GASCOIGNE *and* SIR EDWARD DYER

Eke lullaby my loving boy,
  My little Robin, take thy rest;
Since age is cold and nothing coy,
  Keep close thy coin, for so is best.
With lullaby be thou content,
With lullaby thy lusts relent;
Let others pay which hath mo pence,
Thou art too poor for such expense.

Thus lullaby my youth, mine eyes,
  My will, my ware, and all that was;
I can no more delays devise,
  But, welcome pain, let pleasure pass.
With lullaby now take your leave,
With lullaby your dreams deceive;
And, when you rise with waking eye,
Remember then this lullaby.

G. GASCOIGNE

From Rawlinson MS

My mind to me a kingdom is,
Such present joys therein I find,
That it excels all other bliss
That earth affords, or grows by kind.
    Though much I want which most would have,
    Yet still my mind forbids to crave.

No princely pomp, no wealthy store,
No force to win a victory,
No wily wit to salve a sore,
No shape to feed a loving eye;
    To none of these I yield as thrall;
    For why? My mind doth serve for all.

I see how plenty surfeits oft,
And hasty climbers soon do fall;
I see that those which are aloft,
Mishap doth threaten most of all.
    They get with toil, they keep with fear;
    Such cares my mind could never bear.

SIR E DYER *and* WILLIAM STEVENSON

Content to live, this is my stay,
I seek no more than may suffice.
I press to bear no haughty sway;
Look! what I lack, my mind supplies.
　　Lo thus I triumph like a king;
　　Content with that my mind doth bring.

Some have too much, yet still do crave.
I little have, and seek no more.
They are but poor, though much they have,
And I am rich with little store.
　　They poor, I rich. They beg, I give.
　　They lack, I leave. They pine, I live.

I laugh not at another's loss;
I grudge not at another's pain.
No worldly waves my mind can toss;
My state at one doth still remain.
　　I fear no foe, I fawn no friend.
　　I loathe not life, nor dread my end.

Some weigh their pleasure by their lust;
Their wisdom by their rage of will.
Their treasure is their only trust;
A cloaked craft their store of skill.
　　But all the pleasure that I find
　　Is to maintain a quiet mind.

My wealth is health and perfect ease;
My conscience clear, my choice defence.
I neither seek by bribes to please,
Nor by deceit to breed offence.
　　Thus do I live, thus will I die.
　　Would all did so, as well as I.

SIR E. DYER

From Gammer Gurton's Needle, 1575

I can not eat but little meat,
My stomach is not good;
But sure I think that I can drink
With him that wears a hood.

16

WILLIAM STEVENSON

Though I go bare, take ye no care,
I am nothing a-cold ;
I stuff my skin so full within
Of jolly good ale and old.
Back and side go bare, go bare ;
Both foot and hand go cold ;
But, belly, God send thee good ale enough,
Whether it be new or old.

I love no roast but a nut-brown toast,
And a crab laid in the fire ;
A little bread shall do me stead,
Much bread I not desire.
No frost nor snow, no wind, I trow,
Can hurt me if it would ;
I am so wrapped and throughly lapp'd
Of jolly good ale and old.

And Tyb my wife, that as her life
Loveth well good ale to seek,
Full oft drinks she, till ye may see
The tears run down her cheek ;
Thus doth she troll to me the bowl,
Even as a malt worm should,
And saith, Sweetheart, I took my part
Of this jolly good ale and old.

Now let them drink, till they nod and wink,
Even as good fellows should do ;
They shall not miss to have the bliss
Good ale doth bring men to ;
And all poor souls, that have scour'd bowls,
Or have them lustly troll'd,
God save the lives of them and their wives,
Whether they be young or old.
Back and side go bare, go bare ;
Both foot and hand go cold ;
But, belly, God send thee good ale enough,
Whether it be new or old.

W. Stevenson

NICHOLAS BRETON

From The Will of Wit, 1599

The Song of Care

Come all the world submit yourselves to Care,
And him acknowledge for your chiefest king;
With him no king or keisar may compare,
Who bears so great a sway in everything;
At home, abroad, in peace and eke in war,
Care chiefly stands to either make or mar.

The court he keeps is in a wise conceit,
His house a head where reason rules the wit;
His seat the heart, that hateth all deceit,
His bed the brain that feels no frantic fit,
His diet is the cates of sweet content;
Thus is his life in heavenly pleasure spent.

His kingdom is the whole world round about;
Sorrow his sword to such as do rebel;
His counsel wisdom that decides each doubt;
His skill foresight of things to come to tell;
His chief delight is studies of device
To keep his subjects out of miseries.

Oh courteous King, oh high and mighty Care,
What shall I write in honour of thy name?
But to the world by due desert declare
Thy royal state and thy immortal fame.
Then so I end as I at first begun,
Care is the King of Kings when all is done.

NICHOLAS BRETON

From England's Helicon, 1600

Phillida and Coridon

In the merry month of May,
In a morn, by break of day,
Forth I walk'd by the woodside,
When as May was in his pride.
There I spied all alone
Phillida and Coridon.
Much ado there was, God wot!
He would love and she would not.

BRETON *and* HUMFREY GIFFORD

She said, never man was true;
He said, none was false to you.
He said, he had loved her long;
She said, Love should have no wrong.
Coridon would kiss her then,
She said, Maids must kiss no men,
Till they did for good and all.
Then she made the shepherd call
All the heavens to witness truth,
Never loved a truer youth.
Thus with many a pretty oath
Yea and nay, and faith and troth,
Such as silly shepherds use
When they will not Love abuse,
Love which had been long deluded
Was with kisses sweet concluded;
And Phillida, with garlands gay,
Was made the Lady of the May.

NICHOLAS BRETON

From A Posie of Gilloflowers, 1580

For Soldiers

Ye buds of Brutus' land, courageous youths, now play your
parts,
Unto your tackle stand; abide the brunt with valiant hearts;
For news is carried to and fro, that we must forth to warfare go;
Men muster now in every place, and soldiers are pressed forth
apace.
Faint not, spend blood to do your Queen and country good,
Fair words, good pay, will make men cast all care away.

The time of war is come; prepare your corslet, spear, and
shield.
Methinks I hear the drum strike doleful marches to the field.
Tantara! Tantara! the trumpets sound, which makes our
hearts with joy abound;
The roaring guns are heard afar and everything denounceth
war.
Serve God; stand stout; bold courage brings this gear about;
Fear not, forth run; faint heart fair Lady never won.

GIFFORD *and* THE EARL OF OXFORD

Ye curious Carpet knights, that spend the time in sport and
    play,
Abroad, and see new sights. Your country's cause calls you
    away;
Do not, to make your Ladies game, bring blemish to your
    worthy name;
Away to field, and win renown; with courage beat your
    enemies down;
Stout hearts gain praise, when dastards sail in slander's seas.
Hap what hap shall, we sure shall die but once for all.

Alarm! methinks they cry. Be packing, mates. Be gone
    with speed.
Our foes are very nigh; shame have that man that shrinks
    at need.
Unto it boldly let us stand; God will give right the upper
    hand;
Our cause is good, we need not doubt; in sign of courage
    give a shout.
March forth, be strong; good hap will come ere it be long;
Shrink not, fight well; for lusty lads must bear the bell.

All you that will shun evil, must dwell in warfare every day.
The world, the flesh, and Devil always do seek our soul's
    decay;
Strive with these foes with all your might; so shall you
    fight a worthy fight.
That conquest doth deserve most praise, where vice does yield
    to virtue's ways.
Beat down foul sin; a worthy crown then shall ye win;
If we live well, in Heaven with Christ our souls shall dwell.

H. GIFFORD

From Rawlinson MS

Fond Desire

Come hither, Shepherd swain.
    Sir, what do you require?
I pray thee, shew to me thy name.
    My name is fond DESIRE.

EDWARD DE VERE EARL OF OXFORD

When wert thou born, DESIRE?
    In pomp and pride of May.
By whom, sweet boy, wert thou begot?
    By fond Conceit, men say.

Tell me, who was thy Nurse?
    Fresh Youth, in sugared joy.
What was thy meat and daily food?
    Sad sighs with great annoy.

What hadst thou then to drink?
    Unsavoury lovers' tears.
What cradle wert thou rocked in?
    In hope devoid of fears.

What lulled thee then asleep?
    Sweet speech, which likes me best.
Tell me, where is thy dwelling place?
    In gentle hearts I rest.

What things doth please thee most?
    To gaze on Beauty still.
Whom dost thou think to be thy foe?
    Disdain of my good-will.

Doth company displease?
    Yes surely, many one.
Where doth DESIRE delight to live?
    He loves to live alone.

Doth either time or age
Bring him unto decay?
    No! No! DESIRE both lives and dies
    A thousand times a day.

Then fond DESIRE farewell.
Thou art not mate for me!
I should be loth methinks to dwell
With such a one as thee!

EDWARD DE VERE EARL OF OXFORD

EDWARD DE VERE EARL OF OXFORD

From Byrd's Psalms, Sonnets and Songs, 1588

If women could be fair, and never fond,
Or that their beauty might continue still,
I would not marvel, though they made men bond,
By service long to purchase their good-will;
    But when I see how frail these creatures are,
    I laugh, that men forget themselves so far.

To mark what choice they make, and how they change,
How leaving best, the worst they choose out still;
And how like haggards wild, about they range,
Scorning after reason, to follow will;
    Who would not shake such buzzards from the fist,
    And let them fly, fair fools, which way they list?

Yet for our sport, we fawn and flatter both,
To pass the time when nothing else can please;
And train them on to yield, by subtle oath,
The sweet content that gives such humour ease;
    And then we say when we their follies try,
    To play with fools, Oh what a fool was I.

EDWARD DE VERE EARL OF OXFORD

From England's Helicon, 1600

Ralegh's Reply to Marlowe's Passionate Shepherd

If all the world and love were young,
And truth in every shepherd's tongue,
These pretty pleasures might me move
To live with thee and be thy love.

Time drives the flocks from field to fold,
When rivers rage and rocks grow cold;
And Philomel becometh dumb;
The rest complains of cares to come.

The flowers do fade, and wanton fields
To wayward winter reckoning yields:
A honey tongue, a heart of gall,
Is fancy's spring, but sorrow's fall.

SIR WALTER RALEGH

Thy gowns, thy shoes, thy beds of roses,
Thy cap, thy kirtle, and thy posies,
Soon break, soon wither, soon forgotten,
In folly ripe, in reason rotten.

Thy belt of straw and ivy buds,
Thy coral clasps and amber studs,
All these in me no means can move
To come to thee and be thy love.

But could youth last, and love still breed,
Had joys no date, nor age no need;
Then these delights my mind might move
To live with thee and be thy love.

SIR W. RALEGH

From England's Helicon, 1600

The Shepherd's praise of his sacred Diana

Praised be Diana's fair and harmless light,
Praised be the dews wherewith she moists the ground,
Praised be her beams, the glory of the night,
    Praised be her power, by which all powers abound.

Praised be her nymphs, with whom she decks the woods,
Praised be her knights in whom true honour lives,
Praised be that force by which she moves the floods;
    Let that Diana shine which all these gives.

In heaven queen she is among the spheres,
She mistress-like makes all things to be pure;
Eternity in her oft change she bears;
    She beauty is, by her the fair endure.

Time wears her not, she doth his chariot guide;
Mortality below her orb is placed;
By her the virtue of the stars down slide,
    In her is virtue's perfect image cast.

A knowledge pure it is, her worth to know;
With Circes let them dwell, that think not so.

SIR W. RALEGH

23

SIR WALTER RALEGH

The Lie

Go, soul, the body's guest,
  Upon a thankless arrant ;
Fear not to touch the best ;
  The truth shall be thy warrant :
Go, since I needs must die,
  And give the world the lie.

Say to the court, it glows,
  And shines like rotten wood ;
Say to the church, it shews
  What's good, and doth no good :
If church and court reply,
  Then give them both the lie.

Tell potentates, they live,
  Acting by others' action ;
Not loved, unless they give,
  Not strong, but by a faction :
If potentates reply,
  Give potentates the lie.

Tell men of high condition,
  That manage the estate,
Their purpose is ambition,
  Their practise only hate :
And if they once reply,
  Then give them all the lie.

Tell them that brave it most,
  They beg for more by spending,
Who, in their greatest cost,
  Like nothing but commending :
And if they make reply,
  Then give them all the lie.

SIR WALTER RALEGH

Tell zeal it wants devotion;
 Tell love it is but lust;
Tell time it meets but motion;
 Tell flesh it is but dust:
And wish them not reply,
 For thou must give the lie.

Tell age it daily wasteth;
 Tell honour how it alters;
Tell beauty how she blasteth;
 Tell favour how it falters:
And as they shall reply,
 Give every one the lie.

Tell wit how much it wrangles
 In tickle points of niceness;
Tell wisdom she entangles
 Herself in over-wiseness:
And when they do reply,
 Straight give them both the lie.

Tell physic of her boldness;
 Tell skill it is prevention;
Tell charity of coldness;
 Tell law it is contention:
And as they do reply,
 So give them still the lie.

Tell fortune of her blindness;
 Tell nature of decay;
Tell friendship of unkindness;
 Tell justice of delay:
And if they will reply,
 Then give them all the lie.

Tell arts they have no soundness,
 But vary by esteeming;
Tell schools they want profoundness,
 And stand so much on seeming:
If arts and schools reply,
 Give arts and schools the lie.

SIR WALTER RALEGH

Tell faith it's fled the city;
　Tell how the country erreth;
Tell, manhood shakes off pity;
　Tell, virtue least preferreth:
And if they do reply,
　Spare not to give the lie.

So, when thou hast, as I
　Commanded thee, done blabbing,
Although to give the lie
　Deserves no less than stabbing,
Stab at thee he that will,
　No stab thy soul can kill.

SIR W. RALEGH

From Reliquiae Wottonianae, 1651

Sir Walter Ralegh the night before his death

Even such is time, that takes on trust
Our youth, our joys, our all we have,
And pays us but with age and dust;
Who, in the dark and silent grave,
When we have wand'red all our ways,
Shuts up the story of our days.
But from this earth, this grave, this dust,
My God shall raise me up, I trust.

SIR W. RALEGH

From Ralegh's Remains, 1681

Sir Walter Ralegh's Pilgrimage

Give me my scallop-shell of quiet;
My staff of faith to walk upon;
My scrip of joy, immortal diet;
My bottle of salvation;
My gown of glory (hope's true gage);
And thus I'll take my pilgrimage.
Blood must be my body's only balmer,
No other balm will there be given;
Whil'st my soul, like quiet palmer,
Travelleth towards the land of heaven;

SIR WALTER RALEGH

Over the silver mountains,
Where spring the nectar fountains.
There will I kiss the bowl of bliss,
And drink mine everlasting fill,
Upon every milken hill.
My soul will be a-dry before,
But after, it will thirst no more.
I'll take them first, to quench my thirst,
 And taste of nectar's suckets,
  At those clear wells
  Where sweetness dwells,
Drawn up by saints in crystal buckets.
 Then by that happy blestful day,
More peaceful pilgrims I shall see,
That have cast off their rags of clay,
And walk apparelled fresh like me.
And when our bottles and all we
Are fill'd with immortality,
Then the blessed parts we'll travel,
Strow'd with rubies thick as gravel,
Ceilings of diamonds, sapphire floors,
High walls of coral, and pearly bowers.
From thence to heaven's bribeless hall,
Where no corrupted voices brawl;
No conscience molten into gold,
No forg'd accuser bought or sold,
No cause deferr'd, no vain-spent journey,
For there CHRIST is the KING's attorney;
Who pleads for all without degrees,
And he hath angels, but no fees :
And when the grand twelve million jury
Of our sins, with direful fury,
'Gainst our souls black verdicts give,
Christ pleads his death, and then we live.
Be thou my speaker, (taintless Pleader,
Unblotted Lawyer, true Proceeder !)
Thou would'st salvation even for alms,
Not with a bribed lawyer's palms.
And this is mine eternal plea
To him that made heaven, earth, and sea,

EDMUND SPENSER

That, since my flesh must die so soon,
And want a head to dine next noon,
Just at the stroke, when my veins start and spread,
Set on my soul an everlasting head :
Then am I ready, like a palmer fit,
To tread those blest paths which before I writ.
Of death and judgement, heaven and hell,
Who oft doth think, must needs die well.

Sir W. Ralegh

From The Shepheard's Calender, 1579

April

Ye dayntye Nymphs, that in this blessed brooke
  Doe bathe your brest,
Forsake your watry bowres, and hether looke,
  At my request :
And eke you Virgins, that on Parnasse dwell,
Whence floweth Helicon, the learned well,
  Helpe me to blaze
  Her worthy praise,
Which in her sexe doth all excell.

Of fayre Elisa be your silver song,
  That blessed wight,
The flowre of Virgins : may shee florish long
  In princely plight !
For shee is Syrinx daughter without spotte,
Which Pan, the shepheards God, of her begot :
  So sprong her grace
  Of heavenly race,
No mortall blemishe may her blotte.

See, where she sits upon the grassie greene,
  (O seemely sight !)
Yclad in Scarlot, like a mayden Queene,
  And ermines white :
Upon her head a Cremosin coronet,
With Damaske roses and Daffadillies set :
  Bay leaves betweene,
  And primroses greene,
Embellish the sweete Violet.

EDMUND SPENSER

Tell me, have ye seene her angelick face,
　Like Phœbe fayre ?
Her heavenly haveour, her princely grace,
　Can you well compare?
The Redde rose medled with the White yfere,
In either cheeke depeincten lively chere :
　Her modest eye,
　Her Majestie,
Where have you seene the like but there ?

I sawe Phœbus thrust out his golden hedde,
　Upon her to gaze :
But, when he sawe how broade her beames did spredde,
　It did him amaze.
He blusht to see another Sunne belowe,
Ne durst againe his fyrye face out showe :
　Let him, if he dare,
　His brightnesse compare
With hers, to have the overthrowe.

Shewe thyselfe, Cynthia, with thy silver rayes,
　And be not abasht :
When shee the beames of her beauty displayes,
　O, how art thou dasht !
But I will not match her with Latonaes seede,
Such follie great sorow to Niobe did breede :
　Now she is a stone,
　And makes dayly mone,
Warning all other to take heede.

Pan may be proud that ever he begot
　Such a Bellibone ;
And Syrinx rejoyse that ever was her lot
　To beare such a one.
Soone as my younglings cryen for the dam
To her will I offer a milkwhite Lamb :
　Shee is my goddesse plaine,
　And I her shepherd's swayne,
Albee forswonck and forswatt I am.

EDMUND SPENSER

I see Calliope speede her to the place
   Where my Goddesse shines;
And after her the other Muses trace,
   With their Violines.
Bene they not Bay braunches which they do beare,
All for Elisa in her hand to weare?
   So sweetly they play,
   And sing all the way,
That it a heaven is to heare.

Lo! how finely the Graces can it foote
   To the Instrument:
They dauncen deffly, and singen soote,
   In their meriment.
Wants not a fourth Grace, to make the daunce even?
Let that rowme to my Lady be yeven:
   She shal be a Grace,
   To fyll the fourth place,
And reigne with the rest in heaven.

And whither rennes this bevie of Ladies bright,
   Raunged in a rowe?
They bene all Ladyes of the lake behight,
   That unto her goe.
Chloris, that is the chiefest Nymph of all,
Of Olive braunches beares a Coronall:
   Olives bene for peace,
   When wars doe surcease:
Such for a Princesse bene principall.

Ye shepheards daughters, that dwell on the greene,
   Hye you there apace:
Let none come there but that Virgins bene,
   To adorne her grace:
And, when you come whereas shee is in place,
See that your rudeness doe not you disgrace:
   Binde your fillets faste,
   And girde in your waste,
For more finenesse, with a tawdrie lace.

EDMUND SPENSER

Bring hether the Pincke and purple Cullambine,
  With Gelliflowres ;
Bring Coronations, and Sops in wine,
  Worne of Paramoures :
Strowe me the ground with Daffadowndillies,
And Cowslips, and Kingcups, and loved Lillies :
  The pretie Pawnce,
  And the Chevisaunce,
Shall match with the fayre flowre Delice.

Now ryse up, Elisa, decked as thou art
  In royall aray ;
And now ye daintie Damsells may depart
  Eche one her way.
I feare I have troubled your troupes to longe :
Let dame Elisa thanke you for her song :
  And if you come hether
  When Damsines I gether,
I will part them all you among.

E. SPENSER

Epithalamion, 1595

  Ye learned sisters, which have oftentimes
  Beene to me ayding, others to adorne,
  Whom ye thought worthy of your gracefull rymes,
  That even the greatest did not greatly scorne
  To heare theyr names sung in your simple layes,
  But joyed in theyr praise ;
  And when ye list your owne mishaps to mourne,
  Which death, or love, or fortunes wreck did rayse,
  Your string could soone to sadder tenor turne,
  And teach the woods and waters to lament
  Your dolefull dreriment :
  Now lay those sorrowfull complaints aside ;
  And, having all your heads with girlands crownd,
  Helpe me mine owne loves prayses to resound ;
  Ne let the same of any be envide :
  So Orpheus did for his owne bride !
  So I unto my selfe alone will sing ;
  The woods shall to me answer, and my Eccho ring.

31

EDMUND SPENSER

Early, before the worlds light-giving lampe
His golden beame upon the hils doth spred,
Having disperst the nights unchearefull dampe,
Doe ye awake ; and, with fresh lusty-hed,
Go to the bowre of my beloved love,
My truest turtle dove ;
Bid her awake ; for Hymen is awake,
And long since ready forth his maske to move,
With his bright Tead that flames with many a flake,
And many a bachelor to waite on him,
In theyr fresh garments trim.
Bid her awake therefore, and soone her dight,
For lo ! the wished day is come at last,
That shall, for all the paynes and sorrowes past,
Pay to her usury of long delight :
And, whylest she doth her dight,
Doe ye to her of joy and solace sing,
That all the woods may answer, and your eccho ring.

Bring with you all the Nymphes that you can heare
Both of the rivers and the forrests greene,
And of the sea that neighbours to her neare :
Al with gay girlands goodly wel beseene.
And let them also with them bring in hand
Another gay girland,
For my fayre love, of lillyes and of roses,
Bound truelove wize, with a blew silke riband.
And let them make great store of bridale poses,
And let them eeke bring store of other flowers,
To deck the bridale bowers.
And let the ground whereas her foot shall tread,
For feare the stones her tender foot should wrong,
Be strewed with fragrant flowers all along,
And diapred lyke the discolored mead.
Which done, doe at her chamber dore awayt,
For she will waken strayt;
The whiles doe ye this song unto her sing,
The woods shall to you answer, and your Eccho ring.

Ye Nymphes of Mulla, which with carefull heed
The silver scaly trouts doe tend full well,

EDMUND SPENSER

And greedy pikes which use therein to feed;
(Those trouts and pikes all others doo excell;)
And ye likewise, which keepe the rushy lake,
Where none doo fishes take;
Bynd up the locks the which hang scatterd light,
And in his waters, which your mirror make,
Behold your faces as the christall bright,
That when you come whereas my love doth lie,
No blemish she may spie.
And eke, ye lightfoot mayds, which keepe the dore,
That on the hoary mountayne used to towre;
And the wylde wolves, which seeke them to devoure,
With your steele darts doo chace from comming neer;
Be also present heere,
To helpe to decke her, and to help to sing,
That all the woods may answer, and your eccho ring.

Wake now, my love, awake! for it is time;
The Rosy Morne long since left Tithones bed,
All ready to her silver coche to clyme;
And Phœbus gins to shew his glorious hed.
Hark! how the cheerefull birds do chaunt theyr laies
And carroll of Loves praise.
The merry Larke hir mattins sings aloft;
The Thrush replyes; the Mavis descant playes:
The Ouzell shrills; the Ruddock warbles soft;
So goodly all agree, with sweet consent,
To this dayes merriment.
Ah! my deere love, why doe ye sleepe thus long,
When meeter were that ye should now awake,
T' awayt the comming of your joyous make,
And hearken to the birds love-learned song,
The deawy leaves among!
Nor they of joy and pleasance to you sing,
That all the woods them answer, and theyr eccho ring.

My love is now awake out of her dreames,
And her fayre eyes, like stars that dimmed were
With darksome cloud, now shew theyr goodly beams
More bright then Hesperus his head doth rere.

EDMUND SPENSER

Come now, ye damzels, daughters of delight,
Helpe quickly her to dight:
But first come ye fayre houres, which were begot,
In Joves sweet paradice of Day and Night;
Which doe the seasons of the yeare allot,
And al, that ever in this world is fayre,
Doe make and still repayre:
And ye three handmayds of the Cyprian Queene,
The which doe still adorne her beauties pride
Helpe to addorne my beautifullest bride:
And, as ye her array, still throw betweene
Some graces to be seene;
And, as ye use to Venus, to her sing,
The whiles the woods shal answer, and your eccho ring.

Now is my love all ready forth to come:
Let all the virgins therefore well awayt:
And ye fresh boyes, that tend upon her groome,
Prepare your selves; for he is comming strayt.
Set all your things in seemely good array,
Fit for so joyfull day;
The joyfulst day that ever sunne did see.
Faire Sun! shew forth thy favourable ray,
And let thy lifull heat not fervent be,
For feare of burning her sunshyny face,
Her beauty to disgrace.
O fayrest Phœbus! father of the Muse!
If ever I did honour thee aright,
Or sing the thing that mote thy mind delight,
Doe not thy servants simple boone refuse;
But let this day, let this one day, be myne;
Let all the rest be thine.
Then I thy soverayne prayses loud wil sing,
That all the woods shal answer, and theyr eccho ring.

Harke! how the Minstrils gin to shrill aloud
Their merry Musick that resounds from far,
The pipe, the tabor, and the trembling Croud,
That well agree withouten breach or jar.

EDMUND SPENSER

But, most of all, the Damzels doe delite
When they their tymbrels smyte,
And thereunto doe daunce and carrol sweet,
That all the sences they doe ravish quite ;
The whyles the boyes run up and downe the street,
Crying aloud with strong confused noyce,
As if it were one voyce,
Hymen, iö Hymen, Hymen, they do shout ;
That even to the heavens theyr shouting shrill
Doth reach, and all the firmament doth fill ;
To which the people standing all about,
As in approvance, doe thereto applaud,
And loud advaunce her laud ;
And evermore they Hymen, Hymen sing,
That al the woods them answer, and theyr eccho ring.

Loe ! where she comes along with portly pace,
Lyke Phœbe, from her chamber of the East,
Arysing forth to run her mighty race,
Clad all in white, that seemes a virgin best.
So well it her beseemes, that ye would weene
Some angell she had beene.
Her long loose yellow locks lyke golden wyre,
Sprinckled with perle, and perling flowres atweene,
Doe lyke a golden mantle her attyre ;
And, being crowned with a girland greene,
Seeme lyke some mayden Queene.
Her modest eyes, abashed to behold
So many gazers as on her do stare,
Upon the lowly ground affixed are ;
Ne dare lift up her countenance too bold,
But blush to heare her prayses sung so loud,
So farre from being proud.
Nathlesse doe ye still loud her prayses sing,
That all the woods may answer, and your eccho ring.

Tell me, ye merchants daughters, did ye see
So fayre a creature in your towne before ;
So sweet, so lovely, and so mild as she,
Adornd with beautyes grace and vertues store ?

EDMUND SPENSER

Her goodly eyes lyke Saphyres shining bright,
Her forehead yvory white,
Her cheekes lyke apples which the sun hath rudded,
Her lips lyke cherryes charming men to byte,
Her brest like to a bowle of creame uncrudded,
Her paps lyke lyllies budded,
Her snowie necke lyke to a marble towre;
And all her body like a pallace fayre,
Ascending up, with many a stately stayre,
To honors scat and chastities sweet bowre.
Why stand ye still ye virgins in amaze,
Upon her so to gaze,
Whiles ye forget your former lay to sing,
To which the woods did answer, and your eccho ring?

But if ye saw that which no eyes can see,
The inward beauty of her lively spright,
Garnisht with heavenly guifts of high degree,
Much more then would ye wonder at that sight,
And stand astonisht lyke to those which red
Medusaes mazeful hed.
There dwels sweet love, and constant chastity,
Unspotted fayth, and comely womanhood,
Regard of honour, and mild modesty;
There vertue raynes as Queene in royal throne,
And giveth lawes alone,
The which the base affections doe obay,
And yeeld theyr services unto her will;
Ne thought of thing uncomely ever may
Thereto approch to tempt her mind to ill.
Had ye once seene these her celestial threasures,
And unrevealed pleasures,
Then would ye wonder, and her prayses sing,
That al the woods should answer, and your echo ring.

Open the temple gates unto my love,
Open them wide that she may enter in,
And all the postes adorne as doth behove,
And all the pillours deck with girlands trim,
For to receyve this Saynt with honour dew,
That commeth in to you.

EDMUND SPENSER

With trembling steps, and humble reverence,
She commeth in, before th' Almighties view;
Of her ye virgins learne obedience,
When so ye come into those holy places,
To humble your proud faces:
Bring her up to th' high altar, that she may
The sacred ceremonies there partake,
The which do endlesse matrimony make;
And let the roring Organs loudly play
The praises of the Lord in lively notes;
The whiles, with hollow throates,
The Choristers the joyous Antheme sing,
That al the woods may answere, and their eccho ring.

Behold, whiles she before the altar stands,
Hearing the holy priest that to her speakes,
And blesseth her with his two happy hands,
How the red roses flush up in her cheekes,
And the pure snow, with goodly vermill stayne
Like crimsin dyde in grayne:
That even th' Angels, which continually
About the sacred Altare doe remaine,
Forget their service and about her fly,
Ofte peeping in her face, that seems more fayre,
The more they on it stare.
But her sad eyes, still fastened on the ground,
Are governed with goodly modesty,
That suffers not one looke to glaunce awry,
Which may let in a little thought unsownd.
Why blush ye, love, to give to me your hand,
The pledge of all our band!
Sing, ye sweet Angels, Alleluya sing,
That all the woods may answere, and your eccho ring.

Now al is done: bring home the bride againe;
Bring home the triumph of our victory:
Bring home with you the glory of her gaine,
With joyance bring her and with jollity.
Never had man more joyfull day then this,
Whom heaven would heape with blis,

37

Make feast therefore now all this live-long day;
This day for ever to me holy is.
Poure out the wine without restraint or stay,
Poure not by cups, but by the belly full,
Poure out to all that wull,
And sprinkle all the postes and wals with wine,
That they may sweat, and drunken be withall.
Crowne ye God Bacchus with a coronall,
And Hymen also crowne with wreathes of vine;
And let the Graces daunce unto the rest,
For they can doo it best:
The whiles the maydens doe theyr carroll sing,
To which the woods shall answer, and theyr eccho ring.

Ring ye the bels, ye yong men of the towne,
And leave your wonted labors for this day:
This day is holy; doe ye write it downe,
That ye for ever it remember may.
This day the sunne is in his chiefest hight,
With Barnaby the bright,
From whence declining daily by degrees,
He somewhat loseth of his heat and light,
When once the Crab behind his back he sees.
But for this time it ill ordained was,
To chose the longest day in all the yeare,
And shortest night, when longest fitter weare:
Yet never day so long, but late would passe.
Ring ye the bels, to make it weare away,
And bonefiers make all day;
And daunce about them, and about them sing,
That all the woods may answer, and your eccho ring.

Ah! when will this long weary day have end,
And lende me leave to come unto my love?
How slowly do the houres theyr numbers spend?
How slowly does sad Time his feathers move?
Hast thee, O fayrest Planet, to thy home,
Within the Westerne fome:
Thy tyred steedes long since have need of rest.
Long though it be, at last I see it gloome,

EDMUND SPENSER

And the bright evening-star with golden creast
Appeare out of the East.
Fayre childe of beauty! glorious lampe of love!
That all the host of heaven in rankes doost lead,
And guydest lovers through the nights sad dread,
How chearefully thou lookest from above,
And seemst to laugh atweene thy twinkling light,
As joying in the sight
Of these glad many, which for joy doe sing,
That all the woods them answer, and their echo ring!

Now ceasse, ye damsels, your delights fore-past ;
Enough it is that all the day was youres :
Now day is doen, and night is nighing fast,
Now bring the Bryde into the brydall boures.
The night is come, now soon her disaray,
And in her bed her lay;
Lay her in lillies and in violets,
And silken courteins over her display,
And odourd sheetes, and Arras coverlets.
Behold how goodly my faire love does ly,
In proud humility!
Like unto Maia, when as Jove her took
In Tempe, lying on the flowry gras,
Twixt sleepe and wake, after she weary was,
With bathing in the Acidalian brooke.
Now it is night, ye damsels may be gon,
And leave my love alone,
And leave likewise your former lay to sing :
The woods no more shall answere, nor your echo ring.

Now welcome, night! thou night so long expected,
That long daies labour doest at last defray,
And all my cares, which cruell Love collected,
Hast sumd in one, and cancelled for aye:
Spread thy broad wing over my love and me,
That no man may us see;
And in thy sable mantle us enwrap,
From feare of perrill and foule horror free.
Let no false treason seeke us to entrap,

EDMUND SPENSER

Nor any dread disquiet once annoy
The safety of our joy;
But let the night be calme, and quietsome,
Without tempestuous storms or sad afray:
Lyke as when Jove with fayre Alcmena lay,
When he begot the great Tirynthian groome:
Or lyke as when he with thy selfe did lie
And begot Majesty.
And let the mayds and yongmen cease to sing;
Ne let the woods them answer nor theyr eccho ring.

Let no lamenting cryes, nor dolefull teares,
Be heard all night within, nor yet without:
Ne let false whispers, breeding hidden feares,
Breake gentle sleepe with misconceived dout.
Let no deluding dreames, nor dreadfull sights,
Make sudden sad affrights;
Ne let house-fyres, nor lightnings helpelesse harmes,
Ne let the Pouke, nor other evill sprights,
Ne let mischivous witches with theyr charmes,
Ne let hob Goblins, names whose sence we see not,
Fray us with things that be not:
Let not the shriech Oule nor the Storke be heard,
Nor the night Raven, that still deadly yels;
Nor damned ghosts, cald up with mighty spels,
Nor griesly vultures, make us once affeard:
Ne let th' unpleasant Quyre of Frogs still croking
Make us to wish theyr choking.
Let none of these theyr drery accents sing;
Ne let the woods them answer, nor theyr eccho ring.

But let stil Silence trew night-watches keepe,
That sacred Peace may in assurance rayne,
And tymely Sleep, when it is tyme to sleepe,
May poure his limbs forth on your pleasant playne;
The whiles an hundred little winged loves,
Like divers-fethered doves,
Shall fly and flutter round about your bed,
And in the secret darke, that none reproves,
Their pretty stealthes shal worke, and snares shal spread

EDMUND SPENSER

To filch away sweet snatches of delight,
Conceald through covert night.
Ye sonnes of Venus, play your sports at will!
For greedy pleasure, carelesse of your toyes,
Thinks more upon her paradise of joyes,
Then what ye do, albe it good or ill.
All night therefore attend your merry play,
For it will soone be day:
Now none doth hinder you, that say or sing;
Ne will the woods now answer, nor your Eccho ring.

Who is the same, which at my window peepes?
Or whose is that faire face that shines so bright?
Is it not Cinthia, she that never sleepes,
But walkes about high heaven al the night?
O! fayrest goddesse, do thou not envy
My love with me to spy:
For thou likewise didst love, though now unthought,
And for a fleece of wooll, which privily
The Latmian shepherd once unto thee brought,
His pleasures with thee wrought.
Therefore to us be favorable now;
And sith of wemens labours thou hast charge,
And generation goodly dost enlarge,
Encline thy will t'effect our wishfull vow,
And the chast wombe informe with timely seed,
That may our comfort breed:
Till which we cease our hopefull hap to sing;
Ne let the woods us answere, nor our Eccho ring.

And thou, great Juno! which with awful might
The lawes of wedlock still dost patronize;
And the religion of the faith first plight
With sacred rites hast taught to solemnize;
And eeke for comfort often called art
Of women in their smart;
Eternally bind thou this lovely band,
And all thy blessings unto us impart.
And thou, glad Genius! in whose gentle hand
The bridale bowre and geniall bed remaine,
Without blemish or staine;

EDMUND SPENSER

And the sweet pleasures of theyr loves delight
With secret ayde doest succour and supply,
Till they bring forth the fruitfull progeny;
Send us the timely fruit of this same night.
And thou, fayre Hebe! and thou, Hymen free!
Grant that it may so be.
Til which we cease your further prayse to sing;
Ne any woods shall answer, nor your Eccho ring.

And ye high heavens, the temple of the gods,
In which a thousand torches flaming bright
Doe burne, that to us wretched earthly clods
In dreadful darknesse lend desired light;
And all ye powers which in the same remayne,
More then we men can fayne!
Poure out your blessing on us plentiously,
And happy influence upon us raine,
That we may raise a large posterity,
Which from the earth, which they may long possesse
With lasting happinesse,
Up to your haughty pallaces may mount;
And, for the guerdon of theyr glorious merit,
May heavenly tabernacles there inherit,
Of blessed Saints for to increase the count.
So let us rest, sweet love, in hope of this,
And cease till then our tymely joyes to sing:
The woods no more us answer, nor our eccho ring!

Song! made in lieu of many ornaments,
With which my love should duly have been dect,
Which cutting off through hasty accidents,
Ye would not stay your dew time to expect,
But promist both to recompens;
Be unto her a goodly ornament,
And for short time an endlesse moniment.

E. SPENSER

EDMUND SPENSER

From Daphnaïda, 1591

What man henceforth that breatheth vitall ayre
Will honour heaven, or heavenlie powers adore,
Which so unjustlie doe their judgments share
Mongst earthlie wightes, as to afflict so sore
The innocent, as those which do transgresse,
And do not spare the best or fayrest, more
Than worst or fowlest, but doe both oppresse ?

If this be right, why did they then create
The world so fayre, sith fairenesse is neglected ?
Or whie be they themselves immaculate,
If purest things be not by them respected ?
She faire, shee pure, most faire, most pure shee was,
Yet was by them as thing impure rejected ;
Yet shee in purenesse heaven it selfe did pas.

In purenesse and in all celestiall grace,
That men admire in goodlie womankinde,
She did excell, and seem'd of Angels race,
Living on earth like Angell new divinde,
Adorn'd with wisedome and with chastitie,
And all the dowries of a noble mind,
Which did her beautie much more beautifie.

No age hath bred (since fayre Astræa left
The sinfull world) more vertue in a wight ;
And, when she parted hence, with her she reft
Great hope, and robd her race of bountie quight.
Well may the shepheard lasses now lament ;
For dubble losse by her hath on them light,
To loose both her and bounties ornament.

Ne let Elisa, royall Shepheardesse,
The praises of my parted love envy,
For she hath praises in all plenteousnesse
Powr'd upon her, like showers of Castaly,
By her own Shepheard, Colin, her owne Shepherd,
That her with heavenly hymnes doth deifie,
Of rustick muse full hardly to be betterd.

43

EDMUND SPENSER *and* JOHN LYLY

She is the Rose, the glorie of the day,
And mine the Primrose in the lowly shade:
Mine, ah! not mine; amisse I mine did say:
Not mine, but His, which mine awhile her made;
Mine to be His, with him to live for ay.
O that so faire a flower so soone should fade,
And through untimely tempest fall away!

She fell away in her first ages spring,
Whil'st yet her leafe was greene, and fresh her rinde,
And whil'st her braunch faire blossomes foorth did bring,
She fell away against all course of kinde.
For age to dye is right, but youth is wrong;
She fel away like fruit blowne downe with winde.
Weepe, Shepheard! weepe, to make my undersong.

E. SPENSER

From Sappho and Phao, 1584—1632

The song in making of the arrows

Vulcan My shag-hair Cyclops, come let's ply
Our Lemnian hammers lustily.
      By my wife's sparrows
      I swear these arrows
      Shall singing fly
      Through many a wanton's eye.
These headed are with golden blisses,
These silver ones feather'd with kisses;
      But this of lead
      Strikes a clown dead,
      When in a dance
      He falls in a trance,
To see his black-brow lass not buss him,
And then whines out for death to untruss him.
So, so! our work being done, let's play;
Holiday, boys! cry holiday!

J. LYLY

JOHN LYLY

From Alexander and Campaspe, 1584—1632

Cupid and my Campaspe played
At cards for kisses; Cupid paid.
He stakes his quiver, bow, and arrows,
His mother's doves, and team of sparrows;
Loses them too; then down he throws
The coral of his lip, the rose
Growing on's cheek (but none knows how);
With these the crystal of his brow,
And then the dimple of his chin;
All these did my Campaspe win.
At last he set her both his eyes,
She won; and Cupid blind did rise.
O Love! has she done this to thee?
What shall, alas! become of me?

J LYLY

From Midas, 1592—1632

A song of Daphne to the lute

My Daphne's hair is twisted gold,
Bright stars a-piece her eyes do hold,
My Daphne's brow enthrones the graces,
My Daphne's beauty stains all faces;
On Daphne's cheek grow rose and cherry,
On Daphne's lip a sweeter berry.
Daphne's snowy hand but touched does melt,
And then no heavenlier warmth is felt;
My Daphne's voice tunes all the spheres,
My Daphne's music charms all ears.
     Fond am I thus to sing her praise;
     These glories now are turned to bays.

J. LYLY

From Gallathea, 1592—1632

O yes! O yes! If any maid
Whom leering Cupid has betrayed
To frowns of spite, to eyes of scorn,
And would in madness now see torn
The boy in pieces, let her come
Hither, and lay on him her doom.

45

JOHN LYLY

O yes! O yes! Has any lost
A heart which many a sigh hath cost?
Is any cozened of a tear
Which as a pearl disdain does wear?
Here stands the thief; let her but come
Hither, and lay on him her doom.

Is any one undone by fire,
And turned to ashes through desire?
Did ever any lady weep,
Being cheated of her golden sleep,
Stolen by sick thoughts? The pirate's found,
And in her tears he shall be drown'd.
Read his indictment, let him hear
What he's to trust to; Boy, give ear!

J. LYLY

From Midas, 1592—1632

Sing to Apollo, god of day,
Whose golden beams with morning play,
And make her eyes so brightly shine,
Aurora's face is called divine.
Sing to Phoebus and that throne
Of diamonds which he sits upon.
    Iŏ, paeans let us sing
      To Physic's and to Poesy's king!

Crown all his altars with bright fire,
Laurels bind about his lyre,
A Daphnean coronet for his head,
The Muses dance about his bed.
When on his ravishing lute he plays,
Strew his temple round with bays.
    Iŏ, paeans let us sing
      To the glittering Delian king!

J. LYLY

ANTHONY MUNDAY

From Two Italian Gentlemen, 1584

I serve a mistress whiter than the snow,
Straighter than cedar, brighter than the glass,
Finer in trip and swifter than the roe,
More pleasant than the field of flow'ring grass;
More gladsome to my withering joys that fade
Than winter's sun or summer's cooling shade.

Sweeter than swelling grape of ripest wine,
Softer than feathers of the fairest swan,
Smoother than jet, more stately than the pine,
Fresher than poplar, smaller than my span;
Clearer than beauty's fiery pointed beam,
Or icy crust of crystal's frozen stream.

Yet is she curster than the bear by kind,
And harder hearted than the aged oak,
More glib than oil, more fickle than the wind,
Stiffer than steel no sooner bent, but broke.
Lo thus my service is a lasting sore;
Yet will I serve; although I die therefore.

A. MUNDAY

From The Death of Robert Earl of Huntingdon, 1601

Weep! weep! ye woodmen, wail,
Your hands with sorrow wring!
Your master Robin Hood lies dead,
　　Therefore sigh as you sing.

Here lie his primer and his beads,
His bent bow and his arrows keen,
His good sword and his holy cross;
　　Now cast on flowers fresh and green.

And as they fall, shed tears and say
Wella, well-a-day! wella, well-a-day!
Thus cast ye flowers and sing,
　　And on to Wakefield take your way.

A MUNDAY

47

SIR PHILIP SIDNEY

From Astrophel and Stella, 1591—1598

First Song

Doubt you to whom my Muse these notes intendeth
Which now my breast o'ercharged to music lendeth?
   To you, to you, all song of praise is due:
Only in you my song begins and endeth.

Who hath the eyes which marry state with pleasure?
Who keeps the key of Nature's chiefest treasure?
   To you, to you, all song of praise is due:
Only for you the heaven forgat all measure.

Who hath the lips where wit in fairness reigneth?
Who womankind at once both decks and staineth?
   To you, to you, all song of praise is due:
Only by you Cupid his crown maintaineth.

Who hath the feet whose step of sweetness planteth?
Who else for whom Fame worthy trumpets wanteth?
   To you, to you, all song of praise is due:
Only to you her sceptre Venus granteth.

Who hath the breast whose milk doth passions nourish?
Whose grace is such that when it chides doth cherish?
   To you, to you, all song of praise is due:
Only through you the tree of life doth flourish.

Who hath the hand which without stroke subdueth?
Who long-dead beauty with increase reneweth?
   To you, to you, all song of praise is due:
Only at you all envy hopeless rueth.

Who hath the hair which loosest fastest tieth?
Who makes a man live then glad when he dieth?
   To you, to you, all song of praise is due:
Only of you the flatterer never lieth.

SIR PHILIP SIDNEY

Who hath the voice which soul from senses sunders?
Whose force but yours the bolts of beauty thunders?
  To you, to you, all song of praise is due:
Only with you not miracles are wonders.

Doubt you to whom my Muse these notes intendeth
Which now my breast o'ercharged to music lendeth?
  To you, to you, all song of praise is due:
Only in you my song begins and endeth.

SIR P. SIDNEY

From Astrophel and Stella, 1591—1598

Third Song

If Orpheus' voice had force to breathe such music's love
Through pores of senseless trees, as it could make them move;
If stones good measure danced, the Theban walls to build
To cadence of the tunes which Amphion's lyre did yield;
More cause a like effect at least wise bringeth;
O stones, O trees, learn hearing,—Stella singeth!

If love might sweeten so a boy of shepherd brood,
To make a lizard dull to taste love's dainty food;
If eagle fierce could so in Grecian maid delight,
As his light was her eyes, her death his endless night,—
Earth gave that love; heav'n, I trow, love refineth,—
O birds, O beasts, look, love,—lo, Stella shineth!

The birds, beasts, stones, and trees feel this, and feeling, love;
And if the trees nor stones stir not the same to prove,
Nor beasts nor birds do come unto this blessed gaze,
Know that small love is quick, and great love doth amaze;
They are amazed, but you with reason armed,
O eyes, O ears of men, how are you charmed!

SIR P. SIDNEY

SIR PHILIP SIDNEY

From Astrophel and Stella, 1591—1598

Fourth Song

Only Joy! now here you are,
Fit to hear and ease my care,
Let my whispering voice obtain
Sweet reward for sharpest pain;
Take me to thee, and thee to me.
No, no, no, no, my Dear, let be.

Night hath closed all in her cloak,
Twinkling stars love-thoughts provoke,
Danger hence good care doth keep,
Jealousy itself doth sleep;
Take me to thee, and thee to me.
No, no, no, no, my Dear, let be.

Better place no wit can find,
Cupid's yoke to loose or bind;
Those sweet flowers on fine bed too,
Us in their best language woo:
Take me to thee, and thee to me.
No, no, no, no, my Dear, let be.

This small light the moon bestows
Serves thy beams but to disclose;
So to raise my hap more high,
Fear not else, none can us spy;
Take me to thee, and thee to me.
No, no, no, no, my Dear, let be.

That you heard was but a mouse,
Dumb sleep holdeth all the house:
Yet asleep, methinks they say,
"Young folks, take time while you may:"
Take me to thee, and thee to me.
No, no, no, no, my Dear, let be.

SIR PHILIP SIDNEY

Niggard Time threats, if we miss
This large offer of our bliss,
Long stay, ere he grant the same:
Sweet, then, while each thing doth frame,
Take me to thee, and thee to me.
No, no, no, no, my Dear, let be.

Your fair mother is a-bed,
Candles out and curtains spread;
She thinks you do letters write;
Write, but first let me indite:
Take me to thee, and thee to me.
No, no, no, no, my Dear, let be.

Sweet, alas, why strive you thus?
Concord better fitteth thus;
Leave to Mars the force of hands,
Your power in your beauty stands:
Take me to thee, and thee to me.
No, no, no, no, my Dear, let be.

Woe to me! and do you swear
Me to hate, but I forbear?
Cursed be my destinies all,
That brought me so high to fall!
Soon with my death I will please thee:
No, no, no, no, my Dear, let be.

SIR P. SIDNEY

From **Cottoni Posthuma MS**

Wooing Stuff

Faint Amorist, what! dost thou think
To taste Love's honey, and not drink
One dram of gall? or to devour
A world of sweet and taste no sour?
Dost thou ever think to enter
The Elysian fields that dar'st not venture
In Charon's barge? A lover's mind
Must use to sail with every wind.

SIR PHILIP SIDNEY

He that loves, and fears to try,
Learns his mistress to deny.
Doth she chide thee? 'tis to shew it
That thy coldness makes her do it.
Is she silent? is she mute?
Silence fully grants thy suit.
Doth she pout, and leave the room?
Then she goes to bid thee come.
Is she sick? Why, then be sure
She invites thee to the cure.
Doth she cross thy suit with 'No'?
Tush, she loves to hear thee woo.
Doth she call the faith of man
In question? Nay, she loves thee then;
And if e'er she makes a blot,
She's lost if that thou hitt'st her not.
He that after ten denials
Dares attempt no further trials,
Hath no warrant to acquire
The dainties of his chaste desire.

Sir P. Sidney

From Arcadia and Certain Sonnets, 1598

Dirge

Ring out your bells, let mourning shows be spread;
For Love is dead:
    All Love is dead, infected
With plague of deep disdain:
    Worth, as nought worth, rejected,
And Faith fair scorn doth gain.
    From so ungrateful fancy,
    From such a female frenzy,
    From them that use men thus,
    Good Lord, deliver us!

SIR PHILIP SIDNEY

Weep, neighbours, weep! do you not hear it said
That Love is dead?
      His death-bed, peacock's folly;
His winding-sheet is shame;
      His will, false-seeming wholly;
His sole executor, blame.
          From so ungrateful fancy,
          From such a female frenzy,
          From them that use men thus,
          Good Lord, deliver us!

Let Dirge be sung, and Trentals rightly read,
For Love is dead;
      Sir Wrong his tomb ordaineth
My mistress' marble heart;
      Which epitaph containeth:
"Her eyes were once his dart."
          From so ungrateful fancy,
          From such a female frenzy,
          From them that use men thus,
          Good Lord, deliver us!

Alas, I lie; rage hath this error bred;
Love is not dead;
      Love is not dead, but sleepeth
In her unmatched mind,
      Where she his counsel keepeth,
Till due desert she find.
          Therefore, from so vile fancy,
          To call such wit a frenzy
          Who love can temper thus,
          Good Lord, deliver us!

                     SIR P. SIDNEY

From Arcadia Book III, 1598

O stealing Time, the subject of delay
Delay, the rack of unrefrained desire
What strange design hast thou my hopes to stay,
Mine hopes which do but to mine own aspire?

53

SIR PHILIP SIDNEY

Mine own? O word on whose sweet sound doth prey
My greedy soul with grip of inward fire,
Thy title great I justly challenge may,
Since in such phrase his faith he did attire.
O Time, become the chariot of my joys:
As thou draw'st on, so let my bliss draw near;
Each moment lost, part of my hap destroys.
Thou art the father of occasion dear;
Join with thy son to ease my long annoys:
In speedy help thank-worthy friends appear.

SIR P. SIDNEY

From Arcadia (Wilton House folio Grosart)

To Queen Elizabeth

Her inward worth all outward show transcends,
Envy her merits with regret commends;
Like sparkling gems her virtues draw the sight,
And in her conduct she is always bright.
When she imparts her thoughts, her words have force,
And sense and wisdom flow in sweet discourse.

SIR P. SIDNEY

From Arcadia Book III, 1598

My true-love hath my heart and I have his,
By just exchange—one for the other given;
I hold his dear and mine he cannot miss,
There never was a better bargain driven.
His heart in me keeps me and him in one,
My heart in him his thought and senses guides;
He loves my heart, for once it was his own,
I cherish it because in me it bides.
His heart his wound received from my sight,
My heart was wounded with his wounded heart;
For as from me, on him, his hurt did light,
So still methought, in me, his hurt did smart,
Both equal hurt, in this change sought our bliss,
My true love hath my heart and I have his.

SIR P. SIDNEY

54

SIR PHILIP SIDNEY *and* FULKE GREVILLE

From Arcadia Book III, 1598

O words, which fall like summer dew on me;
O breath, more sweet than is the growing bean;
O tongue, in which all honeyed liquors be;
O voice, that doth the thrush in shrillness stain:
   Do you say still this is her promise due:
   That she is mine, as I to her am true?

Gay hair, more gay than straw when harvest lies;
Lips, red and plump as cherries' ruddy side;
Eyes, fair and great like fair great ox's eyes;
O breast, in which two white sheep swell in pride;
   Join you with me to seal this promise due:
   That she be mine, as I to her am true.

But thou, white skin, as white as curds well pressed,
So smooth, as sleekstone-like, it smooths each part;
And thou, dear flesh, as soft as wool new-dressed,
And yet as hard as brawn made hard by art;
   First four but say, next four their saying seal,
   But you must pay the gage of promised weal.

S<small>IR</small> P. S<small>IDNEY</small>

From Caelica, 1633
XXII

I, with whose colours Myra dressed her head,
I, that wear posies of her own hand-making,
I, that mine own name in the chimneys read
By Myra finely wrought, ere I was waking;
   Must I look on, in hope time coming may
   With change bring back my turn again to play?

I, that on Sunday at the church stile found
A garland sweet, with true-love knots in flowers,
Which I to wear about mine arm was bound,
That each of us might know that all was ours;
   Must I now lead an idle life in wishes?
   And follow Cupid for his loaves and fishes?

FULKE GREVILLE LORD BROOKE

I, that did wear the ring her mother left,
I, for whose love she gloried to be blamed,
I, with whose eyes her eyes committed theft,
I, who did make her blush when I was named;
    Must I lose ring, flowers, blush, theft, and go naked,
    Watching with sighs, till dead love be awaked?

I, that when drowsy Argus fell asleep,
Like jealousy o'erwatched with desire,
Was even warned modesty to keep,
While her breath, speaking, kindled Nature's fire;
    Must I look on a-cold, while others warm them?
    Do Vulcan's brothers in such fine nets arm them?

Was it for this, that I might Myra see,
Washing the waters, with her beauty's white?
Yet would she never write her love to me;
Thinks wit of change, while thoughts are in delight?
    Mad girls must safely love, as they may leave;
    No man can print a kiss; lines may deceive.

FULKE GREVILLE LORD BROOKE

From Caelica, 1633

LXXXVII

When as man's life, the light of human lust,
In socket of his earthly lanthorn burns,
That all this glory unto ashes must,
And generations to corruption turns;
Then fond desires that only fear their end,
Do vainly wish for life, but to amend.

But when this life is from the body fled,
To see itself in that eternal glass
Where time doth end, and thoughts accuse the dead,
Where all to come is one with all that was;
Then living men ask how he left his breath,
That, while he lived, never thought of death.

FULKE GREVILLE LORD BROOKE

FULKE GREVILLE LORD BROOKE

From The Phoenix' Nest, 1593

An epitaph upon the right honourable Sir Philip Sidney

Silence augmenteth grief, writing increaseth rage,
Stal'd are my thoughts, which lov'd and lost the wonder of
    our age,
Yet quickened now with fire, though dead with frost ere now,
Enrag'd I write, I know not what; dead, quick, I know
    not how.

Hard hearted minds relent, and rigour's tears abound,
And envy strangely rues his end, in whom no fault she found;
Knowledge his light hath lost, valour hath slain her knight,
Sidney is dead, dead is my friend, dead is the world's delight.

Place pensive wails his fall, whose presence was her pride,
Time crieth out "My ebb is come; his life was my spring-
    tide."
Fame mourns in that she lost the ground of her reports,
Each living wight laments his lack, and all in sundry sorts.

He was—woe worth that word—to each well-thinking mind,
A spotless friend, a matchless man, whose virtue ever shin'd,
Declaring in his thoughts his life, and that he writ,
Highest conceits, longest foresights, and deepest works of wit.

He only like himself, was second unto none
Where death—though life—we rue, and wrong and all in
    vain do moan;
Their loss, not him, wail they, that fill the world with cries,
Death flew not him, but he made death his ladder to the skies.

Now sink of sorrow I, who live, the more the wrong,
Who wishing death, whom death denies, whose thread is all
    too long,
Who tied to wretched life, who looks for no relief,
Must spend my ever-dying days in never-ending grief.

57

FULKE GREVILLE *and* THOMAS LODGE

Heart's-ease and only I, like parallels, run on,
Whose equal length keep equal breadth, and never meet
in one,
Yet for not wronging him, my thoughts, my sorrow's cell,
Shall not run out, though leak they will, for liking him so
well.

Farewell to you my hopes, my wonted waking dreams,
Farewell, sometimes enjoyed joy, eclipsed are thy beams,
Farewell self pleasing thoughts, which quietness brings forth,
And farewell friendship's sacred league, uniting minds of worth.

And farewell, merry heart, the gift of guiltless minds,
And all sports which, for life's restore, variety assigns;
Let all that sweet is void; in me no mirth may dwell,
Philip, the cause of all this woe, my life's content, farewell.

Now rhyme the son of rage, which art no kin to skill,
And endless grief which deads my life, yet knows not how
to kill,
Go! seek that hapless tomb, which if ye hap to find,
Salute the stones, that keep the limbs, that held so good a
mind.

FULKE GREVILLE LORD BROOKE

From Rosalynd, 1590—1609

First shall the heavens want starry light,
The seas be robbed of their waves,
The day want sun, the sun want bright,
The night want shade, the dead men graves,
The April, flowers and leaf and tree,
Before I false my faith to thee.

First shall the tops of highest hills
By humble plains be overpried,
And poets scorn the Muses' quills,
And fish forsake the water-glide,
And Iris lose her coloured weed,
Before I fail thee at thy need.

THOMAS LODGE

First direful hate shall turn to peace,
And love relent in deep disdain,
And death his fatal stroke shall cease,
And envy pity every pain,
    And pleasure mourn, and sorrow smile,
    Before I talk of any guile.

First Time shall stay his stayless race,
And winter bless his brows with corn,
And snow bemoisten July's face,
And winter, spring, and summer mourn,
    Before my pen, by help of fame,
    Cease to recite thy sacred name.

T. LODGE

From Rosalynd, 1590—1609

Rosalind's Description

Like to the clear in highest sphere,
    Where all imperial glory shines,
Of self-same colours is her hair,
    Whether unfolded or in twines :
      Heigh ho, fair Rosalind !
Her eyes are sapphires set in snow,
    Refining heaven by every wink ;
The gods do fear whenas they glow,
    And I do tremble when I think :
      Heigh ho, would she were mine !

Her cheeks are like the blushing cloud
    That beautifies Aurora's face,
Or like the silver crimson shroud
    That Phœbus' smiling looks doth grace :
      Heigh ho, fair Rosalind !
Her lips are like to budded roses
    Whom ranks of lilies neighbour nigh,
Within which bounds the balm encloses,
    Apt to entice a deity :
      Heigh ho, would she were mine !

THOMAS LODGE

Her neck is like a stately tower
  Where Love himself imprisoned lies,
To watch for glances every hour
  From her divine and sacred eyes:
    Heigh ho, fair Rosalind!
Her paps are centres of delight,
  Her breasts are orbs of heavenly frame,
Where nature moulds the dew of light
  To feed perfection with the same:
    Heigh ho, would she were mine!

With orient pearl, with ruby red,
  With marble white, with sapphire blue,
Her body every way is fed,
  Yet soft in touch and sweet in view:
    Heigh ho, fair Rosalind!
Nature herself her shape admires,
  The gods are wounded in her sight;
And Love forsakes his heavenly fires
  And at her eyes his brand doth light:
    Heigh ho, would she were mine!

Then muse not, Nymphs, though I bemoan
  The absence of fair Rosalind,
Since for her fair there is a fairer none,
  Nor for her virtues so divine:
    Heigh ho, fair Rosalind!
Heigh ho, my heart, would God that she were mine!
                         T. LODGE

From **Rosalynd, 1590—1609**

Rosalind's Madrigal

Love in my bosom, like a bee
    Doth suck his sweet;
Now with his wings he plays with me,
    Now with his feet.
    Within mine eyes he makes his nest,
    His bed amidst my tender breast,
    My kisses are his daily feast;
    And yet he robs me of my rest.
    Ah! wanton will ye?

THOMAS LODGE

And if I sleep, then percheth he,
    With pretty flight,
And makes his pillow of my knee
    The livelong night.
    Strike I my lute, he tunes the string,
    He music plays if so I sing,
    He lends me every lovely thing,
    Yet cruel he my heart doth sting.
    Whist! wanton still ye,

Else I with roses, every day
    Will whip you hence,
And bind you when you long to play
    For your offence.
    I'll shut my eyes to keep you in,
    I'll make you fast it for your sin,
    I'll count your power not worth a pin.
    Alas! what hereby shall I win,
    If he gainsay me?

What if I beat the wanton boy
    With many a rod?
He will repay me with annoy,
    Because a god.
    Then sit you safely on my knee,
    And let thy bower my bosom be,
    Lurk in mine eyes, I like of thee;
    O Cupid, so thou pity me,
    Spare not, but play thee.

                   T. Lodge

From Robert Duke of Normandy, 1591

Pluck the fruit and taste the pleasure,
    Youthful lordings of delight;
Whilst occasion gives you seizure,
    Feed your fancies and your sight.
    After death when you are gone,
    Joy and pleasure is there none.

THOMAS LODGE

Here on earth nothing is stable,
    Fortune's changes well are known;
Whilst as youth doth then enable,
    Let your seeds of joy be sown.
    After death when you are gone
    Joy and pleasure is there none.

Feast it freely with your lovers,
    Blithe and wanton sports do fade,
Whilst that lovely Cupid hovers
    Round about this lovely shade.
    Sport it freely one to one,
    After death is pleasure none.

Now the pleasant spring allureth,
    And both place and time invites;
But alas what heart endureth
    To disclaim his sweet delights?
    After death, when we are gone
    Joy and pleasure is there none.

T. Lodge

From **Phillis, 1593**

Love guards the roses of thy lips,
    And flies about them like a bee;
If I approach, he forward skips,
    And if I kiss, he stingeth me.

Love in thine eyes doth build his bower,
    And sleeps within their pretty shine;
And if I look, the boy will lower,
    And from their orbs shoots shafts divine.

Love works thy heart within his fire,
    And in my tears doth firm the same,
And if I tempt it, will retire,
    And of my plaints doth make a game.

THOMAS LODGE

Love, let me cull her choicest flowers,
  And pity me, and calm her eye;
Make soft her heart, dissolve her lowers,
  Then will I praise thy deity.

But if thou do not, Love, I'll truly serve her
In spite of thee, and by firm faith deserve her.

T. LODGE

From Phillis, 1593

My Phyllis hath the morning sun
  At first to look upon her;
And Phyllis hath morn-waking birds
  Her risings for to honour.
My Phyllis hath prime-feathered flowers
  That smile when she treads on them;
And Phyllis hath a gallant flock
  That leaps since she doth own them.
But Phyllis hath so hard a heart,
  Alas! that she should have it,
As yields no mercy to desert
  Nor grace to those that crave it.
Sweet sun, when thou look'st on,
  Pray her regard my moan;
Sweet birds, when you sing to her,
  To yield some pity woo her;
Sweet flowers, whenas she treads on,
  Tell her, her beauty deads one.
And if in life, her love she nill agree me,
Pray her, before I die, she will come see me.

T. LODGE

From A Margarite of America, 1596

O shady vales, O fair enriched meads,
O sacred woods, sweet fields, and rising mountains;
O painted flowers, green herbs, where Flora treads,
Refreshed by wanton winds and wat'ry fountains!

63

THOMAS LODGE *and* GEORGE PEELE

O all you winged quiristers of wood,
That, perched aloft, your former pains report,
And straight again recount with pleasant mood
Your present joys in sweet and seemly sort.
O all you creatures, whosoever thrive
On mother earth, in seas, by air, or fire,
More blest are you than I here under sun :
Love dies in me, whenas he doth revive
In you; I perish under beauty's ire,
Where after storms, winds, frosts, your life is won.

T LODGE

From The Phoenix' Nest, 1593

For pity, pretty eyes, surcease
To give me war, and grant me peace.
Triumphant eyes, why bear you arms
Against a heart that thinks no harms ?
A heart already quite appalled,
A heart that yields and is enthralled ?

Kill rebels, proudly that resist ;
Not those that in true faith persist,
And conquered serve your Deity.
Will you, alas, command me die ?
Then die I yours, and death my cross ;
But unto you pertains the loss.

T. LODGE

From The Arraignment of Paris, 1584

Oenone. Fair and fair, and twice so fair,
　　　　As fair as any may be ;
　　　　The fairest shepherd on our green,
　　　　A love for any lady.
Paris. Fair and fair, and twice so fair,
　　　　As fair as any may be ;
　　　　Thy love is fair for thee alone,
　　　　And for no other lady.
Oenone. My love is fair, my love is gay,
　　　　As fresh as bin the flowers in May,
　　　　And of my love my roundelay,

GEORGE PEELE

My merry merry merry roundelay,
Concludes with Cupid's curse,
They that do change old love for new,
Pray gods they change for worse !
Oenone. My love can pipe, my love can sing,
My love can many a pretty thing,
And of his lovely praises ring
My merry merry roundelays,
Amen to Cupid's curse,
They that do change old love for new,
Pray gods they change for worse.

G. PEELE

From The Arraignment of Paris, 1584

Melpomene, the muse of tragic songs,
With mournful tunes, in stole of dismal hue,
Assist a silly nymph to wail her woe,
And leave thy lusty company behind.

Thou luckless wreath ! becomes not me to wear
The poplar-tree for triumph of my love ;
Then as my joy, my pride of love is left,
Be thou unclothed of thy lovely green.

And in thy leaves my fortune written be,
And them some gentle wind let blow abroad,
That all the world may see how false of love
False Paris hath to his Œnone been.

G. PEELE

From The Old Wives' Tale, 1595

All ye that lovely lovers be,
Pray you for me ;
Lo, here we come a-sowing, a-sowing,
And sow sweet fruits of love ;
In your sweethearts well may it prove.

*   *   *

Lo, here we come a-reaping, a-reaping,
To reap our harvest fruit.
And thus we pass the year so long,
And never be we mute.

G. PEELE

GEORGE PEELE *and* ROBERT GREENE

From Polyhymnia, 1590

A sonnet

His golden locks time hath to silver turned;
  O time too swift, O swiftness never ceasing!
His youth 'gainst time and age hath ever spurned,
  But spurned in vain; youth waneth by increasing:
Beauty, strength, youth, are flowers but fading seen;
Duty, faith, love, are roots, and ever green.

His helmet now shall make a hive for bees,
  And, lovers' sonnets turned to holy psalms,
A man-at-arms must now serve on his knees,
  And feed on prayers, which are age his alms:
But though from court to cottage he depart,
His saint is sure of his unspotted heart.

And when he saddest sits in homely cell,
  He'll teach his swains this carol for a song,
"Blessed be the hearts that wish my sovereign well,
  Cursed be the souls that think her any wrong!"
Goddess, allow this aged man his right,
To be your beadsman now that was your knight.

G. PEELE

From Perimedes the Blacksmith, 1588

Fair is my love, for April in her face,
  Her lovely breasts September claims his part,
And lordly July in her eyes takes place,
  But cold December dwelleth in her heart:
Blest be the months, that set my thoughts on fire,
Accurst that month that hindereth my desire!

Like Phœbus' fire, so sparkle both her eyes;
  As air perfumed with amber is her breath;
Like swelling waves, her lovely teats do rise;
  As earth her heart, cold, dateth me to death:
Ay me, poor man, that on the earth do live,
When unkind earth death and despair doth give!

ROBERT GREENE

In pomp sits mercy seated in her face;
    Love 'twixt her breasts his trophies doth imprint;
Her eyes shine favour, courtesy, and grace;
    But touch her heart, ah, that is framed of flint!
That fore my harvest in the grass bears grain,
The rock will wear, washed with a winter's rain.

R. Greene

From **Menaphon, 1589**

Sephestia's Song to her Child

Weep not, my wanton, smile upon my knee;
When thou art old there's grief enough for thee.
    Mother's wag, pretty boy,
    Father's sorrow, father's joy;
    When thy father first did see
    Such a boy by him and me,
    He was glad, I was woe;
    Fortune changed made him so
    When he left his pretty boy,
    Last his sorrow, first his joy.

Weep not, my wanton, smile upon my knee;
When thou art old there's grief enough for thee.
    Streaming tears that never stint,
    Like pearl drops from a flint,
    Fell by course from his eyes,
    That one another's place supplies;
    Thus he grieved in every part,
    Tears of blood fell from his heart,
    When he left his pretty boy,
    Father's sorrow, father's joy.

Weep not, my wanton, smile upon my knee;
When thou art old there's grief enough for thee.
    The wanton smiled, father wept,
    Mother cried, baby leapt;

E 2

ROBERT GREENE

More he crowed, more we cried,
Nature could not sorrow hide:
He must go, he must kiss
Child and mother, baby bliss,
For he left his pretty boy,
Father's sorrow, father's joy.
Weep not, my wanton, smile upon my knee;
When thou art old there's grief enough for thee.

R. GREENE

From **Menaphon, 1589**

Doron's description of his Samela

Like to Diana in her summer weed,
Girt with a crimson robe of brightest dye,
                    Goes fair Samela;
Whiter than be the flocks that straggling feed,
When washed by Arethusa faint they lie,
                    Is fair Samela;
As fair Aurora in her morning grey,
Decked with the ruddy glister of her love,
                    Is fair Samela;
Like lovely Thetis on a calmed day,
Whenas her brightness Neptune's fancy move,
                    Shines fair Samela;
Her tresses gold, her eyes like glassy streams,
Her teeth are pearl, the breasts are ivory
                    Of fair Samela;
Her cheeks, like rose and lily, yield forth gleams,
Her brows bright arches framed of ebony:
                    Thus fair Samela
Passeth fair Venus in her bravest hue,
And Juno in the show of majesty,
                    For she's Samela;
Pallas in wit; all three, if you well view,
For beauty, wit, and matchless dignity,
                    Yield to Samela.

R. GREENE

ROBERT GREENE

From **Orpharion, 1590—1599**

Cupid abroad was 'lated in the night,
His wings were wet with ranging in the rain,
Harbour he sought, to me he took his flight,
To dry his plumes; I heard the boy complain;
I oped the door, and granted his desire;
I rose myself, and made the wag a fire.

Looking more narrow by the fire's flame,
I spied his quiver hanging by his back;
Doubting the boy might my misfortune frame,
I would have gone, for fear of further wrack:
But what I drad did me, poor wretch, betide,
For forth he drew an arrow from his side.

He pierced the quick, and I began to start,
A pleasing wound, but that it was too high:
His shaft procured a sharp, yet sugared, smart.
Away he flew; for why? his wings were dry.
But left the arrow sticking in my breast,
That sore I grieved I welcomed such a guest.

R. GREENE

From **Francesco's Fortunes, 1590**

Radagon in Dianam

It was a valley gaudy green,
Where Dian at the fount was seen;
Green it was,
And did pass
All other of Diana's bowers,
In the pride of Flora's flowers.

A fount it was that no sun sees,
Circled in with cypress trees,
Set so nigh
As Phœbus' eye
Could not do the virgins scathe,
To see them naked when they bathe.

69

ROBERT GREENE

She sat there all in white,
Colour fitting her delight:
      Virgins so
      Ought to go,
For white in Armory is placed
To be the colour that is chaste.

Her taffeta cassock might you see
Tucked up above her knee,
      Which did show
      There below
Legs as white as whale's bone,
So white and chaste was never none.

Hard by her, upon the ground,
Sat her virgins in a round
      Bathing their
      Golden hair,
And singing all in notes high,
"Fie on Venus' flattering eye!

"Fie on love, it is a toy;
Cupid witless and a boy;
      All his fires,
      And desires,
Are plagues that God sent down from high,
To pester men with misery."

As thus the virgins did disdain
Lovers' joys and lovers' pain,
      Cupid nigh
      Did espy,
Grieving at Diana's song,
Slyly stole these maids among.

His bow of steel, darts of fire,
He shot amongst them sweet desire,
      Which straight flies
      In their eyes,
And at the entrance made them start,
For it ran from eye to heart.

ROBERT GREENE

Calisto straight supposed Jove
Was fair and frolic for to love;
      Dian she
      'Scaped not free,
For, well I wot, hereupon
She loved the swain Endymion;

Clytia, Phœbus; and Chloris' eye
Thought none so fair as Mercury:
      Venus thus
      Did discuss
By her son in darts of fire,
None so chaste to check desire.

Dian rose with all her maids,
Blushing thus at love's braids.
      With sighs, all
      Show their thrall;
And flinging hence pronounce this saw,
What so strong as love's sweet law?

R. GREENE

From Greene's Groatsworth of Wit bought with a
    million of repentance, 1592—1596

Verses Written in the Poet's Last Illness

Deceiving world, that with alluring toys
Hast made my life the subject of thy scorn,
And scornest now to lend thy fading joÿs
T' outlength my life, whom friends have left forlorn;
How well are they that die ere they be born,
    And never see thy sleights, which few men shun
    Till unawares they helpless are undone!

Oft have I sung of love and of his fire;
But now I find that poet was advised
Which made full feasts increasers of desire,
And proves weak love was with the poor despised;
For when the life with food is not sufficed,
    What thoughts of love, what motion of delight,
    What pleasance can proceed from such a wight?

ROBERT GREENE *and* ANON

Witness my want, the murderer of my wit:
My ravished sense, of wonted fury reft,
Wants such conceit as should in poems fit
Set down the sorrow wherein I am left;
But therefore have high heavens their gifts bereft,
  Because so long they lent them me to use,
  And I so long their bounty did abuse.

O that a year were granted me to live,
And for that year my former wits restored!
What rules of life, what counsel would I give,
How should my sin with sorrow be deplored!
But I must die of every man abhorred:
  Time loosely spent will not again be won;
  My time is loosely spent, and I undone.

R. GREENE

From England's Helicon, 1600

Phillida's Love-call to her Coridon and his replying

Phil.   Coridon, arise, my Coridon!
            Titan shineth clear.
Cor.   Who is it that calleth Coridon?
            Who is it that I hear?
Phil.   Phillida, thy true love, calleth thee.
            Arise then, arise then!
            Arise and keep thy flock with me!
Cor.   Phillida, my true love, is it she?
            I come then, I come then,
            I come and keep my flock with thee.

Phil.   Here are cherries ripe my Coridon;
            Eat them for my sake.
Cor.   Here's my oaten pipe, my lovely one,
            Sport for thee to make.

72

ANON

Phil.   Here are threads, my true love, fine as silk,
        To knit thee, to knit thee,
        A pair of stockings white as milk.
Cor.   Here are reeds, my true love, fine and neat,
        To make thee, to make thee,
        A bonnet to withstand the heat.

Phil.   I will gather flowers, my Coridon,
        To set in thy cap.
Cor.   I will gather pears, my lovely one,
        To put in thy lap.
Phil.   I will buy my true love garters gay,
        For Sundays, for Sundays,
        To wear about his legs so tall.
Cor.   I will buy my true love yellow say
        For Sundays, for Sundays,
        To wear about her middle small.

Phil.   When my Coridon sits on a hill
        Making melody—
Cor.   When my lovely one goes to her wheel,
        Singing cheerily—
Phil.   Sure, methinks, my true love doth excel
        For sweetness, for sweetness,
        Our Pan, that old Arcadian knight.
Cor.   And methinks my true love bears the bell
        For clearness, for clearness,
        Beyond the nymphs that be so bright.

Phil.   Had my Coridon, my Coridon,
        Been alack ! her swain—
Cor.   Had my lovely one, my lovely one
        Been in Ida plain—
Phil.   Cynthia Endymion had refused
        Preferring, preferring,
        My Coridon to play withal.
Cor.   The queen of love had been excused
        Bequeathing, bequeathing,
        My Phillida the golden ball.

ANON

Phil.   Yonder comes my mother, Coridon,
         Whither shall I fly?
Cor.   Under yonder beech, my lovely one,
         While she passeth by.
Phil.   Say to her thy true love was not here;
         Remember, remember,
         To-morrow is another day.
Cor.   Doubt me not, my true love, do not fear;
         Farewell then, farewell then,
         Heaven keep our loves alway.

ANON

From A Poetical Rapsody, 1602—1611

An invective against women

Are women fair? Aye, wondrous fair to see to;
Are women sweet? Yea, passing sweet they be too:
Most fair and sweet to them that inly love them;
Chaste and discreet to all, save those that prove them.

Are women wise? Not wise, but they be witty:
Are women witty? Yea, the more the pity;
They are so witty, and in wit so wily,
That be ye ne'er so wise, they will beguile ye.

Are women fools? Not fools, but fondlings many.
Can women fond be faithful unto any?
When snow-white swans do turn to colour sable,
Then women fond will be both firm and stable.

Are women saints? No saints, nor yet no devils.
Are women good? Not good, but needful evils;
So angel-like, that devils I do not doubt them,
So needful ills, that few can live without them.

Are women proud? Aye, passing proud, and praise them:
Are women kind? Aye, wondrous kind, and please them:
Or so imperious, no man can endure them;
Or so kind-hearted, any may procure them.

ANON

GEORGE CHAPMAN

From Hero and Leander Fifth Sestiad, 1598

Epithalamion Teratos

Come, come, dear Night, Love's mart of kisses,
  Sweet close of his ambitious line,
The fruitful summer of his blisses,
  Love's glory doth in darkness shine.

O come, soft rest of cares, come Night!
  Come naked virtue's only tire,
The reaped harvest of the light
  Bound up in sheaves of sacred fire.
    Love calls to war;
     Sighs his alarms,
    Lips his swords are,
     The field his arms.

Come, Night, and lay thy velvet hand
  On glorious Day's outfacing face.
And all thy crowned flames command
  For torches to our nuptial grace.
    Love calls to war;
     Sighs his alarms,
    Lips his swords are,
     The field his arms.

No need have we of factious Day,
  To cast, in envy of thy peace,
Her balls of discord in thy way;
  Here Beauty's day doth never cease.
    Day is abstracted here,
    And varied in a triple sphere,
Hero, Alcmane, Mya, so outshine thee,
Ere thou come here, let Thetis thrice refine thee.
    Love calls to war;
     Sighs his alarms,
    Lips his swords are,
     The field his arms.

GEORGE CHAPMAN *and* FRANCIS BACON

> The evening star I see;
>   Rise youths, the evening star
>   Helps Love to summon war ;
> Both now embracing be.   G. CHAPMAN

From **Reliquiae Wottonianae, 1651**

The World's a bubble, and the life of man
            Less than a span ;
In his conception wretched, from the womb,
            So to the tomb;
Nurst from his cradle, and brought up to years
            With cares and fears.
    Who then to frail mortality shall trust,
    But limns on water, or but writes in dust.

Yet, whil'st with sorrow here we live opprest,
            What life is best ?
Courts are but only superficial schools,
            To dandle fools :
The rural part is turned into a den
            Of savage men :
    And where's a city from foul vice so free,
    But may be term'd the worst of all the three ?

Domestic cares afflict the husband's bed,
            Or pains his head :
Those that live single, take it for a curse,
            Or do things worse :
These would have children : those that have them, none,
            Or wish them gone :
    What is it, then, to have, or have no wife,
    But single thraldom, or a double strife ?

Our own affections still at home to please,
            Is a disease :
To cross the seas to any foreign soil,
            Peril and toil :
Wars with their noise affright us; when they cease,
            We're worse in peace :
    What then remains, but that we still should cry
    For being born, and, being born, to die ?

                                        FRANCIS BACON

HENRY CONSTABLE

From England's Helicon, 1600

Damelus' Song to his Diaphenia

Diaphenia, like the daffadowndilly,
White as the sun, fair as the lily,
   Heigho, how I do love thee!
I do love thee as my lambs
Are beloved of their dams:
   How blest were I if thou wouldst prove me!

Diaphenia, like the spreading roses,
That in thy sweets all sweets encloses,
   Fair sweet, how I do love thee!
I do love thee as each flower
Love's the sun's life-giving power;
   For dead, thy breath to life might move me.

Diaphenia, like to all things blessed,
When all thy praises are expressed,
   Dear joy, how I do love thee!
As the birds do love the Spring,
Or the bees their careful king:
   Then in requite, sweet virgin, love me!

H. CONSTABLE

From England's Helicon, 1600

To his Flocks

Feed on, my flocks, securely,
Your shepherd watcheth surely:
Run about, my little lambs,
Skip and wanton with your dams,
   Your loving herd with care will tend ye.
Sport on, fair flocks, at pleasure,
Nip Vesta's flow'ring treasure;
I myself will duly hark,
When my watchful dog doth bark;
   From wolf and fox I will defend ye.

H. CONSTABLE

SAMUEL DANIEL

From Certain Small Poems, 1605

Ulysses and the Siren

Siren. Come, worthy Greek ! Ulysses, come,
Possess these shores with me ;
The winds and seas are troublesome,
And here we may be free.
   Here may we sit and view their toil
That travail in the deep,
And joy the day in mirth the while,
And spend the night in sleep.

Ulysses. Fair Nymph, if fame or honour were
To be attained with ease,
Then would I come and rest with thee
And leave such toils as these.
   But here it dwells, and here must I
With danger seek it forth ;
To spend the time luxuriously
Becomes not men of worth.

Siren. Ulysses, O be not deceived
With that unreal name;
This honour is a thing conceived
And rests on others' fame ;
   Begotten only to molest
Our peace and to beguile
(The best thing of our life) our rest,
And give us up to toil.

Ulysses. Delicious Nymph, suppose there were
Nor honour nor report,
Yet manliness would scorn to wear
The time in idle sport.
   For toil doth give a better touch,
To make us feel our joy;
And ease finds tediousness as much
As labour yields annoy.

Siren. Then pleasure likewise seems the shore,
Whereto tends all our toil,
Which you forego to make it more,
And perish oft the while.

SAMUEL DANIEL

Who may desport them diversely
Find never tedious day,
And ease may have variety
As well as action may.

Ulysses. But natures of the noblest frame,
These toils and dangers please,
And they take comfort in the same
As much as you in ease;
    And with the thought of actions past
Are recreated still,
When pleasure leaves a touch at last,
To show that it was ill.

Siren. That doth opinion only cause
That's out of custom bred,
Which makes us many other laws
Than ever Nature did.
    No widows wail for our delights,
Our sports are without blood;
The world, we see, by warlike wights
Receives more hurt than good.

Ulysses. But yet the state of things require
These motions of unrest;
And these great Spirits of high desire
Seem born to turn them best:
    To purge the mischiefs that increase,
And all good order mar,
For oft we see a wicked peace
To be well changed for war.

Siren. Well, well, Ulysses, then I see
I shall not have thee here;
And therefore I will come to thee
And take my fortunes there.
    I must be won that cannot win,
Yet lost were I not won;
For beauty hath created been
To undo, or be undone.

S. DANIEL

SAMUEL DANIEL

From Tethys' Festival, 1610

Are they shadows that we see?
   And can shadows pleasure give?
Pleasures only shadows be,
   Cast by bodies we conceive;
And are made the things we deem
In those figures which they seem.

But these pleasures vanish fast
   Which by shadows are expressed;
Pleasures are not if they last,
   In their passing is their best;
Glory is most bright and gay
In a flash, and so away.

Feed apace, then, greedy eyes,
   On the wonder you behold;
Take it sudden as it flies
   Though you take it not to hold;
When your eyes have done their part,
Thought must length it in the heart.

S. DANIEL

From Hymen's Triumph, 1615

Ah, I remember well—and how can I
But evermore remember well—when first
Our flame began, when scarce we knew what was
The flame we felt; when as we sat and sighed
And looked upon each other, and conceived
Not what we ailed, yet something we did ail,
And yet were well, and yet we were not well,
And what was our disease we could not tell.
Then would we kiss, then sigh, then look; and thus
In that first garden of our simpleness
We spent our childhood. But when years began
To reap the fruit of knowledge, ah, how then
Would she with graver looks, with sweet stern brow,
Check my presumption and my forwardness!
Yet still would give me flowers, still would me show
What she would have me, yet not have me know.

S. DANIEL

SOUTHWELL *and* DRAYTON

From Saint Peter's Complaint, 1615

The Burning Babe

As I, in hoary winter's night, stood shivering in the snow;
Surprised I was with sudden heat, which made my heart to glow;
And lifting up a fearful eye to view what fire was near,
A pretty Babe, all burning bright, did in the air appear;
Who scorched with excessive heat, such floods of tears did shed,
As though his floods should quench his flames, which with
    his tears were bred;
'Alas!' quoth he 'but newly born, in fiery heats I fry,
Yet none approach to warm their hearts, or feel my fire,
    but I.
My faultless breast the furnace is; the fuel wounding thorns;
Love is the fire and sighs the smoke; the ashes shames and
    scorns.
The fuel Justice layeth on; and Mercy blows the coals;
The metal in this Furnace wrought are men's defiled souls,
For which, as now, on fire I am to work them to their good;
So will I melt into a bath, to wash them in my blood!'
With this he vanished out of sight, and swiftly shrunk away,
And straight I called unto mind, that it was Christmas Day.

ROBERT SOUTHWELL

From Poems, 1619

The Crier

Good folk, for gold or hire,
But help me to a crier;
For my poor heart is run astray
After two eyes that passed this way.
    O yes, O yes, O yes!
    If there be any man
    In town or country can
    Bring me my heart again
    I'll please him for his pain.
And by these marks I will you show
That only I this heart do owe.
    It is a wounded heart
    Wherein yet sticks the dart,

MICHAEL DRAYTON

Every piece sore hurt throughout it,
Faith and troth writ round about it.
It was a tame heart and a dear
   And never used to roam;
But having got this haunt I fear
   'Twill hardly stay at home.
For God's sake walking by the way,
   If you my heart do see,
Either impound it for a stray
   Or send it back to me.

M. D<small>RAYTON</small>

From Poems, 1619

To his coy Love

I pray thee leave, love me no more,
   Call home the heart you gave me.
I but in vain that saint adore
   That can, but will not save me.
These poor half kisses kill me quite;
   Was ever man thus served?
Amidst an ocean of delight
   For pleasure to be starved.

Show me no more those snowy breasts,
   With azure riverets branched,
Where, whilst mine eye with plenty feasts,
   Yet is my thirst not stanched.
O, Tantalus! thy pains ne'er tell,
   By me thou art prevented;
'Tis nothing to be plagued in Hell,
   But thus in Heaven tormented.

Clip me no more in those dear arms,
   Nor thy life's comfort call me,
O, these are but too powerful charms,
   And do but more enthral me.
But see how patient I am grown
   In all this coil about thee.
Come nice thing, let thy heart alone,
   I cannot live without thee.

M. D<small>RAYTON</small>

MICHAEL DRAYTON

From Poems, 1606 ?—1619

To the Cambro-Britons and their Harp
His ballad of Agincourt

Fair stood the wind for France
When we our sails advance,
Nor now to prove our chance
    Longer will tarry;
But putting to the main,
At Kaux, the mouth of Seine,
With all his martial train,
    Landed King Harry.

And taking many a fort,
Furnish'd in warlike sort
Marcheth towards Agincourt
    In happy hour;
Skirmishing day by day
With those that stopp'd his way,
Where the French general lay
    With all his power.

Which in his height of pride,
King Henry to deride,
His ransom to provide
    To the King sending;
Which he neglects the while,
As from a nation vile,
Yet with an angry smile,
    Their fall portending.

And turning to his men,
Quoth our brave Henry then,
Though they to one be ten,
    Be not amazed.
Yet, have we well begun,
Battles so bravely won
Have ever to the sun
    By fame been raised.

MICHAEL DRAYTON

And for myself, quoth he,
This my full rest shall be,
England ne'er mourn for me,
    Nor more esteem me.
Victor I will remain,
Or on this earth lie slain,
Never shall she sustain
    Loss to redeem me.

Poictiers and Cressy tell,
When most their pride did swell,
Under our swords they fell,
    No less our skill is,
Than when our grandsire great,
Claiming the regal seat,
By many a warlike feat,
    Lop'd the French lilies.

The Duke of York so dread,
The eager vaward led;
With the main Henry sped
    Amongst his henchmen.
Excester had the rear,
A braver man not there,
O Lord, how hot they were
    On the false Frenchmen.

They now to fight are gone,
Armour on armour shone,
Drum now to drum did groan,
    To hear was wonder;
That with cries they make
The very earth did shake,
Trumpet to trumpet spake
    Thunder to thunder.

Well it thine age became,
O noble Erpingham,
Which didst the signal aim
    To our hid forces;

MICHAEL DRAYTON

When from a meadow by,
Like a storm suddenly,
The English archery
　　Struck the French horses,

With Spanish yew so strong,
Arrows a cloth-yard long,
That like to serpents stung,
　　Piercing the weather.
None from his fellow starts,
But playing manly parts,
And like true English hearts,
　　Stuck close together.

When down their bows they threw
And forth their bilbows drew,
And on the French they flew,
　　Not one was tardy ;
Arms were from shoulders sent,
Scalps to the teeth were rent,
Down the French peasants went,
　　Our men were hardy.

This while our noble king,
His broad sword brandishing,
Down the French host did ding,
　　As to o'erwhelm it ;
And many a deep wound lent,
His arms with blood besprent,
And many a cruel dent
　　Bruised his helmet.

Glo'ster, that duke so good,
Next of the royal blood,
For famous England stood,
　　With his brave brother ;
Clarence, in steel so bright,
Though but a maiden knight,
Yet in that furious fight
　　Scarce such another.

85

MICHAEL DRAYTON

Warwick in blood did wade,
Oxford the foe invade,
And cruel slaughter made,
    Still as they ran up;
Suffolk his axe did ply,
Beaumont and Willoughby
Bare them right doughtily,
    Ferrers and Fanhope.

Upon Saint Crispin's day
Fought was this noble fray,
Which fame did not delay
    To England to carry;
O when shall Englishmen
With such acts fill a pen,
Or England breed again
Such a King Harry?

                    M. DRAYTON

From Poems, 1606 ?—1619

To the Virginian Voyage

You brave heroic minds,
Worthy your country's name,
    That honour still pursue,
    Go, and subdue;
Whilst loitering hinds
Lurk here at home with shame.

Britons, you stay too long,
Quickly aboard bestow you.
    And with a merry gale
    Swell your stretch'd sail,
With vows as strong
As the winds that blow you.

MICHAEL DRAYTON

Your course securely steer,
West and by South forth keep;
    Rocks, lee-shores, nor shoals
    When Eolus scowls,
You need not fear,
So absolute the deep.

And cheerfully at sea,
Success you still entice
    To get the pearl and gold;
    And ours to hold
VIRGINIA
Earth's only Paradise.

Where nature hath in store,
Fowl, venison, and fish;
    And the fruitfull'st soil
    Without your toil,
Three harvests more,
All greater than your wish.

And the ambitious vine
Crowns, with his purple mass,
    The cedar reaching high
    To kiss the sky;
The cypress, pine,
And useful sassafras.

To whom the golden Age
Still Nature's laws doth give,
    Nor other cares attend
    But them to defend
From Winter's age,
That long there doth not live.

When as the luscious smell
Of that delicious land,
    Above the sea that flows,
    The clear wind throws,
Your hearts to swell,
Approaching the dear strand.

MICHAEL DRAYTON *and* ANON

In kenning of the shore,
(Thanks to God first given)
    O, you the happiest men
    Be frolic then!
Let cannons roar,
Frighting the wide heaven!

And in regions far
Such heroes bring ye forth,
    As those from whom we came;
    And plant our name
Under that star
Not known unto our North.

And as there plenty grows
Of Laurel everywhere,
    Apollo's sacred tree,
    You may it see
A poet's brows
To crown, that may sing there.

Thy *Voyages* attend
Industrious HACKLUIT,
    Whose reading shall inflame
    Men to seek fame,
And much commend
To after-Times, thy wit.

M. DRAYTON

From Dowland's **Second Book of Songs or Airs, 1600**

Fine knacks for ladies, cheap, choice, brave, and new!
Good pennyworths, but money cannot move;
I keep a fair, but for the Fair to view!
A beggar may be liberal of love.
  Though all my wares be trash, the heart is true,
                The heart is true,
                The heart is true.

ANON

Great gifts are guiles and look for gifts again,
My trifles come, as treasures from my mind.
It is a precious jewel to be plain,
Sometimes in shell, the orientest pearls we find.
   Of others take a sheaf, of me a grain,
                  Of me a grain,
                  Of me a grain.

Within this pack, pins, points, laces, and gloves !
And divers toys fitting a country fair ;
But my heart, wherein duty serves and loves,
Turtles and twins, court's brood, a heavenly pair ;
   Happy the heart that thinks of no removes,
                  Of no removes,
                  Of no removes.

ANON

From Dowland's Second Book of Songs or Airs, 1600

   I saw my Lady weep;
And Sorrow, proud to be advanced so
In those fair eyes, where all perfections keep.
   Her face was full of woe,
But such a woe (believe me) as wins more hearts
Than mirth can do, with her enticing parts.

   Sorrow was there made fair ;
And Passion wise ; Tears a delightful thing ;
Silence, beyond all speech, a wisdom rare.
   She made her sighs to sing ;
And all things with so sweet a sadness move,
As made my heart at once both grieve and love.

   O ! fairer than aught else
The world can show, leave off in time to grieve.
Enough, enough, your joyful look excels;
   Tears kill the heart, believe.
O ! strive not to be excellent in woe
Which only breeds your beauty's overthrow.

ANON

ANON *and* CHRISTOPHER MARLOWE

From Dowland's Third Book of Songs or Airs, 1603

Weep you no more, sad fountains,
  What need you flow so fast?
Look! how the snowy mountains
  Heaven's sun doth gently waste.
But my Sun's heavenly eyes
    View not your weeping,
    That now lies sleeping
Softly; now softly lies
      Sleeping.

Sleep is a reconciling,
  A rest that peace begets.
Doth not the sun rise smiling
  When fair at e'en he sets?
Rest you; then rest, sad eyes,
    Melt not in weeping;
    While She lies sleeping
Softly; now softly lies
      Sleeping.

Anon

From England's Helicon, 1600

The passionate shepherd to his love

Come live with me and be my love,
And we will all the pleasures prove,
That valleys, groves, hills and fields,
Woods or steepy mountain yields.

And we will sit upon the rocks,
Seeing the shepherds feed their flocks,
By shallow rivers, to whose falls
Melodious birds sing madrigals.

CHRISTOPHER MARLOWE

And I will make thee beds of roses,
And a thousand fragrant posies,
A cap of flowers, and a kirtle,
Embroider'd all with leaves of myrtle.

A gown made of the finest wool
Which from our pretty lambs we pull ;
Fair lined slippers for the cold,
With buckles of the purest gold.

A belt of straw and ivy-buds,
With coral clasps and amber studs :
And if these pleasures may thee move,
Come live with me, and be my love.

The shepherds swains shall dance and sing
For thy delight each May-morning ;
If these delights thy mind may move,
Then live with me, and be my love.

C. MARLOWE

From England's Parnassus, 1600

A fragment

I walk'd along a stream, for pureness rare,
Brighter than sunshine; for it did acquaint
The dullest sight with all the glorious prey
That in the pebble-paved channel lay.
No molten crystal, but a richer mine,
Even Nature's rarest alchymy ran there,
Diamonds resolv'd, and substance more divine,
Through whose bright gliding current might appear
A thousand naked nymphs, whose ivory shine,
Enamelling the banks, made them more dear
Than ever was that glorious palace gate
Where the day-shining Sun, in triumph sate.
Upon this brim the eglantine and rose,
The tamarisk, olive, and the almond tree,
As kind companions in one union grows,
Folding their twining arms, as oft we see

MARLOWE *and* SHAKESPEARE

Turtle-taught lovers either other close,
Lending to dulness feeling sympathy;
And as a costly valance o'er a bed,
So did their garland tops the brook o'erspread.
Their leaves that differ'd both in shape and show,
Though all were green, yet difference such in green,
Like to the chequer'd bent of Iris' bow,
Prided the running main, as it had been......

C. MARLOWE

From Love's Labour's Lost, 1591?

Spring

When daisies pied and violets blue
   And lady-smocks all silver-white
And cuckoo-buds of yellow hue
   Do paint the meadows with delight,
The cuckoo then, on every tree,
Mocks married men; for thus sings he,
                 Cuckoo;
   Cuckoo, cuckoo: O word of fear,
   Unpleasing to a married ear!

When shepherds pipe on oaten straws
   And merry larks are ploughmen's clocks,
When turtles tread, and rooks, and daws,
   And maidens bleach their summer smocks,
The cuckoo then, on every tree,
Mocks married men; for thus sings he,
                 Cuckoo;
   Cuckoo, cuckoo: O word of fear,
   Unpleasing to a married ear!

W. SHAKESPEARE

WILLIAM SHAKESPEARE

From Love's Labour's Lost, 1591 ?

Winter

When icicles hang by the wall,
   And Dick the shepherd blows his nail,
And Tom bears logs into the hall,
   And milk comes frozen home in pail;
When blood is nipp'd, and ways be foul,
Then nightly sings the staring owl
          Tu-whit ;
Tu-who, a merry note,
While greasy Joan doth keel the pot.

When all aloud the wind doth blow,
   And coughing drowns the parson's saw,
And birds sit brooding in the snow,
   And Marian's nose looks red and raw;
When roasted crabs hiss in the bowl,
Then nightly sings the staring owl
          Tu-whit;
Tu-who, a merry note,
While greasy Joan doth keel the pot.

                           W. SHAKESPEARE

From The Two Gentlemen of Verona, 1592 ?

Who is Sylvia? what is she,
   That all our swains commend her ?
Holy, fair, and wise is she ;
   The heaven such grace did lend her,
That she might admired be.

Is she kind as she is fair ?
   For beauty lives with kindness.
Love doth to her eyes repair,
   To help him of his blindness.
And, being help'd, inhabits there.

93

WILLIAM SHAKESPEARE

Then to Sylvia let us sing,
  That Sylvia is excelling;
She excels each mortal thing
  Upon the dull earth dwelling:
To her let us garlands bring.

W. SHAKESPEARE

From A Midsummer Night's Dream, 1595?

Over hill, over dale,
  Thorough bush, thorough brier,
Over park, over pale,
  Thorough flood, thorough fire,
I do wander everywhere,
Swifter than the moon's sphere;
And I serve the fairy queen,
To dew her orbs upon the green.
The cowslips tall her pensioners be:
In their gold coats spots you see;
Those be rubies, fairy favours,
In those freckles live their savours;
I must go seek some dewdrops here,
And hang a pearl in every cowslip's ear.

W. SHAKESPEARE

From The Merchant of Venice, 1596?

Tell me where is fancy bred,
Or in the heart or in the head?
  How begot, how nourished?
      Reply, reply.
It is engender'd in the eyes,
With gazing fed: and fancy dies
In the cradle where it lies.
  Let us all ring fancy's knell:
  I'll begin it,—Ding, dong, bell.
      Ding, dong, bell.

W. SHAKESPEARE

94

WILLIAM SHAKESPEARE

From Much Ado about Nothing, 1599 ?

Sigh no more, ladies, sigh no more,
  Men were deceivers ever,
One foot in sea, and one on shore,
  To one thing constant never;
    Then sigh not so, but let them go,
  And be you blithe and bonny;
Converting all your sounds of woe
  Into Hey nonny, nonny.

Sing no more ditties, sing no moe
  Of dumps so dull and heavy;
The fraud of men was ever so,
  Since summer first was leavy;
    Then sigh not so, but let them go,
  And be you blithe and bonny;
Converting all your sounds of woe
  Into Hey nonny, nonny.

W. SHAKESPEARE

From As You Like It, 1600 ?

Under the greenwood tree
Who loves to lie with me,
And turn his merry note
Unto the sweet bird's throat,
Come hither, come hither, come hither;
  Here shall he see
  No enemy
But winter and rough weather.

Who doth ambition shun,
And loves to live i' the sun,
Seeking the food he eats,
And pleas'd with what he gets,
Come hither, come hither, come hither;
  Here shall he see
  No enemy
But winter and rough weather.

W. SHAKESPEARE

WILLIAM SHAKESPEARE

From **As You Like It, 1600 ?**

Blow, blow, thou winter wind,
Thou art not so unkind
    As man's ingratitude ;
Thy tooth is not so keen,
Because thou art not seen,
    Although thy breath be rude.
Heigh ho! sing heigh ho! unto the green holly :
Most friendship is feigning, most loving mere folly :
    Then heigh ho, the holly !
    This life is most jolly.

Freeze, freeze, thou bitter sky,
That dost not bite so nigh
    As benefits forgot :
Though thou the waters warp,
Thy sting is not so sharp
    As friend remember'd not.
Heigh ho! sing heigh ho! unto the green holly :
Most friendship is feigning, most loving mere folly :
    Then heigh ho, the holly !
    This life is most jolly.

W. SHAKESPEARE

From **As You Like It, 1600 ?**

It was a lover and his lass,
    With a hey, and a ho, and a hey nonino,
That o'er the green cornfield did pass
In the spring time, the only pretty ring time,
When birds do sing, hey ding a ding ding :
    Sweet lovers love the spring.

Between the acres of the rye
These pretty country folks would lie :

This carol they began that hour,
How that a life was but a flower :

WILLIAM SHAKESPEARE

And therefore take the present time,
  With a hey, and a ho, and a hey nonino ;
For love is crowned with the prime
In spring time, the only pretty ring time,
When birds do sing, hey ding a ding ding :
  Sweet lovers love the spring.
                                        W. SHAKESPEARE

From Twelfth Night, 1600 ?

Come away, come away, death,
And in sad cypress let me be laid ;
  Fly away, fly away, breath ;
I am slain by a fair cruel maid.
My shroud of white, stuck all with yew,
        O prepare it !
My part of death, no one so true
        Did share it.

Not a flower, not a flower sweet,
On my black coffin let there be strown ;
  Not a friend, not a friend greet
My poor corpse, where my bones shall be thrown :
A thousand thousand sighs to save,
        Lay me, O where
Sad true lover never find my grave,
        To weep there !
                                        W. SHAKESPEARE

From Twelfth Night, 1600 ?

O mistress mine, where are you roaming ?
O stay and hear, your true-love's coming,
        That can sing both high and low ;
Trip no further, pretty sweeting ;
Journeys end in lovers meeting,
        Every wise man's son doth know.

Y.   G   97

WILLIAM SHAKESPEARE

What is love? 'tis not hereafter;
Present mirth hath present laughter;
    What's to come is still unsure:
In delay there lies no plenty;
Then come kiss me, sweet and twenty,
    Youth's a stuff will not endure.

W. SHAKESPEARE

From **Measure for Measure, 1603?**

Take, O, take those lips away,
That so sweetly were forsworn;
And those eyes, the break of day,
Lights that do mislead the morn:
But my kisses bring again,
       Bring again;
Seals of love, but seal'd in vain,
       Seal'd in vain.

W. SHAKESPEARE

From **The Winter's Tale, 1610?**

Lawn as white as driven snow;
Cyprus black as e'er was crow;
Gloves as sweet as damask roses;
Masks for faces and for noses;
Bugle bracelet, necklace amber,
Perfume for a lady's chamber;
Golden quoifs and stomachers,
For my lads to give their dears:
Pins and poking-sticks of steel,
What maids lack from head to heel:
Come buy of me, come; come buy, come buy;
Buy, lads, or else your lasses cry:
    Come buy.

W. SHAKESPEARE

WILLIAM SHAKESPEARE

From The Winter's Tale, 1610?

> Jog on, jog on, the footpath way,
> And merrily hent the stile-a;
> A merry heart goes all the day,
> Your sad tires in a mile-a.

W. SHAKESPEARE

From Cymbeline, 1610?

> *Gui.* Fear no more the heat o' the sun,
> Nor the furious winter's rages;
> Thou thy worldly task hast done,
> Home art gone and ta'en thy wages:
> Golden lads and girls all must,
> As chimney-sweepers, come to dust.

> *Arv.* Fear no more the frown o' the great,
> Thou art past the tyrant's stroke;
> Care no more to clothe and eat;
> To thee the reed is as the oak:
> The sceptre, learning, physic, must
> All follow this, and come to dust.

> *Gui.* Fear no more the lightning flash,
> *Arv.* Nor the all-dreaded thunder-stone;
> *Gui.* Fear not slander, censure rash;
> *Arv.* Thou hast finished joy and moan;
> *Both.* All lovers young, all lovers must
> Consign to thee, and come to dust.

> *Gui.* No exorciser harm thee!
> *Arv.* Nor no witchcraft charm thee!
> *Gui.* Ghost unlaid forbear thee!
> *Arv.* Nothing ill come near thee!
> *Both.* Quiet consummation have,
> And renowned be thy grave!

W. SHAKESPEARE

G 2

WILLIAM SHAKESPEARE

From **Cymbeline, 1610 ?**

Hark! hark! the lark at heaven's gate sings,
  And Phœbus 'gins arise
His steeds to water at those springs
  On chalic'd flowers that lies;
And winking Mary-buds begin
  To ope their golden eyes;
With everything that pretty is,
  My lady sweet, arise:
      Arise, arise!

W. SHAKESPEARE

From **The Tempest, 1611 ?**

Where the bee sucks, there suck I;
  In a cowslip's bell I lie;
There I couch when owls do cry.
On the bat's back I do fly
After summer merrily.
Merrily, merrily, shall I live now
Under the blossom that hangs on the bough.

W. SHAKESPEARE

From **The Tempest, 1611 ?**

Ariel's Song

Come unto these yellow sands,
  And then take hands:
Courtsied when you have and kissed
  The wild wave whist,
Foot it featly here and there;
And, sweet sprites, the burthen bear.

Burthen.   Hark, hark!
          Bow-wow.
        The watch-dogs bark:
          Bow-wow.

Ariel.   Hark, hark! I hear
The strain of strutting chanticleer
Cry, Cock-a-diddle-dow.

W. SHAKESPEARE

WILLIAM SHAKESPEARE *and* THOMAS NASHE

From The Tempest, 1611?

Full fathom five thy father lies;
   Of his bones are coral made;
Those are pearls that were his eyes;
   Nothing of him that doth fade
But doth suffer a sea-change
Into something rich and strange.
Sea-nymphs hourly ring his knell:
Burthen.   Ding-dong.
Ariel.   Hark now I hear them,—
          Ding-dong, bell.

W. SHAKESPEARE

From Summer's Last Will and Testament, 1600

Spring, the sweet spring, is the year's pleasant king,
Then blooms each thing, then maids dance in a ring,
Cold doth not sting, the pretty birds do sing,
   Cuckoo, jug-jug, pu-we, to-witta-woo.

The palm and may make country houses gay ;
Lambs frisk and play, the shepherds pipe all day ;
And we hear aye birds tune this merry lay,
   Cuckoo, jug-jug, pu-we, to-witta-woo.

The fields breathe sweet, the daisies kiss our feet,
Young lovers meet, old wives a-sunning sit ;
In every street these tunes our ears do greet,
   Cuckoo, jug-jug, pu-we, to-witta-woo.
   Spring, the sweet spring !

T. NASHE

From Summer's Last Will and Testament, 1600

Autumn hath all the summer's fruitful treasure,
Gone is our sport, fled is poor Croydon's pleasure.
Short days, sharp days, long nights come on apace;
Ah, who shall hide us from the winter's face?
Cold doth increase, the sickness will not cease,
And here we lie, God knows, with little ease;
From winter, plague, and pestilence, good Lord, deliver us!

101

NASHE, ESSEX *and* CAMPION

London doth mourn, Lambeth is quite forlorn,
Trades cry, Woe worth that ever they were born!
The want of term is town and city's harm;
Close chambers we do want to keep us warm.
Long banished must we live from our friends.
This low built house will bring us to our ends.
From winter, plague, and pestilence, good Lord, deliver us!

T. NASHE

From Ashmole MS

Verses made in his Trouble

The ways on earth have paths and turnings known;
The ways on sea are gone by needle's light;
The birds of the air the nearest way have flown,
And under earth the moles do cast aright;
A way more hard than these I needs must take,
Where none can teach, nor no man can direct;
Where no man's good for me example makes,
But all men's faults do teach *her* to suspect.
Her thoughts and mine such disproportions have;
All strength of love is infinite in me;
She useth the advantage time and fortune gave
Of worth and power to get the liberty.
Earth, sea, heaven, hell, are subject unto laws,
But I, poor I, must suffer and know no cause.

ROBERT DEVEREUX EARL OF ESSEX

From A Book of Airs, 1601

Follow your Saint, follow with accents sweet.
Haste you sad notes, fall at her flying feet.
There wrapped in cloud of sorrow, pity move,
And tell the ravisher of my soul, I perish for her love.
But if she scorns my never-ceasing pain,
Then burst with sighing in her sight and ne'er return again.

THOMAS CAMPION

All that I sang, still to her praise did tend;
Still she was first, still she my songs did end.
Yet she my love and music both doth fly,
The music that her echo is, and beauty's sympathy;
Then let my notes pursue her scornful flight,
It shall suffice that they were breathed, and died for her
    delight.

                        T. CAMPION

From **A Book of Airs, 1601**

    Thou art not fair for all thy red and white,
    For all those rosy ornaments in thee;
    Thou art not sweet, though made of mere delight,
    Nor fair, nor sweet, unless thou pity me.
    I will not sooth thy fancies; thou shalt prove
    That beauty is no beauty without love.

    Yet love not me; nor seek thou to allure
    My thoughts with beauty, were it more divine.
    Thy smiles and kisses I cannot endure,
    I'll not be wrapt up in those arms of thine.
    Now show it if thou be a woman right,—
    Embrace, and kiss, and love me, in despite.

                        T. CAMPION

From **A Book of Airs, 1601**

    I care not for these ladies,
    That must be wooed and prayed;
    Give me kind Amaryllis,
    The wanton country maid.
    Nature art disdaineth,
    Her beauty is her own.
        Her, when we court and kiss,
        She cries Forsooth, let go!
        But when we come where comfort is,
        She never will say No!

THOMAS CAMPION

If I love Amaryllis
She gives me fruit and flowers;
But if we love these ladies,
We must give golden showers.
Give them gold, that sell love;
Give me the nut-brown lass,
    Who, when we court and kiss,
    She cries Forsooth, let go!
    But when we come where comfort is,
    She never will say No!

These ladies must have pillows
And beds by strangers wrought;
Give me a bower of willows,
Of moss and leaves unbought,
And fresh Amaryllis,
With milk and honey fed,
    Who, when we court and kiss,
    She cries, Forsooth, let go!
    But when we come where comfort is,
    She never will say No!

T. Campion

From A Book of Airs, 1601

When thou must home, to shades of underground,
And there arrived, a new admired guest,
The beauteous spirits do engirt thee round,
White Iope, blithe Helen, and the rest,
To hear the stories of thy finisht love
From that smooth tongue, whose music hell can move;

Then wilt thou speak of banqueting delights,
Of masks and revels which sweet youth did make,
Of tourneys and great challenges of knights,
And all these triumphs for thy beauty's sake.
When thou hast told these honours done to thee,
Then tell, O tell, how thou didst murther me.

T. Campion

THOMAS CAMPION

From A Book of Airs, 1601

My sweetest Lesbia, let us live and love ;
And though the sager sort our deeds reprove,
Let us not weigh them, heaven's great lamps do dive
Into their west, and straight again revive.
But soon as once set is our little light,
Then must we sleep one ever-during night.

If all would lead their lives in love like me,
Then bloody swords and armour should not be.
No drum nor trumpet peaceful sleeps should move,
Unless alarm came from the camp of Love.
But fools do live and waste their little light,
And seek with pain their ever-during night.

When timely death my life and fortune ends,
Let not my hearse be vext with mourning friends.
But let all lovers rich in triumph come,
And with sweet pastimes grace my happy tomb.
And Lesbia, close up thou my little light,
And crown with love my ever-during night.

T. CAMPION

From Observations in the Art of English Poesy, 1602

Rose-cheeked *Laura*, come :
Sing thou smoothly with thy beauty's
Silent music, either other
Sweetly gracing.

Lovely forms do flow
From concent divinely framed :
Heaven is music, and thy beauty's
Birth is heavenly.

These dull notes we sing
Discords need for helps to grace them ;
Only beauty purely loving
Knows no discord,

THOMAS CAMPION

But still moves delight,
Like clear springs renew'd by flowing,
Ever perfect, ever in them-
Selves eternal.

T. CAMPION

From Two Books of Airs, 1613

Though your strangeness frets my heart,
    Yet may not I complain;
    You persuade me ''tis but art;
    That secret love must feign.'
    If another you affect,
    ''Tis but a show, to avoid suspect.'
Is this fair excusing? O, no! all is abusing.

Your wished sight if I desire,
    Suspitions you pretend;
    Causeless you yourself retire;
    While I in vain attend.
    'This a lover whets' you say,
    'Still made more eager by delay.'
Is this fair excusing? O, no! all is abusing.

When another holds your hand,
    You swear, 'I hold your heart.'
    When my rivals close do stand
    And I sit far apart;
    'I am nearer yet than they,
    Hid in your bosom'; as you say.
Is this fair excusing? O, no! all is abusing.

Would my rival then I were,
    Or else your secret friend;
    So much lesser should I fear,
    And not so much attend.
    They enjoy you, every one;
    Yet I must seem your friend alone.
Is this fair excusing? O, no! all is abusing.

T. CAMPION

THOMAS CAMPION

From Two Books of Airs, 1613

Come! you pretty false-ey'd wanton,
  Leave your crafty smiling.
Think you to escape me now,
  With slippery words beguiling?
No, you mocked me the other day;
  When you got loose you fled away;
But, since I have caught you now,
  I'll clip your wings for flying;
Smothering kisses fast I'll heap,
  And keep you so from crying.

Sooner may you count the stars,
  And number hail down-pouring,
Tell the osiers of the Thames,
  Or Goodwin's sands devouring,
Than the thick-showered kisses here,
  Which now thy tired lips must bear.
Such a harvest never was,
  So rich and full of pleasure;
But 'tis spent as soon as reaped,
  So trustless is love's treasure.

Would it were dumb midnight now,
  When all the world lies sleeping;
Would this place some desert were,
  Which no man hath in keeping.
My desires should then be safe,
  And when you cried, then would I laugh:
But if aught might breed offence,
  Love only should be blamed;
I would live your servant still,
  And you my Saint unnamed.

T. CAMPION

THOMAS CAMPION

From **The Third Book of Airs, 1617**

Thrice toss these oaken ashes in the air,
Thrice sit thou mute in this enchanted chair;
And thrice three times tie up this true-love's knot,
And murmur soft 'She will, or she will not.'

Go, burn these poisonous weeds in yon blue fire,
These screech-owl's feathers, and this prickling briar,
This cypress gathered at a dead man's grave;
That all thy fears and cares an end may have.

Then come you Fairies, dance with me a round;
Melt her hard heart with your melodious sound.
In vain are all the charms I can devise,
She hath an Art to break them with her eyes.

T. CAMPION

From **The Third Book of Airs, 1617**

Never love unless you can
Bear with all the faults of man.
Men sometimes will jealous be,
Though but little cause they see,
    And hang the head as discontent,
    And speak what straight they will repent.

Men that but one Saint adore,
Make a show of love to more;
Beauty must be scorned in none,
Though but truly served in one.
    For what is courtship but disguise?
    True hearts may have dissembling eyes.

Men when their affairs require,
Must awhile themselves retire;
Sometimes hunt, and sometimes hawk,
And not ever sit and talk.
    If these and such like you can bear
    Then like, and love, and never fear.

T. CAMPION

THOMAS CAMPION *and* SIR HENRY WOTTON

From The Third Book of Airs, 1617

Now winter nights enlarge
The number of their hours ;
And clouds their storms discharge
Upon the airy towers.
Let now the chimneys blaze,
And cups o'er flow with wine,
Let well-tuned words amaze
With harmony divine.
Now yellow waxen lights
Shall wait on honey love ;
While youthful revels, masques, and courtly sights,
Sleep's leaden spells remove.

This time doth well dispense
    With lovers' long discourse ;
Much speech hath some defence,
    Though beauty no remorse.
All do not all things well ;
    Some measures comely tread,
Some knotted riddles tell,
    Some poems smoothly read.
The summer hath his joys,
    And winter his delights ;
Though love and all his pleasures are but toys,
    They shorten tedious nights.

                              T. CAMPION

From Reliquiae Wottonianae, 1651

On his Mistress.   The Queen of Bohemia.

You meaner beauties of the night,
That poorly satisfy our eyes,
More by your number, than your light,
You common people of the skies ;
    What are you when the sun shall rise ?

109

SIR HENRY WOTTON *and* T. HEYWOOD

You curious chanters of the wood,
That warble forth Dame Nature's lays,
Thinking your voices understood
By your weak accents; what's your praise,
  When Philomel her voice shall raise?

You violets that first appear,
By your pure purple mantles known,
Like the proud virgins of the year,
As if the spring were all your own;
  What are you when the rose is blown?

So, when my mistress shall be seen
In form and beauty of her mind,
By virtue first, then choice, a Queen,
Tell me if she were not design'd
  The eclipse and glory of her kind?

Sir H. Wotton

From The Rape of Lucrece, 1608—1630

Pack clouds, away, and welcome, day,
  With night we banish sorrow.
Sweet air, blow soft; mount, lark, aloft
  To give my love good-morrow.
Wings from the wind to please her mind,
  Notes from the lark I'll borrow;
Bird, prune thy wing. Nightingale, sing,
  To give my love good-morrow.
    To give my love good-morrow,
    Notes from them all I'll borrow.

Wake from thy nest, robin red-breast,
  Sing, birds, in every furrow.
And from each bill let music shrill
  Give my fair love good-morrow!
Blackbird and thrush in every bush,
  Stare, linnet, and cocksparrow,
You pretty elves, amongst yourselves
  Sing my fair love good-morrow.
    To give my love good-morrow,
    Sing, birds, in every furrow!

Thomas Heywood

BEN JONSON

From **Cynthia's Revels, 1601—1616**

Slow, slow, fresh fount, keep time with my salt tears;
  Yet slower yet; O, faintly gentle springs;
List to the heavy part the music bears,
  Woe weeps out her division when she sings.
      Droop herbs and flowers,
      Fall grief in showers,
      Our beauties are not ours;
       O, I could still,
Like melting snow upon some craggy hill,
      Drop, drop, drop, drop,
Since nature's pride is now a withered daffodil.

BEN JONSON

From **Cynthia's Revels, 1601—1616**

O, that joy so soon should waste!
      Or so sweet a bliss
      As a kiss
Might not for ever last!
So sugar'd, so melting, so soft, so delicious,
  The dew that lies on roses,
    When the morn herself discloses,
      Is not so precious.
O rather than I would it smother,
Were I to taste such another,
      It should be my wishing
      That I might die kissing.

BEN JONSON

From **Cynthia's Revels, 1601—1616**

    Queen and huntress, chaste and fair,
    Now the sun is laid to sleep,
    Seated in thy silver chair,
    State in wonted manner keep:
      Hesperus entreats thy light,
      Goddess, excellently bright.

BEN JONSON

Earth, let not thy envious shade
Dare itself to interpose;
Cynthia's shining orb was made
Heav'n to clear, when day did close:
    Bless us then with wished sight,
    Goddess excellently bright.

Lay thy bow of pearl apart,
And thy crystal-shining quiver;
Give unto the flying hart
Space to breathe, how short soever:
    Thou that mak'st a day of night,
    Goddess excellently bright.

BEN JONSON

From Volpone, 1607

Come, my Celia, let us prove,
While we may, the sports of love;
Time will not be ours for ever:
He at length our good will sever.
Spend not then his gifts in vain.
Suns that set, may rise again;
But if once we lose this light,
'Tis with us perpetual night.
Why should we defer our joys?
Fame and rumour are but toys.
Cannot we delude the eyes
Of a few poor household spies?
Or his easier ears beguile,
Thus removed by our wile?
'Tis no sin love's fruits to steal,
But the sweet thefts to reveal:
To be taken, to be seen,
These have crimes accounted been.

BEN JONSON

BEN JONSON

From **The Silent Woman, 1609—1616**

> Still to be neat, still to be drest,
> As you were going to a feast;
> Still to be powdered, still perfumed;
> Lady it is to be presumed,
> Though art's hid causes are not found,
> All is not sweet, all is not sound.
>
> Give me a look, give me a face,
> That makes simplicity a grace;
> Robes loosely flowing, hair as free;
> Such sweet neglect more taketh me,
> Than all the adulteries of art,
> They strike mine eyes, but not my heart.

BEN JONSON

From **The Forest, folio 1616**

To Celia

> Drink to me only with thine eyes,
>   And I will pledge with mine;
> Or leave a kiss but in the cup,
>   And I'll not look for wine.
> The thirst that from the soul doth rise,
>   Doth ask a drink divine;
> But might I of Jove's nectar sup,
>   I would not change for thine.
>
> I sent thee late a rosy wreath,
>   Not so much honouring thee,
> As giving it a hope that there
>   It could not wither'd be;
> But thou thereon didst only breathe
>   And sent'st it back to me;
> Since when it grows, and smells, I swear,
>   Not of itself, but thee.

BEN JONSON

BEN JONSON

From **The Forest,** folio 1616

To Heaven

Good and great God! can I not think of Thee,
But it must straight my melancholy be?
Is it interpreted in me disease,
That laden with my sins, I seek for ease?
O! be Thou witness, that the reins dost know
And hearts of all, if I be sad for show,
And judge me after, if I dare pretend
To aught but grace, or aim at other end.
As Thou art all, so be Thou all to me,
First, midst, and last, converted One and Three;
My Faith, my Hope, my Love; and in this state,
My Judge, my Witness, and my Advocate.
Where have I been this while exiled from Thee,
And whither rapt, now Thou but stoop'st to me?
Dwell, dwell here still! O! being everywhere,
How can I doubt to find Thee ever here?
I know my state, both full of shame and scorn,
Conceived in sin, and unto labour born,
Standing with fear, and must with horror fall,
And destined unto judgment after all.
I feel my griefs too, and there scarce is ground
Upon my flesh to inflict another wound.
Yet dare I not complain or wish for death,
With holy PAUL, lest it be thought the breath
Of discontent; or that these prayers be
For weariness of life, not love of Thee.

BEN JONSON

From **Epigrams,** folio 1616

Epitaph on Elizabeth, L. H

Would'st thou hear what man can say
In a little? Reader, stay.
Underneath this stone doth lie
As much beauty as could die,

BEN JONSON

Which in life did harbour give
To more virtue than doth live.
If, at all, she had a fault
Leave it buried in this vault.
One name was Elizabeth,
The other let it sleep with death.
Fitter, where it died, to tell,
Than that it lived at all.   Farewell.

BEN JONSON

From Pan's Anniversary, 1624—1640

1. Of Pan we sing, the best of singers, Pan,
    That taught us swains how first to tune our lays,
    And on the pipe, more airs than Phoebus can.
Chorus. Hear! O you groves, and hills resound his praise.

2. Of Pan we sing, the best of leaders, Pan,
    That leads the Naiads and the Dryads forth,
    And to their dances more than Hermes can.
Chorus. Hear! O you groves, and hills resound his worth.

3. Of Pan we sing, the best of hunters, Pan,
    That drives the hart to seek unused ways,
    And in the chase more than Silvanus can.
Chorus. Hear! O you groves, and hills resound his praise.

4. Of Pan we sing, the best of shepherds, Pan,
    That keeps our flocks and us, and both leads forth
    To better pastures than great Pales can.
Chorus. Hear! O you groves, and hills resound his worth.
    And while his powers and praises thus we sing,
    The valleys let rebound, and all the rivers ring.

BEN JONSON

From The New Inn, 1629—1631

It was a beauty that I saw
So pure, so perfect, as the frame
Of all the universe was lame
To that one figure, could I draw,
Or give least line of it a law!

BEN JONSON

A skein of silk without a knot,
A fair march made without a halt,
A curious form without a fault,
A printed book without a blot,
All beauty, and without a spot !

BEN JONSON

From **Underwoods**, folio **1640**

Her man described by her own dictamen

Of your trouble, Ben, to ease me,
I will tell what man would please me.
I would have him, if I could,
Noble, or of greater blood.
Titles, I confess, do take me,
And a woman God did make me.
French to boot, at least in fashion,
And his manners of that nation.
Young I'd have him too, and fair,
Yet a man ; with crisped hair
Cast in thousand snares and rings
For love's fingers and his wings ;
Chestnut colour, or more slack,
Gold, upon a ground of black.
Venus and Minerva's eyes,
For he must look wanton-wise.

   Eyebrows bent like Cupid's bow,
Front an ample field of snow ;
Even nose and cheek withal,
Smooth as is the billiard ball.
Chin as woolly as the peach ;
And his lip should kissing teach,
Till he cherished too much beard,
And made Love or me a-feard.
He would have a hand as soft
As the down, and show it oft ;
Skin as smooth as any rush,
And so thin to see a blush

BEN JONSON

Rising through it ere it came.
All his blood should be a flame
Quickly fired as in beginners
In Love's school, and yet no sinners.
　'Twere too long to speak of all;
What we harmony do call
In a body should be there.
Well he should his clothes, too, wear;
Yet no tailor help to make him;
Drest, you still for man should take him·
And not think he had eat a stake,
Or were set up in a brake.
　Valiant he should be as fire,
Shewing danger more than ire.
Bounteous as the clouds to earth,
And as honest as his birth.
All his actions to be such,
As to do nothing too much;
Nor o'er-praise, nor yet condemn,
Nor out-value, nor contemn;
Nor do wrongs, nor wrongs receive,
Nor tie knots, nor knots unweave;
And from baseness to be free,
As he durst love Truth and me.
　　　Such a man with every part,
　　　I could give my very heart;
　　　But of one if short he came,
　　　I can rest me where I am.

BEN JONSON

From The Celebration of Charis, folio 1640

Her Triumph

See the chariot at hand here of Love,
　Wherein my Lady rideth!
Each that draws is a swan or a dove,
　And well the car Love guideth.
As she goes, all hearts do duty
　　　　　Unto her beauty;

BEN JONSON

And enamour'd do wish, so they might
                  But enjoy such a sight,
That they still were to run by her side,
Through swords, through seas, whither she would ride.

Do but look on her eyes, they do light
  All that Love's world compriseth!
Do but look on her hair, it is bright
  As Love's star when it riseth!
Do but mark, her forehead's smoother
              Than words that soothe her:
And from her arched brows such a grace
             Sheds itself through the face,
As alone there triumphs to the life
All the gain, all the good of the elements' strife.

Have you seen but a bright lily grow
  Before rude hands have touch'd it?
Have you mark'd but the fall of the snow
  Before the soil hath smutch'd it?
Have you felt the wool of the beaver?
             Or swan's down ever?
Or have smelt o' the bud of the briar?
             Or the nard in the fire?
Or have tasted the bag of the bee?
O so white! O so soft! O so sweet is she!

BEN JONSON

From **Underwoods**, folio **1640**

Against Jealousy

Wretched and foolish jealousy,
How cam'st thou thus to enter me?
    I ne'er was of this kind,
    Nor have I yet the narrow mind
    To vent that poor desire,
That others should not warm them at my fire.
    I wish the sun should shine
On all men's fruit and flowers as well as mine.

118

BEN JONSON

But under the disguise of love,
Thou say'st thou only cam'st to prove
    What my affections were.
    Think'st thou that love is helped by fear?
    Go! get thee quickly forth,
Love's sickness, and his noted want of worth.
    Seek doubting men to please,
I ne'er will owe my health to a disease.

BEN JONSON

From **Underwoods,** folio 1640

An Ode to Sir Lucius Cary and Sir H. Morison

For what is life, if measured by the space
    Not by the act?
Or masked man, if valued by his face,
    Above his fact?
    Here's one outlived his peers,
    And told forth fourscore years;
    He vexed time, and busied the whole state;
    Troubled both foes and friends;
    But ever to no ends:
    What did this stirrer, but die late?
How well at twenty had he fallen or stood!
For three of his fourscore, he did no good.

    It is not growing like a tree
    In bulk, doth make men better be;
Or standing long an oak, three hundred year,
To fall a log at last, dry, bald, and sear:
    A lily of a day
    Is fairer far in May,
    Although it fall and die that night;
    It was the plant, and flower of light.
In small proportions we just beauties see;
And in short measures, life may perfect be.

BEN JONSON

BEN JONSON *and* JOHN DONSON

From Wit's Recreations, 1641

On the death of Mary Countess of Pembroke

Underneath this sable hearse
Lies the subject of all verse,
SIDNEY's sister, PEMBROKE's mother;
Death, ere thou hast killed another,
Fair and learn'd, good as she,
Time shall throw a dart at thee.

BEN JONSON

From Poems, 1633—1669

The Good-Morrow

I wonder, by my troth, what thou and I
Did, till we loved? were we not wean'd till then?
But suck'd on country pleasures, childishly?
Or snorted we in the Seven Sleepers' den?
'Twas so; but this, all pleasures fancies be;
If ever any beauty I did see,
Which I desired, and got, 'twas but a dream of thee.

And now good-morrow to our waking souls,
Which watch not one another out of fear;
For love all love of other sights controls,
And makes one little room an everywhere.
Let sea-discoverers to new worlds have gone;
Let maps to other, worlds on worlds have shown;
Let us possess one world; each hath one, and is one.

My face in thine eye, thine in mine appears,
And true plain hearts do in the faces rest;
Where can we find two better hemispheres
Without sharp north, without declining west?
Whatever dies, was not mix'd equally;
If our two loves be one, or thou and I
Love so alike that none can slacken, none can die.

J. DONNE

JOHN DONNE

From Poems, 1633—1669

The Undertaking

I have done one braver thing
    Than all the Worthies did ;
And yet a braver thence doth spring,
    Which is, to keep that hid.

It were but madness now to impart
    The skill of specular stone,
When he, which can have learn'd the art
    To cut it, can find none.

So, if I now should utter this,
    Others—because no more
Such stuff to work upon there is—
    Would love but as before.

But he who loveliness within
    Hath found, all outward loathes,
For he who colour loves, and skin,
    Loves but their oldest clothes.

If, as I have, you also do
    Virtue in woman see,
And dare love that, and say so too,
    And forget the He and She ;

And if this love, though placed so,
    From profane men you hide,
Which will no faith on this bestow,
    Or, if they do, deride ;

Then you have done a braver thing
    Than all the Worthies did ;
And a braver thence will spring,
    Which is, to keep that hid.

J. DONNE

121

JOHN DONNE

From Poems, 1633—1669

Song

Sweetest love, I do not go
  For weariness of thee,
Nor in hope the world can show
  A fitter love for me;
    But since that I
At the last must part, 'tis best,
Thus to use myself in jest
  By feigned deaths to die.

Yesternight the sun went hence,
  And yet is here to-day;
He hath no desire nor sense,
  Nor half so short a way;
    Then fear not me,
But believe that I shall make
Speedier journeys, since I take
  More wings and spurs than he.

O how feeble is man's power,
  That if good fortune fall,
Cannot add another hour,
  Nor a lost hour recall;
    But come bad chance,
And we join to it our strength,
And we teach it art and length,
  Itself o'er us to advance.

When thou sigh'st, thou sigh'st not wind,
  But sigh'st my soul away;
When thou weep'st, unkindly kind,
  My life's blood doth decay.
    It cannot be
That thou lovest me as thou say'st,
If in thine my life thou waste,
  That art the best of me.

JOHN DONNE

Let not thy divining heart
  Forethink me any ill;
Destiny may take thy part,
  And may thy fears fulfil.
    But think that we
Are but turn'd aside to sleep.
They who one another keep
  Alive, ne'er parted be.

J. DONNE

From Poems, 1633—1669

Love's Deity

I long to talk with some old lover's ghost,
  Who died before the god of love was born.
I cannot think that he, who then loved most
  Sunk so low as to love one which did scorn.
But since this god produced a destiny,
And that vice-nature, custom, lets it be,
  I must love her that loves not me.

Sure, they which made him god, meant not so much,
  Nor he in his young godhead practised it.
But when an even flame two hearts did touch,
  His office was indulgently to fit
Actives to passives. Correspondency
Only his subject was; it cannot be
  Love, till I love her, who loves me.

But every modern god will now extend
  His vast prerogative as far as Jove.
To rage, to lust, to write to, to commend,
  All is the purlieu of the god of love.
O! were we waken'd by this tyranny
To ungod this child again, it could not be
  I should love her, who loves not me.

JOHN DONNE

Rebel and atheist too, why murmur I,
    As though I felt the worst that love could do?
Love may make me leave loving, or might try
    A deeper plague, to make her love me too;
Which, since she loves before, I'm loth to see.
Falsehood is worse than hate; and that must be,
    If she whom I love, should love me.

J. DONNE

From Poems, 1633—1669

The Relic

When my grave is broke up again
Some second guest to entertain,
    —For graves have learn'd that woman-head,
    To be to more than one a bed—
        And he that digs it, spies
A bracelet of bright hair about the bone,
        Will not he let us alone,
And think that there a loving couple lies,
Who thought that this device might be some way
To make their souls at the last busy day
Meet at this grave, and make a little stay?

If this fall in a time, or land,
Where mass-devotion doth command,
    Then he that digs us up will bring
    Us to the bishop or the king,
        To make us relics; then
Thou shalt be a Mary Magdalen, and I
        A something else thereby;
All women shall adore us, and some men.
And, since at such time miracles are sought,
I would have that age by this paper taught
What miracles we harmless lovers wrought.

JOHN DONNE

First we loved well and faithfully,
Yet knew not what we loved, nor why;
Difference of sex we never knew,
No more than guardian angels do;
    Coming and going we
Perchance might kiss, but not between those meals;
    Our hands ne'er touch'd the seals,
Which nature, injured by late law, sets free.
These miracles we did; but now alas!
All measure, and all language, I should pass,
Should I tell what a miracle she was.

J. DONNE

From Poems, 1633—1669

*Elegy on his Mistress when she wished to accompany
him in the guise of a page*

By our first strange and fatal interview,
By all desires which thereof did ensue,
By our long starving hopes, by that remorse
Which my words' masculine persuasive force
Begot in thee, and by the memory
Of hurts, which spies and rivals threaten'd me,
I calmly beg. But by thy father's wrath,
By all pains, which want and divorcement hath,
I conjure thee, and all the oaths which I
And thou have sworn to seal joint constancy,
Here I unswear, and overswear them thus;
Thou shalt not love by ways so dangerous.
Temper, O fair love, love's impetuous rage;
Be my true mistress still, not my feign'd page.
I'll go, and, by thy kind leave, leave behind
Thee, only worthy to nurse in my mind
Thirst to come back; O! if thou die before,
My soul from other lands to thee shall soar.
Thy else almighty beauty cannot move
Rage from the seas, nor thy love teach them love,

JOHN DONNE

Nor tame wild Boreas' harshness; thou hast read
How roughly he in pieces shivered
Fair Orithea, whom he swore he loved.
Fall ill or good, 'tis madness to have proved
Dangers unurged; feed on this flattery,
That absent lovers one in th' other be.
Dissemble nothing, not a boy, nor change
Thy body's habit, nor mind; be not strange
To thyself only. All will spy in thy face
A blushing womanly discovering grace.
Richly clothed apes are call'd apes, and as soon
Eclipsed as bright, we call the moon the moon.
Men of France, changeable chameleons,
Spitals of diseases, shops of fashions,
Love's fuellers, and the rightest company
Of players, which upon the world's stage be,
Will quickly know thee, and no less, alas!
Th' indifferent Italian, as we pass
His warm land, well content to think thee page,
Will hunt thee with such lust, and hideous rage,
As Lot's fair guests were vex'd. But none of these,
Nor spongy hydroptic Dutch shall thee displease,
If thou stay here. O stay here, for for thee
England is only a worthy gallery,
To walk in expectation, till from thence
Our greatest king call thee to his presence.
When I am gone, dream me some happiness;
Nor let thy looks our long-hid love confess;
Nor praise, nor dispraise me, nor bless nor curse
Openly love's force, nor in bed fright thy nurse
With midnight's startings, crying out, O! O!
Nurse, O! my love is slain; I saw him go
O'er the white Alps alone; I saw him, I,
Assail'd, fight, taken, stabb'd, bleed, fall, and die.
Augur me better chance, except dread Jove
Think it enough for me to have had thy love.

J. DONNE

JOHN DONNE *and* ANON

From Poems, 1633—1669

A Hymn to God the Father

Wilt Thou forgive that sin where I begun,
　Which was my sin, though it were done before?
Wilt Thou forgive that sin, through which I run,
　And do run still, though still I do deplore?
　　When Thou hast done, Thou hast not done,
　　　For I have more.

Wilt Thou forgive that sin which I have won
　Others to sin, and made my sin their door?
Wilt Thou forgive that sin which I did shun
　A year or two, but wallowed in a score?
　　When Thou hast done, Thou hast not done,
　　　For I have more.

I have a sin of fear, that when I have spun
　My last thread, I shall perish on the shore;
But swear by Thyself, that at my death Thy Son
　Shall shine as he shines now, and heretofore;
　　And, having done that, Thou hast done;
　　　I fear no more.

J. DONNE

From R. *Jones's* First Book of Songs, 1601

If fathers knew but how to leave
　Their children wit, as they do wealth,
And could constrain them to receive
　That physic which brings perfect health,
The world would not admiring stand
A woman's face and woman's hand.

Women confess they must obey,
　We men will needs be servants still;
We kiss their hands, and what they say
　We must commend be it ne'er so ill:
Thus we, like fools, admiring stand
Her pretty foot and pretty hand.

ANON

We blame their pride which we increase
  By making mountains of a mouse;
We praise because we know we please;
  Poor women are too credulous
To think that we admiring stand
A foot, or face, or foolish hand.

ANON

From R. Jones's Ultimum Vale, 1608

Think'st thou, Kate, to put me down
With a 'No' or with a frown?
Since Love holds my heart in bands
I must do as Love commands.

Love commands the hands to dare
When the tongue of speech is spare,
Chiefest lesson in Love's school,
'Put it in adventure, fool!'

Fools are they that fainting flinch
For a squeak, a scratch, a pinch;
Women's words have double sense;
'Stand away,' a simple fence.

If thy mistress swear she'll cry,
Fear her not, she'll swear and lie;
Such sweet oaths no sorrow bring
Till the prick of conscience sting.

ANON

From Capt. Tobias Hume's First Part of Airs, 1605

Fain would I change that note
  To which fond love hath charmed me
Long long to sing by rote,
  Fancying that that harmed me.
Yet when this thought doth come,
'Love is the perfect sum
    Of all delight,'
I have no other choice
Either for pen or voice,
    To sing or write.

ANON *and* RICHARD BARNFIELD

O Love! they wrong thee much
    That say thy sweet is bitter,
When thy ripe fruit is such
    As nothing can be sweeter.
Fair house of joy and bliss,
Where truest pleasure is,
      I do adore thee;
I know thee what thou art;
I serve thee with my heart;
      And fall before thee.

ANON

From Ford's Music of Sundry kinds, 1607

There is a Lady sweet and kind,
Was never face so pleased my mind;
I did but see her passing by,
And yet I love her till I die.

Her gesture, motion, and her smiles,
Her wit, her voice, my heart beguiles,
Beguiles my heart, I know not why,
And yet I love her till I die.

   *   *   *   *   *

Cupid is winged and doth range,
Her country so my love doth change;
But change she earth or change she sky,
Yet will I love her till I die.

ANON

From The Passionate Pilgrim, 1599

My flocks feed not, my ewes breed not,
My rams speed not, all is amiss;
Love is dying, faith's defying,
Heart's renying, causer of this.
All my merry jigs are quite forgot,
All my lady's love is lost, God wot;

RICHARD BARNFIELD *and* FRANCIS DAVISON

Where her faith was firmly fixed in love,
There a 'Nay' is placed without remove.
One silly cross wrought all my loss;
   O frowning Fortune, cursed fickle dame!
For now I see inconstancy
   More in women than in men remain.

In black mourn I, all fears scorn I,
Love hath forlorn me, living in thrall.
Heart is bleeding, all help needing;
O cruel speeding, fraughted with gall.
My shepherd's pipe can sound no deal,
My wether's bell rings doleful knell;
My curtail dog that wont to have played,
Plays not at all, but seems afraid;
With sighs so deep, procures to weep,
   In howling wise, to see my doleful plight.
How sighs resound, through heartless ground,
   Like a thousand vanquish'd men in bloody fight.

Clear wells spring not, sweet birds sing not,
Green plants bring not forth their dye.
Herds stand weeping, flocks all sleeping,
Nymphs back peeping, fearfully.
All our pleasure known to us poor swains,
All our merry meetings on the plains,
All our evening sport from us is fled,
All our love is lost, for love is dead.
Farewell sweet love, thy like ne'er was
   For a sweet content, the cause of all my woe,
Poor Corydon must live alone
   Other help for him I see that there is none!

R. B<small>ARNFIELD</small>

From A Poetical Rapsody, 1602—1611

Lady! you are with beauties so enriched
   Of body and of mind,
   As I can hardly find
Which of them all hath most my heart bewitched.

Whether your skin so white, so smooth, so tender,
    Or face well formed and fair,
    Or heart-ensnaring hair,
Or dainty hand, or leg and foot so slender;

Or whether your sharp wit and lively spirit,
    Where pride can find no place,
    Or your enchanting grace,
Or speech which doth true eloquence inherit.

Most lovely all, and each of them doth move me
    More than words can express;
    But yet I must confess
I love you most, because you please to love me.

F. Davison

From A Poetical Rapsody, 1602—1611

Love the only price of Love

The fairest pearls that northern seas do breed,
For precious stones from eastern coasts are sold.
Nought yields the earth that from exchange is free'd,
Gold values all, and all things value gold.
    Where goodness wants an equal change to make,
    There greatness serves or number place doth take.

No mortal thing can bear so high a price,
But that with mortal thing it may be bought.
The corn of Sicil buys the western spice,
French wine of us, of them our cloth is sought.
    No pearls, no gold, no stones, no corn, no spice,
    No cloth, no wine, of love can pay the price.

What thing is love, which nought can countervail?
Nought save itself, ev'n such a thing is love.
All worldly wealth in worth as far doth fail,
As lowest earth doth yield to heaven above.
    Divine is love, and scorneth worldly pelf,
    And can be bought with nothing, but with self.

I 2

A. W

Such is the price my loving heart would pay,
Such is the pay thy love doth claim as due.
Thy due is love, which I, poor I, assay
In vain assay to quite with friendship true;
  True is my love, and true shall ever be,
  And truest love is far too base for thee.

Love but thyself, and love thyself alone,
For, save thyself, none can thy love requite.
All mine thou hast, but all as good as none,
My small desert must take a lower flight.
  Yet if thou wilt vouchsafe my heart such bliss,
  Accept it for thy prisoner as it is.

A. W

A defiance to disdainful love

Now have I learn'd with much ado at last
  By true disdain to kill desire;
This was the mark at which I shot so fast,
  Unto this height I did aspire.
Proud love, now do thy worst and spare not,
For thee and all thy shafts I care not.

What hast thou left wherewith to move my mind?
  What life to quicken dead desire?
I count thy words and oaths as light as wind,
  I feel no heat in all thy fire.
Go change thy bow, and get a stronger,
Go break thy shafts and buy thee longer.

In vain thou bait'st thy hook with beauty's blaze,
  In vain thy wanton eyes allure;
These are but toys for them that love to gaze,
  I know what harm thy looks procure.
Some strange conceit must be devised,
Or thou and all thy skill despised.

A. W

A. W *and* THOMAS DEKKER

From A Poetical Rapsody, 1602—1611

Dispraise of love and lovers' follies

If love be life, I long to die,
  Live they that list for me;
And he that gains the most thereby,
  A fool at least shall be.
But he that feels the sorest fits,
'Scapes with no less than loss of wits;
    Unhappy life they gain,
    Which love do entertain.

In day by feigned looks they live,
  By lying dreams in night;
Each frown a deadly wound doth give,
  Each smile a false delight.
If't hap their lady pleasant seem,
It is for other's love they deem;
    If void she seem of joy,
    Disdain doth make her coy.

Such is the peace that lovers find,
  Such is the life they lead.
Blown here and there with every wind,
  Like flowers in the mead;
Now war, now peace, now war again,
Desire, despair, delight, disdain;
    Though dead, in midst of life,
    In peace, and yet at strife.

A. W

From Patient Grissell, 1603

Art thou poor, yet hast thou golden slumbers?
        O sweet content.
Art thou rich, yet is thy mind perplex'd?
        O punishment.
Dost thou laugh to see how fools are vex'd
To add to golden numbers, golden numbers?

THOMAS DEKKER

O sweet content, O sweet, O sweet content.
  Work apace, apace, apace, apace;
  Honest labour bears a lovely face;
Then hey nonny nonny, hey nonny nonny!

Canst drink the waters of the crisped spring?
          O sweet content.
Swimm'st thou in wealth, yet sink'st in thine own tears?
          O punishment.
Then he that patiently want's burden bears,
No burden bears, but is a king, a king.
O sweet content, O sweet, O sweet content.
  Work apace, apace, apace, apace;
  Honest labour bears a lovely face;
Then hey nonny nonny, hey nonny nonny!

T. DEKKER

From **Patient Grissell, 1603**

    Golden slumbers kiss your eyes,
    Smiles awake you when you rise;
    Sleep pretty wantons do not cry,
    And I will sing a lullaby;
    Rock them, rock them, lullaby.

    Care is heavy, therefore sleep you;
    You are care, and care must keep you;
    Sleep pretty wantons, do not cry,
    And I will sing a lullaby;
    Rock them, rock them, lullaby.

T. DEKKER

From **Patient Grissell, 1603**

Beauty arise! show forth thy glorious shining.
Thine eyes feed love, for them he standeth pining.
Honour and youth attend to do their duty
To thee, their only sovereign beauty.

THOMAS DEKKER

Beauty arise! whilst we thy servants sing
Io to Hymen, wedlock's jocund king.
Io to Hymen, Io, Io, sing,
Of wedlock, love, and youth, is Hymen king!

Beauty arise! thy glorious lights display,
Whilst we sing Io, glad to see this day.
Io to Hymen, Io, Io, sing,
Of wedlock, love, and youth, is Hymen king!

T. DEKKER

From The Sun's Darling, 1623—1656

Haymakers, rakers, reapers, and mowers,
    Wait on your summer queen.
Dress up with musk-rose her eglantine bowers,
    Daffodils strew the green.
        Sing, dance, and play,
        'Tis holiday.
The Sun does bravely shine
On our ears of corn.
        Rich as a pearl
        Comes every girl,
This is mine, this is mine, this is mine;
Let us die, ere away they be borne.

Bow to the Sun, to our queen, and that fair one,
    Come to behold our sports.
Each bonny lass here is counted a rare one,
    As those in princes' courts.
        These and we
        With country glee,
Will teach the woods to resound,
And the hills with echo's Hollo!
        Skipping lambs
        Their bleating dams
'Mongst kids shall trip it round;
For joy thus our wenches we follow.

THOMAS DEKKER

Wind, jolly huntsmen, your neat bugles shrilly,
    Hounds make a lusty cry;
Spring up, you falconers, the partridges freely,
    Then let your brave hawks fly.
        Horses amain
        Over ridge, over plain,
    The dogs have the stag in chase;
    'Tis a sport to content a king.
        So, ho! ho! through the skies
        How the proud bird flies,
    And sousing kills with a grace.
Now the deer falls; hark! how they ring.

T. DEKKER

From The Sun's Darling, 1623—1656

Cast away care! he that loves sorrow
Lengthens not a day, nor can buy to-morrow.
Money is trash, and he that will spend it,
Let him drink merrily, Fortune will send it.
    Merrily, merrily, merrily, oh, ho!
    Play it off stiffly, we may not part so.

Wine is a charm, it heats the blood too,
Cowards it will arm, if the wine be good too;
Quickens the wit, and makes the back able,
Scorns to submit to the watch or constable.
    Merrily, merrily, merrily, oh, ho!
    Play it off stiffly, we may not part so.

Pots fly about, give us more liquor,
Brothers of a rout, our brains will flow quicker,
Empty the cask, score up, we care not,
Fill all the pots again, drink on and spare not.
    Merrily, merrily, merrily, oh, ho!
    Play it off stiffly, we may not part so.

T. DEKKER

THOMAS MIDDLETON

From The Witch, 1613?

Now I'm furnished for the flight,
Now I go, now I fly,
Malkin my sweet spirit and I.
O, what a dainty pleasure 'tis
To ride in the air
When the moon shines fair,
And sing and dance and toy and kiss.
Over woods, high rocks, and mountains,
Over seas, our mistress' fountains,
Over steeples, towers, and turrets,
We fly by night, 'mongst troops of spirits.
No ring of bells to our ears sounds,
No howls of wolves, no yelp of hounds.
No, not the noise of water's breach,
Or cannon's throat our height can reach.

T. MIDDLETON

From A Chaste Maid in Cheapside, 1630

Weep eyes, break heart,
My love and I must part.
Cruel fates true love do soonest sever ;
O, I shall see thee, never, never, never.
O, happy is the maid whose life takes end
Ere it knows parent's frown or loss of friend.
Weep eyes, break heart,
My love and I must part.

T. MIDDLETON

THOMAS MIDDLETON

From **The Widow, 1652**

How round the world goes, and everything that's in it,
The tides of gold and silver ebb and flow in a minute.
From the usurer to his sons, there a current swiftly runs,
From the sons to queans in chief, from the gallant to the thief,
From the thief unto his host, from the host to husbandmen,
From the country to the court, and so it comes to us again.
   How round the world goes, and everything that's in it,
   The tides of gold and silver ebb and flow in a minute.

T. Middleton ?

From **More Dissemblers besides Women, 1657**

Gipsy Captain.
        We sport in tents,
        Then rouse betimes and steal our dinners.
        Our store is never taken
        Without pigs, hens, or bacon,
        And that's good meat for sinners :
        At wakes and fairs we cozen
        Poor country folks by dozen ;
        If one have money, he disburses ;
        Whilst some tell fortunes, some pick purses ;
        Rather than be out of use,
        We'll steal garters, hose, or shoes,
        Boots, or spurs, with jingling rowels,
        Shirts, or napkins, smocks, or towels.
        Come live with us, come live with us,
          All you that love your eases ;
        He that's a gipsy
        May be drunk or tipsy
          At what hour he pleases.
All.   We laugh, we quaff, we roar, we scuffle ;
        We cheat, we drab, we filch, we shuffle.

T. Middleton

JOHN FLETCHER

From The Faithful Shepherdess, 1609 ?

Shepherds all, and maidens fair,
Fold your flocks up, for the air
'Gins to thicken, and the sun
Already his great course hath run.
See the dew-drops how they kiss
Every little flower that is ;
Hanging on their velvet heads
Like a rope of crystal beads.
See the heavy clouds low falling,
And bright Hesperus down calling
The dead night from under ground,
At whose rising mists unsound,
Damps and vapours fly apace,
Hovering o'er the wanton face
Of these pastures, where they come,
Striking dead both bud and bloom.
Therefore from such danger lock
Every one his loved flock,
And let your dogs lie loose without,
Lest the wolf come as a scout
From the mountain, and ere day
Bear a lamb or kid away;
Or the crafty thievish fox
Break upon your simple flocks.
To secure your selves from these,
Be not too secure in ease ;
Let one eye his watches keep,
Whilst the t'other eye doth sleep ;
So you shall good shepherds prove,
And for ever hold the love
Of our great god. Sweetest slumbers
And soft silence fall in numbers
On your eyelids ; so farewell,
Thus I end my evening's knell.

J. Fletcher

JOHN FLETCHER

From The Faithful Shepherdess, 1609 ?

Now whilst the moon doth rule the sky,
And the stars, whose feeble light
Give a pale shadow to the night,
Are up, great Pan commanded me
To walk this grove about, whilst he
In a corner of the wood,
Where never mortal foot hath stood,
Keeps dancing, music, and a feast,
To entertain a lovely guest,
Where he gives her many a rose,
Sweeter than the breath that blows
The leaves ; grapes, berries of the best,
I never saw so great a feast.
But to my charge ; here must I stay,
To see what mortals lose their way,
And by a false fire seeming bright,
Train them in, and leave them right.
Then must I watch if any be
Forcing of a chastitie.
If I find it, then in haste
Give my wreathed horn a blast ;
And the fairies all will run,
Wildly dancing by the moon,
And will pinch him to the bone,
Till his lustful thoughts be gone.

J. FLETCHER

From The Faithful Shepherdess, 1609 ?

River God. Fairest Virgin, now adieu ;
I must make my waters fly,
Lest they leave their channels dry,
And beasts that come unto the spring
Miss their morning's watering,

JOHN FLETCHER

Which I would not; for of late
All the neighbour people sate
On my banks, and from the fold
Two white lambs of three weeks old
Offered to my deity:
For which this year they shall be free
From raging floods, that as they pass
Leave their gravel in the grass:
Nor shall their meads be overflown,
When their grass is newly mown.

Amoret.   For thy kindness to me shown,
Never from thy banks be blown
Any tree with windy force
'Cross thy streams to stop thy course:
May no beast that comes to drink,
With his horns cast down thy brink;
May none that for thy fish do look
Cut thy banks to dam thy brook;
Barefoot may no neighbour wade
In thy cool streams, wife nor maid,
When the spawns on stones do lie,
To wash their hemp, and spoil the fry.

J. FLETCHER

From The Faithful Shepherdess, 1609?

All ye woods, and trees, and bowers,
All ye virtues and ye powers
That inhabit in the lakes,
In the pleasant springs or brakes,
> Move your feet
> To our sound,
> Whilst we greet
> All this ground,
With his honour and his name
That defends our flocks from blame.

JOHN FLETCHER

He is great and he is just,
He is ever good, and must
Thus be honoured. Daffadillies,
Roses, pinks, and loved lilies,
 Let us fling,
 Whilst we sing,
 Ever holy,
 Ever holy,
Ever honour'd, ever young,
Thus great Pan is ever sung.

J. FLETCHER

From The Faithful Shepherdess, 1609?

Thou divinest, fairest, brightest,
Thou most powerful maid and whitest,
Thou most virtuous and most blessed,
Eyes of stars, and golden tressed
Like Apollo, tell me, sweetest,
What new service now is meetest
For the Satyr? Shall I stray
In the middle air and stay
The sailing rack, or nimbly take
Hold by the moon, and gently make
Suit to the pale queen of the night
For a beam to give thee light?
Shall I dive into the sea,
And bring thee coral, making way
Through the rising waves that fall
In snowy fleeces; dearest, shall
I catch the wanton fawns, or flies,
Whose woven wings the summer dyes
Of many colours? Get thee fruit?
Or steal from heaven old Orpheus' lute?
All these I'll venture for and more
To do her service all these woods adore.

J. FLETCHER

JOHN FLETCHER

From **King Henry VIII, Shakespeare** folio 1623

Orpheus with his lute made trees,
And the mountain-tops that freeze,
 Bow themselves when he did sing.
To his music plants and flowers
Ever sprung; as sun and showers
 There had made a lasting spring.

Every thing that heard him play,
Even the billows of the sea,
 Hung their heads and then lay by.
In sweet music is such art,
Killing care and grief of heart
 Fall asleep, or hearing, die.

        J. FLETCHER

From **The Tragedy of Valentinian,** folio 1647

Now the lusty spring is seen,
 Golden yellow, gaudy blue,
Daintily invite the view.
 Everywhere on every green
Roses blushing as they blow
 And enticing men to pull;
Lilies whiter than the snow,
 Woodbines of sweet honey full.
  All love's emblems, and all cry,
  'Ladies, if not pluckt, we die.'

Yet the lusty spring hath stayed,
 Blushing red and purest white
Daintily to love invite
 Every woman, every maid;
Cherries kissing as they grow,
 And inviting men to taste,
Apples even ripe below,
 Winding gently to the waist.
  All love's emblems, and all cry,
  'Ladies, if not pluckt, we die.'

        J. FLETCHER

JOHN FLETCHER

From The Tragedy of Valentinian, folio 1647

Hear ye ladies that despise
  What the mighty Love has done.
Fear examples, and be wise,
  Fair Calisto was a nun.
Leda sailing on the stream,
  To deceive the hopes of man,
Love accounting but a dream,
  Doted on a silver swan.
Danae in a brazen tower
  Where no love was, loved a shower.

Hear ye ladies that are coy,
  What the mighty Love can do.
Fear the fierceness of the boy,
  The chaste moon he makes to woo.
Vesta kindling holy fires
  Circled round about with spies,
Never dreaming loose desires,
  Doting at the altar dies.
    Ilion in a short hour, higher
    He can build and once more fire.

J. Fletcher

From The Tragedy of Valentinian, folio 1647

Care charming sleep, thou easer of all woes,
Brother to death, sweetly thyself dispose
On this afflicted prince ; fall like a cloud
In gentle showers, give nothing that is loud,
Or painful to his slumbers ; easy, sweet,
And as a purling stream, thou son of night,
Pass by his troubled senses ; sing his pain
Like hollow murmuring wind, or silver rain.
Into this prince, gently, oh, gently slide,
And kiss him into slumbers like a bride.

J. Fletcher

JOHN FLETCHER

From The Tragedy of Valentinian, folio 1647

> God Lyeus ever young,
> Ever honour'd, ever sung,
> Stained with blood of lusty grapes,
> In a thousand lusty shapes
> Dance upon the mazer's brim,
> In the crimson liquor swim:
> From thy plenteous hand divine
> Let a river run with wine:
> > God of youth, let this day here
> > Enter neither care nor fear.
>
> > > J. FLETCHER

From The Mad Lover, folio 1647

Orpheus. Charon, O, Charon,
Thou wafter of the souls to bliss or bane.
Charon. Who calls the ferryman of hell?
Orph.   Come near,
And say who lives in joy and who in fear.
Char. Those that die well, eternal joy shall follow;
Those that die ill, their own foul fate shall swallow.
Orph. Shall thy black bark those guilty spirits stow
That kill themselves for love?
Char.   O no, no,
My cordage cracks when such great sins are near,
No wind blows fair, nor I myself can steer.
Orph. What lovers pass and in Elyzium reign?
Char. Those gentle loves that are beloved again.
Orph. This soldier loves and fain would die to win,
Shall he go on?
Char.   No, 'tis too foul a sin.
He must not come aboard; I dare not row,
Storms of despair and guilty blood will blow.
Orph. Shall time release him, say?
Char.   No, no, no, no.
Nor time nor death can alter us, nor prayer;
My boat is destiny, and who then dare,

JOHN FLETCHER

> But those appointed, come aboard? Live still,
> And love by reason, mortal, not by will.
> *Orph.* And when thy mistress shall close up thine eyes,
> *Char.* Then come aboard and pass,
> *Orph.* Till when be wise,
> *Char.* Till when be wise.
>
> J. FLETCHER

From **The Mad Lover**, folio 1647

Arm, arm, arm, arm, the scouts are all come in,
Keep your ranks close, and now your honours win.
Behold from yonder hill the foe appears,
Bows, bills, glaves, arrows, shields and spears,
Like a dark wood he comes, or tempest pouring;
O view the wings of horse the meadows scouring:
The vant-guard marches bravely; hark the drums—dub, dub.
　　They meet, they meet, now the battle comes:
　　　　See how the arrows fly,
　　　　That darken all the sky.
　　　　Hark how the trumpets sound,
　　　　Hark how the hills rebound—tara, tara, tara.
Hark how the horses charge; in boys, in boys in—tara, tara.
　　The battle totters; now the wounds begin;
　　　　O how they cry,
　　　　O how they die!
　　Room for the valiant Memnon armed with thunder,
　　　See how he breaks the ranks asunder.
　　They fly, they fly, Eumenes has the chase,
　　And brave Polybius makes good his place.
　　　　To the plains, to the woods,
　　　　To the rocks, to the floods,
　　They fly for succour. Follow, Follow, Follow. Hey, hey.
　　　　Hark how the soldiers hollo!
　　　　Brave Diocles is dead,
　　　　And all his soldiers fled,
　　　　The battle's won, and lost,
　　　　That many a life hath cost.

J. FLETCHER

JOHN FLETCHER

From **The Spanish Curate,** folio 1679

Let the bells ring, and let the boys sing,
    The young lasses skip and play;
Let the cups go round, till round goes the ground,
    Our learned old vicar will stay.

Let the pig turn merrily, merrily, ah!
    And let the fat goose swim;
For verily, verily, verily, ah!
    Our vicar this day shall be trim.

The stewed cock shall crow, cock-a-loodle-loo,
    A loud cock-a-loodle shall he crow;
The duck and the drake shall swim in a lake
    Of onions and claret below.

Our wives shall be neat, to bring in our meat
    To thee our most noble adviser;
Our pains shall be great, and bottles shall sweat,
    And we ourselves will be wiser.

We'll labour and swink, we'll kiss and we'll drink,
    And tithes shall come thicker and thicker;
We'll fall to our plough, and get children enough,
    And thou shalt be learned old vicar.
J. Fletcher

From **The Spanish Curate,** folio 1679

Dearest do not you delay me,
    Since thou knowest I must be gone;
Wind and tide, 'tis thought, doth stay me,
    But 'tis wind that must be blown
    From that breath, whose native smell
    Indian odours far excel.

Oh then speak, thou fairest fair,
    Kill not him that vows to serve thee,
But perfume this neighbouring air;
    Else dull silence sure will starve me.
    'Tis a word that's quickly spoken
    Which being restrained, a heart is broken.
J. Fletcher

JOHN FLETCHER

From **The Nice Valour,** folio **1647**

Hence all you vain delights,
As short as are the nights
Wherein you spend your folly.
There's nought in this life sweet
If man were wise to see't
  But only melancholy,
  Oh, sweetest melancholy.
Welcome folded arms, and fixed eyes,
A sigh that piercing mortifies,
A look that's fastened to the ground,
A tongue chained up without a sound.

Fountain-heads and pathless groves,
Places which pale passion loves;
Moonlight walks when all the fowls
Are warmly housed, save bats and owls;
  A midnight bell, a parting groan,
  These are the sounds we feed upon.
Then stretch our bones in a still gloomy valley,
Nothing's so dainty sweet as lovely melancholy.

J. FLETCHER

From **The Nice Valour,** folio **1647**

Oh, how my lungs do tickle, ha, ha, ha!
Oh, how my lungs do tickle, oh, oh, ho, ho!
  Set a sharp jest
  Against my breast,
 Then how my lungs do tickle.
  As nightingales
  And things in cambric rails
 Sing best against a prickle.
  Ha, ha, ha, ha!
  Ho, ho, ho, ho, ha!
 Laugh, laugh, laugh, laugh!
  Wide, loud, and vary.

JOHN FLETCHER

A smile is for a simpering novice,
    One that ne'er tasted caviare,
Nor knows the smack of dear anchovies.
    Ha, ha, ha, ha, ha!
    Ho, ho, ho, ho, ho!
A giggling waiting wench for me,
That shows her teeth, how white they be.
A thing not fit for gravity,
For theirs are foul, and hardly three.
    Ha, ha, ha!
    Ho, ho, ho!
Democritus, thou ancient fleerer,
How I miss thy laugh and ha' since.
There you named the famous jeerer,
That ever jeered in Rome or Athens.
    Ha, ha, ha!
    Ho, ho, ho!
How brave lives he that keeps a fool,
    Although the rate be deeper.
But he that is his own fool, sir,
    Does live a great deal cheaper.
Sure I shall burst, burst, quite break,
    Thou art so witty;
'Tis rare to break at court,
    For that belongs to the city.
Ha, ha! my spleen is almost worn
    To the last laughter.
Oh, keep a corner for a friend;
    A jest may come hereafter.

J. FLETCHER

From The Two Noble Kinsmen, 1634

Roses, their sharp spines being gone,
Not royal in their smells alone,
    But in their hue;
Maiden pinks of odour faint,
Daisies smell-less, yet most quaint,
    And sweet thyme true;

149

JOHN FLETCHER

Primrose, first-born child of Ver,
Merry springtime's harbinger,
     With her bells dim;
Oxlips in their cradles growing,
Marigolds on death-beds blowing,
     Larks'-heels trim;
All dear Nature's children sweet,
Lie 'fore bride and bridegroom's feet,
     Blessing their sense.
Not an angel of the air,
Bird melodious, or bird fair,
     Be absent hence.
The crow, the slanderous cuckoo, nor
The boding raven, nor chough hoar,
     Nor chattering pie,
May on our bride-house perch or sing,
Or with them any discord bring,
     But from it fly.

J. FLETCHER

From The Elder Brother, 1637

Beauty, clear and fair,
     Where the air
Rather like a perfume dwells,
     Where the violet and the rose
     The blue veins in blush disclose,
And come to honour nothing else.

Where to live near,
     And planted there,
Is to live, and still live new;
     Where to gain a favour is
     More than light, perpetual bliss,
Make me live by serving you.

Dear again back recall
     To this light
A stranger to himself and all;
     Both the wonder and the story
     Shall be yours, and eke the glory;
I am your servant and your thrall.

J. FLETCHER

FLETCHER *and* BEAUMONT AND FLETCHER

From The Bloody Brother, 1639

Drink to-day and drown all sorrow,
You shall perhaps not do it to-morrow.
Best while you have it, use your breath,
There is no drinking after death.

Wine works the heart up, wakes the wit,
There is no cure 'gainst age but it.
It helps the head-ache, cough, and tisic,
And is for all diseases physic.

Then let us swill boys for our health,
Who drinks well loves the commonwealth.
And he that will to bed go sober
Falls with the leaf still in October.

J. FLETCHER

From The Woman Hater, 1607

Come, sleep, and with thy sweet deceiving,
    Lock me in delight awhile;
Let some pleasing dreams beguile
All my fancies; that from thence
I may feel an influence,
All my powers of care bereaving.

Though but a shadow, but a sliding,
    Let me know some little joy.
We that suffer long annoy
Are contented with a thought,
Through an idle fancy wrought:
Oh, let my joys have some abiding.

BEAUMONT AND FLETCHER

BEAUMONT AND FLETCHER

From The Maid's Tragedy, 1619—1622

> Lay a garland on my hearse
>   Of the dismal yew;
> Maidens, willow branches bear;
>   Say, I died true.
>
> My love was false, but I was firm
>   From my hour of birth.
> Upon my buried body, lie
>   Lightly, gentle earth.

Beaumont and Fletcher

From The Maid's Tragedy, 1619—1622

> Cynthia to thy power and thee
>   We obey.
> Joy to this great company;
>   And no day
> Come to steal this night away,
> Till the rites of love are ended,
> And the lusty bridegroom say,
> Welcome, light, of all befriended.
>
> Pace out, you watery powers below;
>   Let your feet,
> Like the galleys when they row,
>   Even beat.
> Let your unknown measures, set
> To the still winds, tell to all
> That gods are come, immortal, great,
> To honour this great nuptial.

Beaumont and Fletcher

FRANCIS BEAUMONT and JOHN WEBSTER

From **Poems, 1652**

On the Tombs in Westminster

Mortality, behold and fear
What a change of flesh is here !
Think how many royal bones
Sleep within these heaps of stones;
Here they lie, had realms and lands,
Who now want strength to stir their hands,
Where from their pulpits seal'd with dust
They preach, 'In greatness is no trust.'
Here's an acre sown indeed
With the richest royallest seed
That the earth did e'er suck in
Since the first man died for sin:
Here the bones of birth hath cried
'Though gods they were, as men they died !'
Here are sands, ignoble things,
Dropt from the ruin'd sides of kings:
  Here's a world of pomp and state
  Buried in dust, once dead by fate.

F. BEAUMONT

From **The White Devil, 1612**

Call for the robin-redbreast and the wren,
Since o'er shady groves they hover,
And with leaves and flowers do cover
The friendless bodies of unburied men.
Call unto his funeral dole
The ant, the field-mouse, and the mole,
To rear him hillocks that shall keep him warm,
And, when gay tombs are robbed, sustain no harm;
But keep the wolf far thence that's foe to men,
For with his nails he'll dig them up again.

J. WEBSTER

153

JOHN WEBSTER *and* JOHN FORD

From The Devil's Law-Case, 1623

All the flowers of the spring
Meet to perfume our burying;
These have but their growing prime,
And man does flourish but his time.
Survey our progress from our birth;
We are set, we grow, we turn to earth.
Courts adieu, and all delights,
All bewitching appetites.
Sweetest breath and clearest eye,
Like perfumes, go out and die.
And consequently this is done
As shadows wait upon the sun.
Vain the ambition of kings
Who seek by trophies and dead things
To leave a living name behind,
And weave but nets to catch the wind.

J. WEBSTER

From The Broken Heart, 1633

Oh, no more, no more, too late
  Sighs are spent; the burning tapers
Of a life as chaste as fate
    Pure as are unwritten papers
Are burnt out; no heat, no light
Now remains; 'tis ever night.
    Love is dead; let lovers' eyes,
    Locked in endless dreams,
    The extremes of all extremes,
    Ope no more, for now love dies.
Now love dies, implying
Love's martyrs must be ever, ever dying.

J. FORD

154

NATHANIEL FIELD *and* JAMES SHIRLEY

From Amends for Ladies, 1618

Rise, lady mistress, rise !
  The night hath tedious been ;
No sleep hath fallen into my eyes
  Nor slumbers made me sin.
Is not she a saint then, say,
Thought of whom keeps sin away?

Rise, madam, rise and give me light,
  Whom darkness still will cover
And ignorance, darker than night,
  Till thou smile on thy lover.
All want day till thy beauty rise ;
For the grey morn breaks from thine eyes.

N. FIELD

From The School of Compliment, 1631

Woodmen, shepherds, come away,
    This is Pan's great holiday;
      Throw off cares,
With your heaven-aspiring airs
      Help us to sing,
While valleys with your echoes ring.

Nymphs that dwell within these groves,
    Leave your arbours, bring your loves,
      Gather posies,
Crown your golden hair with roses ;
      As you pass
Foot like fairies on the grass.

Joy crown our bowers ; Philomel
    Leave of Tereus' rape to tell.
      Let trees dance
As they at Thracian lyre did once.
      Mountains play,
This is shepherds' holiday.

J. SHIRLEY

JAMES SHIRLEY

From **The Witty Fair One, 1633**

> Love, a thousand sweets distilling,
> And with nectar bosoms filling,
> Charm all eyes that none may find us,
>   Be above, before, behind us.
> And, while we thy pleasures taste,
>   Enforce time itself to stay,
> And by forelock hold him fast
>   Lest occasion slip away.

J. Shirley

From **The Imposture, 1652**

> You virgins that did late despair
> To keep your wealth from cruel men,
> Tie up in silk your careless hair,
> Soft peace is come again.
>
> Now lovers' eyes may gently shoot
> A flame that will not kill;
> The drum was angry, but the lute
> Shall whisper what you will.
>
> Sing Iŏ, Iŏ, for his sake
> Who hath restored your drooping heads;
> With choice of sweetest flowers make
> A garden where he treads;
>
> Whilst we whole groves of laurel bring,
> A petty triumph to his brow,
> Who is the master of our spring
> And all the bloom we owe.

J. Shirley

JAMES SHIRLEY

From **The Imposture, 1652**

O fly, my soul; what hangs upon
    Thy drooping wings,
    And weighs them down
With love of gaudy mortal things?

The sun is now i' th' east; each shade
    As he doth rise
    Is shorter made
That earth may lessen to our eyes.

Oh, be not careless then, and play
    Until the star of peace
Hide all his beams in dark recess.
Poor pilgrims needs must lose their way
When all the shadows do increase.

                      J. SHIRLEY

From **Cupid and Death, 1653**

Victorious men of earth, no more
  Proclaim how wide your empires are;
Though you bind in every shore
  And your triumphs reach as far
    As night or day,
Yet you, proud monarchs, must obey
And mingle with forgotten ashes, when
Death calls ye to the crowd of common men.

Devouring Famine, Plague, and War,
  Each able to undo mankind,
Death's servile emissaries are;
  Nor to these alone confined,
    He hath at will
  More quaint and subtle ways to kill;
A smile or kiss, as he will use the art,
Shall have the cunning skill to break a heart.

                      J. SHIRLEY

JAMES SHIRLEY *and* ANON

From The Contention of Ajax and Ulysses, 1659

The glories of our blood and state
    Are shadows, not substantial things;
There is no armour against fate;
    Death lays his icy hand on kings:
        Sceptre and crown
        Must tumble down,
And in the dust be equal made
With the poor crooked scythe and spade.

Some men with swords may reap the field,
    And plant fresh laurels where they kill:
But their strong nerves at last must yield;
    They tame but one another still:
        Early or late
        They stoop to fate,
And must give up their murmuring breath
When they, pale captives, creep to death.

The garlands wither on your brow;
    Then boast no more your mighty deeds;
Upon Death's purple altar now
    See where the victor-victim bleeds:
        Your heads must come
        To the cold tomb;
Only the actions of the just
Smell sweet, and blossom in their dust.

J. SHIRLEY

From Wit Restored, 1658

The Constant Lover

I know as well as you she is not fair,
Nor hath she sparkling eyes, or curled hair;
Nor can she brag of virtue or of truth,
Or anything about her, save her youth.
She is woman too, and to no end
I know, I verses write and letters send;

ANON

And nought I do can to compassion move her;
All this I know, yet cannot choose but love her.
Yet am not blind, as you and others be,
Who think and swear they little Cupid see
Play in their mistress' eyes, and that there dwell
Roses on cheeks, and that her breasts excel
The whitest snow, as if that love were built
On fading red and white, the body's quilt;
And that I cannot love unless I tell
Wherein or on what part my love doth dwell.
Vain heretics you be, for I love more
Than ever any did that told wherefore;
Then trouble me no more, nor tell me why:
'Tis, because she is she, and I am I.

ANON

From Wit Restored, 1658

Phillada flouts me

Oh what a pain is love!
How shall I bear it?
She will inconstant prove,
I greatly fear it.
She so torments my mind,
That my strength faileth;
And wavers with the wind,
As a ship that saileth.
Please her the best I may,
She looks another way,
Alack! and well-a-day!
     Phillada flouts me.

All the fair yesterday,
She did pass by me;
She looked another way
And would not spy me.
I wooed her for to dine
But could not get her.
Will had her to the wine,
He might entreat her.

159

ANON

With *Daniel* she did dance,
On me she looked askance.
O thrice unhappy chance!
    Phillada flouts me.

Fair maid, be not so coy,
Do not disdain me.
I am my mother's joy;
Sweet, entertain me.
She'll give me, when she dies,
All that is fitting;
Her poultry and her bees,
And her geese sitting.
A pair of mattress beds,
And a bag full of shreds.
And yet for all these goods
    Phillada flouts me.

She hath a clout of mine,
Wrought with good Coventry,
Which she keeps for a sign
Of my fidelity.
But i' faith, if she flinch,
She shall not wear it.
To *Tibb* my t'other wench,
I mean to bear it.
And yet it grieves my heart,
So soon from her to part.
Death strikes me with his dart.
    Phillada flouts me.

Thou shalt eat curds and cream
All the year lasting;
And drink the crystal stream
Pleasant in tasting.
Wig and whey whilst thou burst,
And ramble berry;
Pie-lid and pastry crust,
Pears, plums, and cherry.

ANON *and* THOMAS RANDOLPH

Thy raiment shall be thin
Made of a weaver's skin.
Yet all's not worth a pin,
    Phillada flouts me.

Fair maiden, have a care,
And in time take me.
I can have those as fair
If you forsake me.
For *Doll* the dairymaid
Laughed on me lately,
And wanton *Winifrid*
Favours me greatly.
One throws milk on my clothes,
T'other plays with my nose.
What wanton signs are those?
    Phillada flouts me.

I cannot work and sleep
All at a season;
Love wounds my heart so deep,
Without all reason.
I 'gin to pine away
With grief and sorrow;
Like to a fatted beast
Penned in a meadow.
I shall be dead I fear,
Within this thousand year.
And all for very fear!
    Phillada flouts me.

ANON

From Aristippus, 1630

We care not for money riches or wealth,
    Old sack is our money, old sack is our health.
      Then let's flock hither
      Like birds of a feather,
To drink, to fling,
To laugh and sing,
    Conferring our notes together,
    Conferring our notes together.

THOMAS RANDOLPH

Come let us laugh, let us drink, let us sing;
The winter with us is as good as the spring.
    We care not a feather
    For wind or for weather,
But night and day
We sport and play,
    Conferring our notes together,
    Conferring our notes together.

T. RANDOLPH

From Annalia Dubrensia, 1636

Mr Robert Dover's Olympic games upon Cotswold Hills

Colin.   Early in May up got the jolly rout,
        Call'd by the lark, and spread the fields about:
        One, for to breathe himself, would coursing be
        From this same beech to yonder mulberry;
        A second leaped his supple nerves to try;
        A third was practising his melody;
        This a new jig was footing; others were
        Busied at wrestling, or to throw the bar,
        Ambitious which should bear the bell away,
        And kiss the nut-brown lady of the May.
        This stirr'd 'em up; a jolly swain was he
        Whom Peg and Susan after victory
        Crown'd with a garland they had made beset
        With daisies, pinks, and many a violet,
        Cowslip, and gilliflower. Rewards, though small,
        Encourage virtue, but if none at all
        Meet her, she languisheth, and dies, as now
        Where worth's denied the honour of a bough.
        And, Thenot, this the cause I read to be
        Of such a dull and general lethargy.
Thenot. Ill thrive the lout that did their mirth gainsay!
        Wolves haunt his flocks that took those sports away!

THOMAS RANDOLPH

Colin.　Some melancholy swains about have gone
To teach all zeal their own complexion:
Choler they will admit sometimes, I see,
But phlegm and sanguine no religions be.
These teach that dancing is a Jezebel,
And barley-break the ready way to hell;
The morrice-idols, Whitsun-ales, can be
But profane relics of a jubilee!
These, in a zeal t' express how much they do
The organs hate, have silenced bagpipes, too,
And harmless May-poles, all are rail'd upon,
As if they were the towers of Babylon.
Some think not fit there should be any sport
I' th' country, 'tis a dish proper to th' Court.
Mirth not becomes 'em; let the saucy swain
Eat beef and bacon, and go sweat again.
Besides, what sport can in the pastimes be,
When all is but ridiculous foppery?

T. RANDOLPH

From Poems, 1638

From witty men and mad
All poetry conception had.
No sires but these will poetry admit:
Madness or wit.
This definition poetry doth fit:
It is a witty madness, or mad wit.
Only these two poetic heat admits:
A witty man, or one that's out of 's wits.

T. RANDOLPH

THOMAS RANDOLPH

From Poems, 1638

An Elegie

I have a mistress, for perfections rare
In every eye, but in my thoughts most fair.
Like tapers on the altar shine her eyes;
Her breath is the perfume of sacrifice.
And wheresoe'er my fancy would begin,
Still her perfection lets religion in.
We sit and talk, and kiss away the hours
As chastely as the morning dews kiss flowers.
I touch her, like my beads, with devout care,
And come unto my courtship as my prayer.

T. RANDOLPH

From Poems, 1638

Ode to Master Anthony Stafford, to hasten him into the country

Come, spur away,
I have no patience for a longer stay,
But must go down
And leave the chargeable noise of this great town.
I will the country see,
Where old simplicity,
Though hid in grey,
Doth look more gay
Than foppery in plush and scarlet clad.
Farewell, you city-wits, that are
Almost at civil war;
'Tis time that I grow wise, when all the world grows mad.

More of my days
I will not spend to gain an idiot's praise;
Or to make sport
For some slight puny of the Inns-of-Court.
Then, worthy Stafford, say
How shall we spend the day?

164

THOMAS RANDOLPH

With what delights
Shorten the nights?
When from this tumult we are got secure,
    Where mirth with all her freedom goes,
    Yet shall no finger lose;
Where every word is thought, and every thought is pure.

    There from the tree
We'll cherries pluck, and pick the strawberry;
    And every day
Go see the wholesome country girls make hay,
    Whose brown hath lovelier grace
    Than any painted face,
    That I do know
    Hyde Park can show.
Where I had rather gain a kiss than meet
    (Though some of them in greater state
    Might court my love with plate)
The beauties of the Cheap, the wives of Lombard Street.

    But think upon
Some other pleasures; these to me are none.
    Why do I prate
Of women, that are things against my fate?
    I never mean to wed
    That torture to my bed.
    My muse is she
    My love shall be.
Let clowns get wealth and heirs; when I am gone,
    And the great bugbear, grisly death,
    Shall take this idle breath,
If I a poem leave, that poem is my son.

    Of this no more;
We'll rather taste the bright Pomona's store;
    No fruit shall 'scape
Our palates, from the damson to the grape.
    Then full we'll seek a shade,
    And hear what music's made;

THOMAS RANDOLPH

How Philomel
Her tale doth tell,
And how the little birds do fill the quire:
The thrush and blackbird lend their throats
Warbling melodious notes;
We will all sports enjoy which others but desire.

Ours is the sky
Where at what fowl we please our hawk shall fly:
Nor will we spare
To hunt the crafty fox or timorous hare;
But let our hounds run loose
In any grounds they'll choose,
The buck shall fall,
The stag, and all:
Our pleasures must from their own warrants be;
For to my muse, if not to me,
I'm sure all game is free:
Heaven, earth, are all but parts of her great royalty.

And when we mean
To taste of Bacchus' blessings now and then,
And drink by stealth
A cup or two to noble Barkley's health,
I'll take my pipe and try
The Phrygian melody;
Which he that hears
Lets through his ears
A madness to distemper all the brain.
Then I another pipe will take
And Doric music make,
To civilise with graver notes our wits again.

T. RANDOLPH

THOMAS RANDOLPH

From **Poems, 1638**

A dialogue betwixt a nymph and a shepherd

Nymph. Why sigh you, swain? this passion is not common,
Is't for kids or lambkins?
Shep.   For a woman.
Nymph. How fair is she that on so sage a brow
Prints lowering looks?
Shep.   Just such a toy as thou.
Nymph. Is she a maid?
Shep.   What man can answer that?
Nymph. Or widow?
Shep.   No.
Nymph.   What then?
Shep.   I know not what;
Saint-like she looks, a Syren if she sing.
Her eyes are stars, her mind is everything.
Nymph. If she be fickle, shepherd, leave to woo,
Or fancy me.
Shep.   No, thou art woman, too.
Nymph. But I am constant.
Shep.   Then thou art not fair.
Nymph. Bright as the morning.
Shep.   Wavering as the air.
Nymph. What grows upon this cheek?
Shep.   A pure carnation.
Nymph. Come, take a kiss.
Shep.   O sweet, O sweet temptation!
Chorus. Ah, Love! and canst thou never lose the field?
Where Cupid lays a siege, the town must yield.
He warms the chiller blood with glowing fire,
And thaws the icy frost of cold desire.

T. RANDOLPH

PETER HAUSTED

From The Rival Friends, 1632

Have you a desire to see
The glorious Heaven's epitome?
Or an abstract of the spring?
Adonis' garden? or a thing
    Fuller of wonder? Nature's shop displayed,
    Hung with the choicest pieces she has made?
        Here behold it open laid.

Or else would you bless your eyes
With a type of paradise?
Or behold how poets feign
Jove to sit amidst his train?
    Or see (what made Actaeon rue)
    Diana 'mongst her virgin crew?
        Lift up your eyes and view.

P. HAUSTED

168

DESCRIPTIVE AND NARRATIVE
POEMS

From Venus and Adonis, 1593

Wat

And when thou hast on foot the purblind hare,
Mark the poor wretch, to overshoot his troubles
How he outruns the wind and with what care
He cranks and crosses with a thousand doubles:
 The many musets through the which he goes
 Are like a labyrinth to amaze his foes.

Sometime he runs among a flock of sheep,
To make the cunning hounds mistake their smell,
And sometime where earth-delving conies keep,
To stop the loud pursuers in their yell,
 And sometime sorteth with a herd of deer;
 Danger deviseth shifts, wit waits on fear;

For there his smell with others being mingled,
The hot scent-snuffing hounds are driv'n to doubt,
Ceasing their clamorous cry till they have singled
With much ado the cold fault cleanly out;
 Then do they spend their mouths; Echo replies,
 As if another chase were in the skies.

By this, poor Wat, far off upon a hill,
Stands on his hinder legs with listening ear,
To hearken if his foes pursue him still:
Anon their loud alarums he doth hear;
 And now his grief may be compared well
 To one sore sick that hears the passing-bell.

Then shalt thou see the dew-bedabbled wretch
Turn, and return, indenting with the way;
Each envious brier his weary legs doth scratch,
Each shadow makes him stop, each murmur stay:
 For misery is trodden on by many
 And being low never relieved by any.

W. SHAKESPEARE

MICHAEL DRAYTON

From Endimion and Phoebe, 1594?

The Progress of Endymion

And now at length the joyful time drew on,
She meant to honour her Endymion,
And glorify him on that stately mount,
Whereof the Goddess made so great account.
She sends Jove's winged herald to the woods,
The neighbour fountains, and the bordering floods,
Charging the nymphs which did inhabit there,
Upon a day appointed to appear,
And to attend her sacred Majesty
In all their pomp and great solemnity,
Having obtained great Phoebus' free consent
To further her divine and chaste intent;
Which thus imposed as a thing of weight,
In stately troops appear before her straight,
The Fawns and Satyrs from the tufted brakes,
Their bristly arms wreath'd all about with snakes;
Their sturdy loins with ropes of ivy bound,
Their horned heads with woodbine chaplets crown'd,
With cypress javelins, and about their thighs
The flaggy hair disorder'd loosely flies:
Th' Oriades, like to the Spartan maid,
In murrie-scyndall gorgeously arrayed:
With gallant green scarves girded in the waist,
Their flaxen hair with silken fillets lac'd,
Woven with flowers in sweet lascivious wreaths,
Moving like feathers as the light air breathes;
With crowns of myrtle, glorious to behold,
Whose leaves are painted with pure drops of gold:
With trains of fine bisse checker'd all with frets
Of dainty pinks and precious violets,
In branched buskins of fine cordiwin,
With spangled garters down unto the shin,
Fring'd with fine silk, of many a sundry kind,
Which like to pennons waved with the wind;

MICHAEL DRAYTON

The Hamadriads from their shady bowers,
Deck'd up in garlands of the rarest flowers,
Upon the backs of milk-white bulls were set,
With horn and hoof, as black as any jet,
Whose collars were great massy golden rings,
Led by their swains in twisted silken strings;
Then did the lovely Driades appear,
On dappled stags, which bravely mounted were,
Whose velvet palms with nosegays rarely dight,
To all the rest bred wonderful delight;
And in this sort accompanied with these,
In triumph rid the wat'ry Niades,
Upon sea-horses trapt with shining fins,
Arm'd with their mail impenetrable skins,
Whose scaly crests like rain-bows bended high,
Seem to control proud Iris in the sky;
Upon a chariot was Endymion laid,
In snowy tissue gorgeously arrayed,
Of precious ivory cover'd o'er with lawn,
Which by four stately unicorns was drawn.
Of ropes of orient pearl their traces were,
Pure as the path which doth in heaven appear,
With rarest flowers enchas'd and over-spread,
Which serv'd as curtains to this glorious bed,
Whose seat of crystal in the sun-beams shone,
Like thunder-breathing Jove's celestial throne.
Upon his head a coronet install'd,
Of one entire and mighty emerald,
With richest bracelets on his lily wrists,
Of hellitropium link'd with golden twists;
A bevy of fair swans which flying over,
With their large wings him from the sun do cover,
And easily wafting as he went along,
Do lull him still with their enchanting song,
Whilst all the nymphs on solemn instruments,
Sound dainty music to their sweet laments.

M. DRAYTON

EDMUND SPENSER

From The Faerie Queene, 1609

Two cantos of mutability

VII vii 28

So forth issew'd the Seasons of the yeare.
First, lusty Spring, all dight in leaves of flowres
That freshly budded and new bloosmes did beare,
(In which a thousand birds had built their bowres
That sweetly sung to call forth Paramours)
And in his hand a javelin he did beare,
And on his head (as fit for warlike stoures)
A guilt engraven morion he did weare;
That as some did him love, so others did him feare.

Then came the jolly Sommer, being dight
In a thin silken cassock coloured greene,
That was unlyned all, to be more light;
And on his head a girlond well beseene
He wore, from which, as he had chauffed been,
The sweat did drop; and in his hand he bore
A boawe and shaftes, as he in forrest greene
Had hunted late the Libbard or the Bore,
And now would bathe his limbes with labor heated sore.

Then came the Autumne all in yellow clad,
As though he joyed in his plentious store,
Laden with fruits that made him laugh, full glad
That he had banisht hunger, which to-fore
Had by the belly oft him pinched sore:
Upon his head a wreath, that was enrold
With ears of corne of every sort, he bore;
And in his hand a sickle he did holde,
To reape the ripened fruits the which the earth had yold.

Lastly, came Winter cloathed all in frize,
Chattering his teeth for cold that did him chill;
Whil'st on his hoary beard his breath did freese,
And the dull drops, that from his purpled bill
As from a limbeck did adown distill.

EDMUND SPENSER

In his right hand a tipped staffe he held,
With which his feeble steps he stayed still;
For he was faint with cold, and weak with eld,
That scarse his loosed limbes he hable was to weld.

*   *   *   *   *   *   *

And after these there came the Day and Night,
Riding together both with equall pase,
Th' one on a Palfrey blacke, the other white;
But Night had covered her uncomely face
With a blacke veile, and held in hand a mace,
On top whereof the moon and stars were pight;
And sleep and darknesse round about did trace:
But Day did beare upon his scepters hight
The goodly Sun encompast all with beames bright.

Then came the Howres, faire daughters of high Jove
And timely Night; the which were all endewed
With wondrous beauty fit to kindle love;
But they were virgins all, and love eschewed
That might forslack the charge to them foreshewed
By mighty Jove; who did them porters make
Of heavens gate (whence all the gods issued)
Which they did daily watch, and nightly wake
By even turnes, ne ever did their charge forsake.

And after all came Life, and lastly Death;
Death with most grim and griesly visage seene,
Yet is he nought but parting of the breath;
Ne ought to see, but like a shade to weene,
Unbodied, unsoul'd, unheard, unseene:
But Life was like a faire young lusty boy,
Such as they faine Dan Cupid to have beene,
Full of delightfull health and lively joy,
Deckt all with flowres, and wings of gold fit to employ.

E. SPENSER

MICHAEL DRAYTON

From Nimpnidia, 1627

Queen Mab and Oberon

Her chariot ready straight is made,
Each thing therein is fitting laid,
That she by nothing might be stayed,
    For nought must be her letting;
Four nimble gnats the horses were,
Their harnesses of gossamere,
Fly Cranion her charioteer
    Upon the coach-box getting.

Her chariot of a snail's fine shell,
Which for the colours did excel,
The fair Queen Mab becoming well,
    So lively was the limning;
The seat the soft wool of the bee,
The cover (gallantly to see)
The wing of a pied butterfly;
    I trow 'twas simple trimming.

The wheels composed of crickets' bones,
And daintily made for the nonce,
For fear of rattling on the stones,
    With thistle-down they shod it;
For all her maidens much did fear
If Oberon had chanc'd to hear
That Mab his Queen should have been there,
    He would not have abode it.

She mounts her chariot with a trice,
Nor would she stay for no advice,
Until her maids that were so nice,
    To wait on her were fitted,
But ran herself away alone;
Which when they heard, there was not one
But hasted after to be gone,
    As she had been diswitted.

MICHAEL DRAYTON

Hop and Mop and Drop so clear,
Pip and Trip and Skip that were
To Mab, their sovereign, ever dear,
    Her special maids of honour;
Fib and Tib and Pink and Pin,
Tick and Quick and Jill and Jin,
Tit and Nit and Wap and Win,
    The train that wait upon her.

Upon a grasshopper they got
And, what with amble and with trot,
For hedge nor ditch they spared not,
    But after her they hie them;
A cobweb over them they throw,
To shield the wind if it should blow,
Themselves they wisely could bestow,
    Lest any should espy them.

But let us leave Queen Mab a while,
Through many a gate, o'er many a stile,
That now had gotten by this wile,
    Her dear Pigwiggin kissing;
And tell how Oberon doth fare,
Who grew as mad as any hare,
When he had sought each place with care,
    And found his Queen was missing.

By grisly Pluto he doth swear;
He rent his clothes and tore his hair,
And as he runneth here and there
    An acorn cup he greeteth,
Which soon he taketh by the stalk,
About his head he lets it walk,
Nor doth he any creature balk,
    But lays on all he meeteth.

The Tuscan Poet doth advance
The frantic Paladin of France,
And those more ancient do enhance
    Alcides in his fury,

175

And others Aiax Telamon,
But to this time there hath been none
So Bedlam as our Oberon,
    Of which I dare assure you.

And first encountering with a Wasp,
He in his arms the fly doth clasp
As though his breath he forth would grasp,
    Him for Pigwiggin taking:
'Where is my wife, thou rogue?' quoth he;
'Pigwiggin, she is come to thee;
Restore her, or thou diest by me!'
    Whereat the poor Wasp quaking

Cries, 'Oberon, great Fairy King,
Content thee, I am no such thing:
I am a Wasp, behold my sting!'
    At which the Fairy started;
When soon away the Wasp doth go,
Poor wretch, was never frighted so;
He thought his wings were much too slow,
    O'erjoyed they so were parted.

He next upon a Glow-worm light,
(You must suppose it now was night)
Which, for her hinder part was bright,
    He took to be a devil,
And furiously doth her assail
For carrying fire in her tail;
He thrashed her rough coat with his flail;
    The mad King feared no evil.

'Oh!' quoth the Glow-worm, 'hold thy hand,
Thou puissant King of Fairy-land!
Thy mighty strokes who may withstand?
    Hold, or of life despair I!'
Together then herself doth roll,
And tumbling down into a hole
She seemed as black as any coal;
    Which vext away the Fairy.

MICHAEL DRAYTON

From thence he ran into a hive:
Amongst the bees he letteth drive,
And down their combs begins to rive,
    All likely to have spoiled,
Which with their wax his face besmeared,
And with their honey daubed his beard:
It would have made a man afeared
    To see how he was moiled.

A new adventure him betides;
He met an Ant, which he bestrides,
And post thereon away he rides,
    Which with his haste doth stumble;
And came full over on her snout,
Her heels so threw the dirt about,
For she by no means could get out,
    But over him doth tumble.

And being in this piteous case,
And all be-slurried head and face,
On runs he in this wild-goose chase,
    As here and there he rambles
Half blind, against a molehole hit,
And for a mountain taking it,
For all he was out of his wit
    Yet to the top he scrambles.

And being gotten to the top,
Yet there himself he could not stop,
But down on the other side doth chop,
    And to the foot came rumbling;
So that the grubs, therein that bred,
Hearing such turmoil overhead,
Thought surely they had all been dead;
    So fearful was the jumbling.

*   *   *   *   *

MICHAEL DRAYTON

Pigwiggin arms

And quickly arms him for the field,
A little cockle-shell his shield,
Which he could very bravely wield,
    Yet could it not be pierced:
His spear a bent both stiff and strong,
And well near of two inches long:
The pile was of a horse-fly's tongue,
    Whose sharpness nought reversed.

And puts him on a coat of mail,
Which was of a fish's scale,
That when his foe should him assail,
    No point should be prevailing:
His rapier was a hornet's sting;
It was a very dangerous thing,
For if he chanced to hurt the King,
    It would be long in healing.

His helmet was a beetle's head,
Most horrible and full of dread,
That able was to strike one dead,
    Yet did it well become him;
And for a plume a horse's hair
Which, being tossed with the air,
Had force to strike his foe with fear,
    And turn his weapon from him.

Himself he on an earwig set,
Yet scarce he on his back could get,
So oft and high he did curvet,
    Ere he himself could settle:
He made him turn, and stop, and bound,
To gallop and to trot the round,
He scarce could stand on any ground,
    He was so full of mettle.

M. DRAYTON

MICHAEL DRAYTON

From **The Muses' Elizium, 1630**

The Description of Elizium

A paradise on earth is found,
Though far from vulgar sight,
Which with those pleasures doth abound
That it Elizium hight.

Where in delights that never fade,
The Muses lulled be,
And sit at pleasure in the shade
Of many a stately tree,

Which no rough tempest makes to reel
Nor their straight bodies bows,
Their lofty tops do never feel
The weight of winter's snows;

In groves that evermore are green,
No falling leaf is there,
But Philomel (of birds the queen)
In music spends the year.

The merle upon her myrtle perch
There to the mavis sings,
Who from the top of some curl'd birch
Those notes redoubled rings.

There daisies damask every place
Nor once their beauties lose,
That when proud Phœbus hides his face,
Themselves they scorn to close.

The pansy and the violet here,
As seeming to descend,
Both from one root, a very pair,
For sweetness yet contend,

And pointing to a pink to tell
Which bears it, it is loath
To judge it; but replies, for smell
That it excels them both.

MICHAEL DRAYTON

Wherewith displeased they hang their heads
So angry soon they grow,
And from their odoriferous beds
Their sweets at it they throw.

The winter here a summer is,
No waste is made of time,
Nor doth the autumn ever miss
The blossoms of the prime.

The flower that July forth doth bring,
In April here is seen,
The primrose that puts on the spring,
In July decks each green.

The sweets for sovereignty contend,
And so abundant be,
That to the very earth they lend
And bark of every tree:

Rills rising out of every bank,
In wild meanders strain,
And playing many a wanton prank
Upon the speckled plain,

In gambols and lascivious gyres
Their time they still bestow,
Nor to their fountains none retires,
Nor on their course will go.

Those brooks with lilies bravely deckt,
So proud and wanton made,
That they their courses quite neglect
And seem as though they stayed

Fair Flora in her state to view
Which through those lilies looks,
Or as those lilies lean'd to show
Their beauties to the brooks.

MICHAEL DRAYTON

That Phœbus in his lofty race,
Oft lays aside his beams
And comes to cool his glowing face
In these delicious streams.

Oft spreading vines climb up the cleeves,
Whose ripen'd clusters there
Their liquid purple drop, which drives
A vintage through the year.

Those cleeves whose craggy sides are clad
With trees of sundry suits,
Which make continual summer glad,
Even bending with their fruits,

Some ripening, ready some to fall,
Some blossom'd, some to bloom,
Like gorgeous hangings on the wall
Of some rich princely room.

Pomegranates, lemons, citrons, so
Their laded branches bow,
Their leaves in number that outgo
Nor roomth will them allow.

There in perpetual summer's shade
Apollo's prophets sit,
Among the flowers that never fade,
But flourish like their wit ;

To whom the nymphs upon their lyres
Tune many a curious lay,
And with their most melodious quires
Make short the longest day.

The thrice three Virgins heavenly clear
Their trembling timbrels sound,
Whilst the three comely Graces there
Dance many a dainty round.

MICHAEL DRAYTON

Decay nor age there nothing knows,
There is continual youth,
As time on plant or creatures grows,
So still their strength renew'th.

The poet's paradise this is,
To which but few can come,
The Muses' only bower of bliss,
Their dear Elizium.

Here happy souls, (their blessed bowers
Free from the rude resort
Of beastly people) spend the hours
In harmless mirth and sport.

Then on to the Elizian plains
Apollo doth invite you,
Where he provides with pastoral strains,
In nymphals to delight you.

M. DRAYTON

SONNETS

From Tottel's Songs and Sonnets, 1557

The lover's life compared to the Alps

Like unto these unmeasurable mountains
So is my painful life, the burden of ire;
For high be they, and high is my desire;
And I of tears, and they be full of fountains;
Under craggy rocks they have barren plains,
Hard thoughts in me my woful mind doth tire:
Small fruit and many leaves their tops do attire,
With small effect great trust in me remains;
The boistous winds oft their high boughs do blast,
Hot sighs in me continually be shed;
Wild beasts in them, fierce love in me is fed;
Unmovable am I, and they steadfast.
     Of singing birds they have the tune and note,
     And I always plaints passing through my throat.

SIR T. WYATT

The lover abused renounceth love

My love to scorn, my service to retain,
Therein, methought, you used cruelty;
Since with good will I lost my liberty
[To follow her which causeth all my pain.]
Might never woe yet cause me to refrain,
But only this, which is extremity;
To give me nought, alas, nor to agree
That, as I was, your man I might remain:
But since that thus ye list to order me,
That would have been your servant true and fast,
Displease you not, my doting time is past;
And with my loss to leave I must agree:
     For as there is a certain time to rage,
     So is there time such madness to assuage.

SIR T. WYATT

SIR T. WYATT *and* THE EARL OF SURREY

*The lover compareth his state to a ship in perilous
storm tossed on the sea*

My galley charged with forgetfulness,
Through sharp seas, in winter nights, doth pass
'Tween rock and rock; and eke my foe, alas,
That is my lord, steereth with cruelness;
And every hour, a thought in readiness,
As though that death were light in such a case,
An endless wind doth tear the sail apace
Of forced sighs, and trusty fearfulness;
A rain of tears, a cloud of dark disdain,
Have done the wearied cords great hinderance:
Wreathed with error, and with ignorance;
The stars be hid that lead me to this pain.
  Drown'd is reason that should be my comfort,
  And I remain, despairing of the port.

SIR T. WYATT

From Tottel's Songs and Sonnets, 1557

*Description of Spring wherein each thing renews
save only the lover*

The soote season, that bud and bloom forth brings,
With green hath clad the hill and eke the vale:
The nightingale with feathers new she sings;
The turtle to her make hath told her tale:
Summer is come for every spray now springs,
The hart hath hung his old head on the pale:
The buck in brake his winter coat he flings:
The fishes float with new repaired scale:
The adder all her slough away she slings;
The swift swallow pursueth the flies smale;
The busy bee her honey now she mings:
Winter is worne that was the flowers' bale:
  And thus I see among these pleasant things
  Each care decays, and yet my sorrow springs.

HENRY HOWARD EARL OF SURREY

HENRY HOWARD EARL OF SURREY

A complaint by night of the lover not beloved

Alas, so all things now do hold their peace.
Heaven and earth disturbed in nothing :
The beasts, the air, the birds their song do cease :
The nightes car the stars about doth bring :
Calme is the Sea, the waves work less and less :
So am not I, whom love alas doth wring,
Bringing before my face the great increase
Of my desires, whereat I weep and sing,
In joy and woe, as in a doubtful ease.
For my sweet thoughts sometime do pleasure bring :
But bye and bye the cause of my disease
Gives me a pang, that inwardly doth sting,
    When that I think what grief it is again,
    To live and lack the thing should rid my pain.

HENRY HOWARD EARL OF SURREY

Vow to love faithfully howsoever he be rewarded

Set me whereas the sun doth parch the green,
Or where his beams do not dissolve the ice :
In temperate heat where he is felt and seen :
In presence prest of people mad or wise.
Set me in high, or yet in low degree :
In longest night, or in the shortest day :
In clearest sky, or where clouds thickest be :
In lusty youth, or when my hairs are grey.
Set me in heaven, in earth, or else in hell,
In hill, or dale, or in the foaming flood :
Thrall, or at large, alive where so I dwell :
Sicke or in health : in evil fame or good.
    Hers will I be, and only with this thought
    Content my self, although my chance be nought.

HENRY HOWARD EARL OF SURREY

SIR PHILIP SIDNEY

From Astrophel and Stella, 1591—1598

I

Loving in truth, and fain in verse my love to show,
That she, dear she, might take some pleasure of my pain,
Pleasure might cause her read, reading might make her know,
Knowledge might pity win, and pity grace obtain,
I sought fit words to paint the blackest face of woe;
Studying inventions fine, her wits to entertain;
Oft turning others' leaves, to see if thence would flow
Some fresh and fruitful showers upon my sun-burned brain.
But words came halting forth, wanting Invention's stay;
Invention, Nature's child, fled step-dame Study's blows;
And others' feet still seemed but strangers in my way.
Thus, great with child to speak, and helpless in my throes,
    Biting my truant pen, beating myself for spite,
    'Fool,' said my Muse to me, 'Look in thy heart, and
      write.'

SIR P. SIDNEY

XXXI

With how sad steps, O Moon, thou climb'st the skies,
How silently, and with how wan a face!
What! may it be that even in heav'nly place
That busy archer his sharp arrows tries?
Sure, if that long with love acquainted eyes
Can judge of love, thou feel'st a lover's case.
I read it in thy looks; thy languished grace
To me, that feel the like, thy state descries.
Then ev'n of fellowship, O Moon, tell me,
Is constant love deemed there but want of wit?
Are beauties there as proud as here they be?
Do they above love to be loved, and yet
    Those lovers scorn whom that love doth possess?
    Do they call virtue there ungratefulness?

SIR P. SIDNEY

SIR PHILIP SIDNEY

XXXIX

Come, sleep! O sleep, the certain knot of peace,
The baiting-place of wit, the balm of woe,
The poor man's wealth, the prisoner's release,
Th' indifferent judge between the high and low;
With shield of proof shield me from out the prease
Of those fierce darts despair at me doth throw:
O make in me those civil wars to cease,
I will good tribute pay, if thou do so.
Take thou of me smooth pillows, sweetest bed,
A chamber deaf to noise and blind to light,
A rosy garland and a weary head:
And if these things, as being thine by right,
 Move not thy heavy grace, thou shalt in me
 Livelier than elsewhere Stella's image see.

Sir P. Sidney

LIV

Because I breathe not love to every one,
Nor do not use set colours for to wear,
Nor nourish special locks of vowed hair,
Nor give each speech a full point of a groan,
The courtly nymphs, acquainted with the moan
Of them who in their lips Love's standard bear,
'What, he!' say they of me: 'now I dare swear
He cannot love; no, no, let him alone.'
And think so still, so Stella know my mind!
Profess in deed I do not Cupid's art;
But you, fair maids, at length this true shall find,
That his right badge is but worn in the heart;
 Dumb swans, not chattering pies, do lovers prove;
 They love indeed who quake to say they love.

Sir P. Sidney

SIR PHILIP SIDNEY

LXXIV

I never drank of Aganippe well,
Nor ever did in shade of Tempe sit,
And Muses scorn with vulgar brains to dwell,
Poor layman I, for sacred rites unfit.
Some do I hear of poets' fury tell,
But—God wot—wot not what they mean by it;
And this I swear by blackest brook of hell,
I am no pick-purse of another's wit.
How falls it, then, that with so smooth an ease
My thoughts I speak; and what I speak doth flow
In verse, and that my verse best wits doth please?
'Guess we the cause?   What, is it this?'   Fie, no!
    'Or so?'   Much less.   'How then?'   Sure thus it is,
    My lips are sweet, inspired with Stella's kiss.

SIR P. SIDNEY

LXXXIV

Highway! since you my chief Parnassus be,
And that my Muse, to some ears not unsweet,
Tempers her words to trampling horses' feet
More oft than to a chamber melody,
Now blessed you, bear onward blessed me
To her, where I my heart, safe-left, shall meet;
My Muse and I must you of duty greet
With thanks and wishes, wishing thankfully.
Be you still fair, honoured by public heed;
By no encroachment wronged, nor time forgot;
Nor blamed for blood, nor shamed for sinful deed;
And that you know I envy you no lot
    Of highest wish, I wish you so much bliss,
    Hundreds of years you Stella's feet may kiss!

SIR P. SIDNEY

SIR PHILIP SIDNEY

XC

Stella, think not that I by verse seek fame,
Who seek, who hope, who love, who live but thee;
Thine eyes my pride, thy lips mine history;
If thou praise not, all other praise is shame.
Nor so ambitious am I as to frame
A nest for my young praise in laurel tree.
In truth I swear I wish not there should be
Graved in mine epitaph a poet's name.
Ne, if I would, could I just title make
That any laud to me thereof should grow,
Without my plumes from others' wings I take.
For nothing from my wit or will doth flow,
　　Since all my words thy beauty doth endite,
　　And love doth hold my hand, and makes me write.

SIR P. SIDNEY

XCII

Be your words made, good sir, of Indian ware,
That you allow them me by so small rate?
Or do you cutted Spartans imitate?
Or do you mean my tender ears to spare,
That to my questions you so total are?
When I demand of Phoenix Stella's state,
You say forsooth 'You left her well of late.'
O God! think you that satisfies my care?
I would know whether she did sit or walk,
How clothed, how waited on, sighed she, or smiled,
Whereof, with whom, how often did she talk,
With what pastime time's journey she beguiled,
　　If her lips deigned to sweeten my poor name?
　　Say all, and all well said, still say the same.

SIR P. SIDNEY

SIR PHILIP SIDNEY

CIII

O happy Thames, that didst my Stella bear!
I saw thyself with many a smiling line
Upon thy cheerful face, joy's livery wear,
While those fair planets on thy streams did shine.
The boat for joy could not to dance forbear,
While wanton winds, with beauties so divine
Ravished, stayed not, till in her golden hair
They did themselves—O sweetest prison!—twine.
And fain those Æol's youth there would their stay
Have made, but, forc'd by Nature still to fly,
First did with puffing kiss those locks display:
She, so dishevelled, blushed : from window I
    With sight thereof cried out, 'O, fair disgrace,
    Let Honour's self to thee grant highest place!'

Sir P. Sidney

CVII

Stella, since thou so right a princess art
Of all the powers which life bestows on me,
That ere by them ought undertaken be,
They first resort unto that sovereign part;
Sweet, for a while give respite to my heart,
Which pants as though it still should leap to thee;
And on my thoughts give thy lieutenancy
To this great cause, which needs both use and art.
And as a queen who from her presence sends
Whom she employs, dismiss from thee my wit,
Till it have wrought what thy own will attends.
On servant's shame oft master's blame doth sit.
    O let not fools in me thy works reprove
    And scorning say 'See what it is to love!'

Sir P. Sidney

SIR PHILIP SIDNEY *and* FULKE GREVILLE

From Arcadia and Certain Sonnets, 1598

Leave me, O love! which reachest but to dust,
And thou, my mind, aspire to higher things:
Grow rich in that which never taketh rust;
Whatever fades but fading pleasure brings.
Draw in thy beams, and humble all thy might
To that sweet yoke where lasting freedoms be,
Which breaks the clouds, and opens forth the light
That doth both shine, and give us sight to see.
O take fast hold! let that light be thy guide,
In this small course which birth draws out to death,
And think how evil becometh him to slide,
Who seeketh heaven, and comes of heavenly breath.
    Then farewell, world, thy uttermost I see,
    Eternal Love maintain thy life in me.

SIR P. SIDNEY

From Caelica, 1633

XVII

Cynthia, whose glories are at full for ever,
Whose beauties draw forth tears, and kindle fires,
Fires, which kindled once are quenched never,
So beyond hope your worth bears up desires;
Why cast you clouds on your sweet looking eyes?
Are you afraid they show me too much pleasure?
Strong Nature decks the grave wherein it lies;
Excellence can never be expressed in measure.
Are you afraid, because my heart adores you,
The world will think I hold Endymion's place?
Hippolytus, sweet Cynthia, kneel'd before you,
Yet did you not come down to kiss his face.
    Angels enjoy the heavens' inward quires;
    Stargazers only multiply desires.

FULKE GREVILLE LORD BROOKE

191

THOMAS WATSON

From Hekatompathia, 1582

XXXIII

In this sonnet the author is of opinion, that his mistress (by the fatal appointment of destiny) was from the beginning reserved to live in these times, and to be the only governess and subject of his thoughts: whereas, if either she had been born when *Paris* was to give sentence upon *Ida* for bestowing the Golden Apple, she had (as he supposeth) been preferred before *Juno*, *Pallas*, and *Venus*, and moreover supplied that place in the love of king *Priam's* son which *Helen* of *Greece* obtained; or if she had then lived when *Bacchus* took *Ariadne* to wife, she had been conveyed in her stead unto that place in heaven where now the crown of *Ariadne* called *Corona Gnosia* doth shine continually, being beautified with great variety of lightsome stars.

> When Priam's son in midst of Ida plain
> Gave one the price, and other two the foile,
> If she for whom I still abide in pain
> Had lived then within the Troyan soil,
> > No doubt but hers had been the golden ball,
> > Helen had scaped rape, and Troy his fall.
> Or if my dame had then enjoyed life
> When Bacchus sought for Ariadne's love,
> No doubt but she had only been his wife,
> And flown from hence to sit with gods above:
> > For she exceeds his choice of Crete so far
> > As Phoebus doth excel a twinkling star.
> But from the first all fates have thus assigned,
> That she should live in these our latter days,
> I think to bear a sway within my mind
> And feed my thoughts with friendly sweet delays;
> > If so it be, let me attend my chance,
> > And fortune pipe when I begin to dance.

T. WATSON

THOMAS WATSON *and* SIR WALTER RALEGH

XXXVII

The author in this passion doth by manner of secret comparison prefer his beloved before all other women whatsoever : and persuadeth upon the examples of all sorts of Gods (whom love hath overtaken at one time or other) that the worthiness of his mistress being well considered, his own fondness in love must of force be in itself excusable.

If Jove himself be subject unto love
And range the woods to find a mortal prey ;
If Neptune from the seas himself remove,
And seek on sands with earthly wights to play:
  Then may I love my peerless choice by right,
  Who far excels each other mortal wight.
If Pluto could by love be drawn from hell,
To yield himself a silly virgin's thrall ;
If Phoebus could vouchsafe on earth to dwell,
To win a rustic maid unto his call ;
  Then how much more should I adore the sight
  Of her, in whom the heavens themselves delight ?
If country Pan might follow nymphs in chase,
And yet through love remain devoid of blame ;
If Satyrs were excus'd for seeking grace
To joy the fruits of any mortal dame ;
  Then why should I once doubt to love her still,
  On whom ne Gods nor men can gaze their fill ?
             T. WATSON

From The Faerie Queene, 1590

 A vision upon this conceit of the Faerie Queene

Methought I saw the grave where Laura lay
Within that temple where the vestal flame
Was wont to burn ; and passing by that way
To see that buried dust of living fame,
Whose tomb fair love and fairer virtue kept,
All suddenly I saw the Fairy Queen,
At whose approach the soul of Petrarch wept,
And from henceforth those graces were not seen ;
For they this Queen attended in whose stead
Oblivion laid him down on Laura's hearse.

RALEGH, BARNES *and* LODGE

Hereat the hardest stones were seen to bleed,
And groans of buried ghosts the heavens did pierce;
Where Homer's spright did tremble all for grief,
And curst th' access of that celestial thief.

Sir W. Ralegh

From **Parthenophil and Parthenophe, 1593**
XCIII

Begs Love, which whilom was a deity?
I list no such proud beggars at my gate.
For alms, he 'mongst cold Arctic folk doth wait,
And sunburnt Moors in contrariety,
Yet sweats nor freezes more. Then is it piety
To be remorseful at his bare estate?
His reach, he racketh at a higher rate.
He joins with proudest in society.
His eyes are blind forsooth; and men must pity
A naked poor boy, which doth no man harm.
He is not blind, such beggar boys be witty,
For he marks, hits and wounds hearts with his arm;
    Nor coldest North can stop his naked race,
    For where he comes, he warmeth every place.

Barnabe Barnes

From **Phillis, 1593**
I

O, pleasing thoughts, apprentices of love,
Fore-runners of desire, sweet mithridates
The poison of my sorrows to remove,
With whom my hopes and fear full oft debates;
Enrich yourselves and me by your self riches,
Which are the thoughts you spend on heaven-bred beauty,
Rouse you my muse beyond our poets' pitches,
And working wonders, yet say all is duty;
Use you no eaglets' eyes, nor phoenix' feathers,
To tower the heaven from whence heaven's wonder sallies.
For why? Your sun sings sweetly to her weathers,
Making a spring of winter in the valleys.
    Show to the world, though poor and scant my skill is,
    How sweet thoughts be, that are but thought on Phillis.

T. Lodge

THOMAS LODGE *and* GILES FLETCHER

XX

Some praise the looks, and others praise the locks,
Of their fair queens in love, with curious words.
Some laud the breast where love his treasure locks,
All like the eye that life and love affords.
But none of these frail beauties and unstable
Shall make my pen riot in pompous style;
More greater gifts shall my grave muse enable,
Whereat severer brows shall never smile.
I praise her honey-sweeter eloquence,
Which from the fountain of true wisdom floweth,
Her modest mien that matcheth excellence,
Her matchless faith which from her virtue groweth.
    And could my style her happy virtues equal,
    Time had no power her glories to enthral.

T. Lodge

From Licia, 1593

XXVIII

In time the strong and stately turrets fall;
In time the rose and silver lilies die;
In time the monarchs captive are and thrall;
In time the sea and rivers are made dry.
The hardest flint in time doth melt asunder;
Still living fame in time doth fade away;
The mountains proud we see in time come under;
And earth, for age, we see in time decay.
The sun in time forgets for to retire
From out the east where he was wont to rise;
The basest thoughts we see in time aspire;
And greedy minds in time do wealth despise.
    Thus all, sweet fair, in time must have an end,
    Except thy beauty, virtues, and thy friend.

G. Fletcher

HENRY CONSTABLE

From Diana, 1594

IX

My lady's presence makes the roses red,
Because to see her lips they blush for shame :
The lilies' leaves, for envy, pale became,
And her white hands in them this envy bred.
The marigold the leaves abroad doth spread,
Because the sun's and her power is the same ;
The violet of purple colour came,
Dyed in the blood she made my heart to shed.
In brief, all flowers from her their virtue take :
From her sweet breath their sweet smells do proceed,
The living heat which her eye-beams doth make,
Warmeth the ground, and quickeneth the seed.
   The rain wherewith she watereth the flowers
   Falls from mine eyes, which she dissolves in showers.

            H. Constable

From An Apology for Poetry, 1595

To Sir Philip Sidney's Soul

Give pardon, blessed soul, to my bold cries,
If they, importune, interrupt thy song,
Which now with joyful notes thou sing'st among
The angel-quiristers of the heavenly skies.
Give pardon eke, sweet soul, to my slow eyes
That since I saw thee now it is so long,
And yet the tears that unto thee belong
To thee as yet they did not sacrifice.
I did not know that thou wert dead before ;
I did not feel the grief I did sustain ;
The greater stroke astonisheth the more ;
Astonishment takes from us sense of pain ;
   I stood amazed when others' tears begun,
   And now begin to weep when they have done.

            H. Constable

196

SAMUEL DANIEL

From Delia, 1594

XIX

Restore thy tresses to the golden ore ;
Yield Cytherea's son those arcs of love ;
Bequeath the heavens the stars that I adore ;
And to the orient do thy pearls remove ;
Yield thy hands' pride unto the ivory white ;
To Arabian odours give thy breathing sweet ;
Restore thy blush unto Aurora bright ;
To Thetis give the honour of thy feet ;
Let Venus have thy graces her resigned ;
And thy sweet voice give back unto the spheres ;
But yet restore thy fierce and cruel mind
To Hyrcan tigers and to ruthless bears.
    Yield to the marble thy hard heart again ;
    So shalt thou cease to plague, and I to pain.

S. DANIEL

XXXIV

Look, Delia, how we 'steem the half-blown rose,
The image of thy blush and summer's honour ;
Whilst in her tender green she doth inclose
The pure sweet beauty Time bestows upon her.
No sooner spreads her glory in the air,
But straight her full-blown pride is in declining ;
She then is scorned that late adorned the fair.
So clouds thy beauty after fairest shining ;
No April can revive thy withered flowers,
Whose blooming grace adorns thy glory now :
Swift speedy Time, feathered with flying hours,
Dissolves the beauty of the fairest brow.
    O let not then such riches waste in vain,
    But love whilst that thou may'st be loved again.

S. DANIEL

SAMUEL DANIEL

XLIX

Care-charmer Sleep, son of the sable Night,
Brother to Death in silent darkness born,
Relieve my languish, and restore the light,
With dark forgetting of my cares return,
And let the day be time enough to mourn
The shipwreck of my ill-adventured youth :
Let waking eyes suffice to wail their scorn,
Without the torment of the night's untruth.
Cease, dreams, the imagery of our day-desires,
To model forth the passions of the morrow ;
Never let rising sun approve you liars,
To add more grief to aggravate my sorrow :
    Still let me sleep, embracing clouds in vain,
    And never wake to feel the day's disdain.

S. DANIEL

L

Let others sing of Knights and Paladines
In aged accents and untimely words ;
Paint shadows in imaginary lines
Which well the reach of their high wits records ;
But I must sing of thee, and those fair eyes
Authentic shall my verse in time to come ;
When yet the unborn shall say, 'Lo, where she lies
Whose beauty made him speak that else was dumb.'
These are the arks, the trophies I erect,
That fortify thy name against old age ;
And these thy sacred virtues must protect
Against the dark, and Time's consuming rage.
    Though the error of my youth they shall discover,
    Suffice they shew I lived, and was thy lover.

S. DANIEL

MICHAEL DRAYTON

From Idea, 1594—1619

IV

Bright star of beauty, on whose eyelids sit
A thousand nymph-like and enamoured graces,
The goddesses of memory and wit
Which there in order take their several places;
In whose dear bosom sweet delicious Love
Lays down his quiver, which he once did bear,
Since he that blessed paradise did prove,
And leaves his mother's lap to sport him there :
Let others strive to entertain with words,
My soul is of a braver mettle made;
I hold that vile which vulgar wit affords,
In me's that faith which time cannot invade.
    Let what I praise be still made good by you :
    Be you most worthy, whilst I am most true.

M. DRAYTON

VII

Love in a humour played the prodigal,
And bade my senses to a solemn feast;
Yet more to grace the company withal,
Invites my heart to be the chiefest guest :
No other drink would serve this glutton's turn
But precious tears distilling from mine eyne,
Which with my sighs this epicure doth burn,
Quaffing carouses in this costly wine ;
Where, in his cups o'ercome with foul excess,
Straightways he plays a swaggering ruffian's part,
And at the banquet in his drunkenness
Slew his dear friend, my kind and truest heart ;
    A gentle warning, friends, thus may you see,
    What 'tis to keep a drunkard company.

M. DRAYTON

MICHAEL DRAYTON

XLIV

Whilst thus my pen strives to eternize thee,
Age rules my lines with wrinkles in my face,
Where, in the map of all my misery,
Is modelled out the world of my disgrace;
Whilst in despite of tyrannizing times,
Medea-like, I make thee young again,
Proudly thou scorn'st my world-out-wearing rhymes,
And murtherest virtue with thy coy disdain:
And though in youth my youth untimely perish
To keep thee from oblivion and the grave,
Ensuing ages yet my rhymes shall cherish,
Where I entombed my better part shall save;
    And though this earthly body fade and die,
    My name shall mount upon eternity.

M. Drayton

LIII

Clear Ankor, on whose silver sanded shore
My soul-shrined saint, my fair Idea, lies;
O blessed brook, whose milk-white swans adore
The crystal stream refined by her eyes,
Where sweet myrrh-breathing zephyr in the spring
Gently distils his nectar-dropping showers,
Where nightingales in Arden sit and sing
Amongst the dainty dew-impearled flowers;
Say thus, fair brook, when thou shalt see thy queen,
Lo, here thy shepherd spent his wandering years,
And in these shades, dear nymph, he oft hath been,
And here to thee he sacrificed his tears:
    Fair Arden, thou my Tempe art alone,
    And thou, sweet Ankor, art my Helicon.

M. Drayton

MICHAEL DRAYTON *and* EDMUND SPENSER

LXI

Since there's no help, come let us kiss and part.
Nay, I have done, you get no more of me,
And I am glad, yea, glad with all my heart,
That thus so cleanly I myself can free;
Shake hands for ever, cancel all our vows,
And when we meet at any time again,
Be it not seen in either of our brows
That we one jot of former love retain;
Now at the last gasp of Love's latest breath,
When, his pulse failing, Passion speechless lies,
When Faith is kneeling by his bed of death,
And Innocence is closing up his eyes,
    Now if thou would'st, when all have given him over,
    From death to life thou might'st him yet recover.

M. DRAYTON

From Amoretti, 1595

III

The soverayne beauty which I doo admyre,
Witnesse the world how worthy to be prayzed!
The light whereof hath kindled heavenly fyre
In my fraile spirit, by her from basenesse raysed;
That, being now with her huge brightnesse dazed,
Base thing I can no more endure to view:
But, looking still on her, I stand amazed
At wondrous sight of so celestiall hew.
So when my toung would speak her praises dew,
It stopped is with thoughts astonishment;
And, when my pen would write her titles true,
It ravisht is with fancies wonderment:
    Yet in my hart I then both speake and write
    The wonder that my wit cannot endite.

E. SPENSER

EDMUND SPENSER

XV

Ye tradefull Merchants, that, with weary toyle,
Do seeke most pretious things to make your gain;
And both the Indias of their treasure spoile;
What needeth you to seeke so farre in vaine?
For loe, my love doth in her selfe containe
All this worlds riches that may farre be found:
If Saphyres, loe, her eies be Saphyres plaine;
If Rubies, loe, hir lips be Rubies sound;
If Pearles, hir teeth be Pearles, both pure and round;
If Yvorie, her forehead Yvory weene;
If Gold, her locks are finest Gold on ground;
If Silver, her faire hands are Silver sheene:
    But that which fairest is, but few behold,
    Her mind adornd with vertues manifold.

E. Spenser

XXV

How long shall this lyke dying lyfe endure,
And know no end of her owne mysery,
But wast and weare away in termes unsure,
Twixt feare and hope depending doubtfully!
Yet better were attonce to let me die,
And shew the last ensample of your pride;
Then to torment me thus with cruelty,
To prove your powre, which I too well have tride.
But yet if in your hardned brest ye hide
A close intent at last to shew me grace;
Then all the woes and wrecks which I abide,
As meanes of blisse I gladly wil embrace;
    And wish that more and greater they might be,
    That greater meede at last may turne to mee.

E. Spenser

EDMUND SPENSER

XXVII

Faire Proud! now tell me, why should faire be proud,
Sith all worlds glorie is but drosse uncleane,
And in the shade of death it selfe shall shroud,
However now thereof ye little weene!
That goodly Idoll, now so gay beseene,
Shall doffe her fleshes borrowd fayre attyre,
And be forgot as it had never beene;
That many now much worship and admire!
Ne any then shall after it inquire,
Ne any mention shall thereof remaine,
But what this verse, that never shall expyre,
Shall to you purchas with her thankles paine!
        Faire! be no lenger proud of that shall perish;
        But that, which shall you make immortall, cherish.

E. SPENSER

XXXIV

Lyke as a ship, that through the Ocean wyde,
By conduct of some star, doth make her way;
Whenas a storme hath dimd her trusty guyde,
Out of her course doth wander far astray!
So I, whose star, that wont with her bright ray
Me to direct, with cloudes is over-cast,
Doe wander now, in darknesse and dismay,
Through hidden perils round about me plast;
Yet hope I well that, when this storme is past,
My Helice, the lodestar of my lyfe,
Will shine again, and looke on me at last,
With lovely light to cleare my cloudy grief,
        Till then I wander carefull, comfortlesse,
        In secret sorrow, and sad pensivenesse.

E. SPENSER

EDMUND SPENSER

LXIII

After long stormes and tempests sad assay,
Which hardly I endured heretofore,
In dread of death, and daungerous dismay,
With which my silly barke was tossed sore:
I doe at length descry the happy shore,
In which I hope ere long for to arryve :
Fayre soyle it seemes from far, and fraught with store
Of all that deare and daynty is alyve.
Most happy he ! that can at last atchyve
The joyous safety of so sweet a rest ;
Whose least delight sufficeth to deprive
Remembrance of all paines which him opprest.
 All paines are nothing in respect of this ;
 All sorrowes short that gaine eternall blisse.

E. SPENSER

LXIX

The famous warriors of anticke world
Used Trophees to erect in stately wize ;
In which they would the records have enrold
Of theyr great deeds and valorus emprize.
What trophee then shall I most fit devize,
In which I may record the memory
Of my loves conquest, peerelesse beauties prise,
Adorn'd with honour, love, and chastity !
Even this verse, vowd to eternity,
Shall be thereof immortall moniment ;
And tell her prayse to all posterity,
That may admire such worlds rare wonderment ;
 The happy purchase of my glorious spoile,
 Gotten at last with labour and long toyle.

E. SPENSER

SPENSER *and* GRIFFIN

LXX

Fresh Spring, the herald of loves mighty king,
In whose cote-armour richly are displayed
All sorts of flowers, the which on earth do spring,
In goodly colours gloriously arrayed ;
Goe to my love, where she is carelesse layd,
Yet in her winters bowre not well awake ;
Tell her the joyous time wil not be staid,
Unlesse she doe him by the forelock take ;
Bid her therefore her selfe soone ready make,
To wayt on Love amongst his lovely crew;
Where every one, that misseth then her make,
Shall be by him amearst with penance dew.
   Make hast, therefore, sweet love, whilest it is prime ;
   For none can call againe the passed time.

E. SPENSER

From Fidessa, 1596

LI

Work, work apace, you blessed Sisters three,
In restless twining of my fatal thread.
O, let your nimble hands at once agree,
To weave it out and cut it off with speed.
Then shall my vexed and tormented ghost
Have quiet passage to the Elysian rest ;
And sweetly over death and fortune boast,
In everlasting triumphs with the blest.
But ah ! (too well I know) you have conspired
A lingering death for him that loatheth life,
As if with woes he never could be tired.
For this, you hide your all-dividing knife.
   One comfort yet the heavens have assigned me,
   That I must die, and leave my griefs behind me.

BARTHOLOMEW GRIFFIN

205

RICHARD LINCHE *and* RICHARD BARNFIELD

From Diella, 1596

XXVIII

Weary with serving where I naught could get,
I thought to cross great Neptune's greatest seas
To live in exile; but my drift was let
By cruel Fortune, spiteful of such ease.
The ship I had to pass in, was my mind;
Greedy desire was topsail of the same;
My tears were surges, sighs did serve for wind;
Of all my ship despair was chiefest frame.
Sorrow was master, care the cable rope;
Grief was the mainmast, Love the captain of it;
He that did rule the helm was foolish hope,
But beauty was the rock that my ship split,
   Which since hath made such shipwreck of my joy,
   That still I swim in th' ocean of annoy.

R. Linche

From Poems in divers Humours, 1598

In praise of Music and Poetry

If music and sweet poetry agree,
As they must needs, the sister and the brother;
Then must the love be great twixt thee and me,
Because thou lovs't the one, and I the other.
Dowland to thee is dear, whose heavenly touch
Upon the lute doth ravish human sense;
Spenser to me, whose deep conceit is such
As passing all conceit needs no defence.
Thou lov'st to hear the sweet melodious sound
That Phoebus' lute, the queen of music, makes;
And I in deep delight am chiefly drowned,
Whenas himself to singing he betakes.
   One god is god of both as poets feign,
   One knight loves both, and both in thee remain.

R. Barnfield

WILLIAM SHAKESPEARE

From Sonnets, 1609

XVIII

Shall I compare thee to a summer's day ?
Thou art more lovely and more temperate :
Rough winds do shake the darling buds of May,
And summer's lease hath all too short a date :
Sometime too hot the eye of heaven shines,
And often is his gold complexion dimm'd :
And every fair from fair sometime declines,
By chance or nature's changing course untrimm'd.
But thy eternal summer shall not fade
Nor lose possession of that fair thou owest ;
Nor shall Death brag thou wander'st in his shade,
When in eternal lines to time thou growest.
    So long as men can breathe, or eyes can see,
    So long lives this, and this gives life to thee.

W. SHAKESPEARE

XXIX

When, in disgrace with fortune and men's eyes,
I all alone beweep my outcast state,
And trouble deaf heaven with my bootless cries,
And look upon myself, and curse my fate ;
Wishing me like to one more rich in hope,
Featured like him, like him with friends possess'd,
Desiring this man's art and that man's scope,
With what I most enjoy contented least ;
Yet in these thoughts myself almost despising,
Haply I think on thee, and then my state,
Like to the lark at break of day arising
From sullen earth, sings hymns at heaven's gate ;
    For thy sweet love remember'd such wealth brings
    That then I scorn to change my state with kings.

W. SHAKESPEARE

WILLIAM SHAKESPEARE

XXX

When to the sessions of sweet silent thought
I summon up remembrance of things past,
I sigh the lack of many a thing I sought,
And with old woes new wail my dear time's waste;
Then can I drown an eye, unused to flow,
For precious friends hid in death's dateless night,
And weep afresh love's long since cancelled woe,
And moan the expense of many a vanish'd sight.
Then can I grieve at grievances foregone,
And heavily from woe to woe tell o'er
The sad account of fore-bemoaned moan,
Which I new pay as if not paid before:
  But if the while I think on thee, dear friend,
  All losses are restored, and sorrows end.

W. Shakespeare

XXXII

If thou survive my well-contented day
When that churl Death my bones with dust shall cover,
And shalt by fortune once more re-survey
These poor rude lines of thy deceased lover;
Compare them with the bettering of the time,
And though they be outstripp'd by every pen,
Reserve them for my love, not for their rhyme,
Exceeded by the height of happier men.
O then vouchsafe me but this loving thought:
' Had my friend's Muse grown with this growing age,
A dearer birth than this his love had brought,
To march in ranks of better equipage:
  But since he died, and poets better prove,
  Theirs for their style I'll read, his for his love.'

W. Shakespeare

WILLIAM SHAKESPEARE

XXXIII

Full many a glorious morning have I seen
Flatter the mountain-tops with sovereign eye,
Kissing with golden face the meadows green,
Gilding pale streams with heavenly alchemy ;
Anon permit the basest clouds to ride
With ugly rack on his celestial face,
And from the forlorn world his visage hide,
Stealing unseen to west with this disgrace :
Even so my sun one early morn did shine
With all-triumphant splendour on my brow ;
But out, alack ! he was but one hour mine ;
The region cloud hath mask'd him from me now.
  Yet him for this my love no whit disdaineth ;
  Suns of the world may stain when heaven's sun staineth.

W. SHAKESPEARE

LIV

O, how much more doth beauty beauteous seem
By that sweet ornament which truth doth give !
The rose looks fair, but fairer we it deem
For that sweet odour which doth in it live.
The canker-blooms have full as deep a dye
As the perfumed tincture of the roses,
Hang on such thorns and play as wantonly
When summer's breath their masked buds discloses ;
But, for their virtue only is their show,
They live unwooed and unrespected fade,
Die to themselves. Sweet roses do not so ;
Of their sweet deaths are sweetest odours made ;
  And so of you, beauteous and lovely youth,
  When that shall fade, my verse distills your truth.

W. SHAKESPEARE

WILLIAM SHAKESPEARE

LXIV

When I have seen by Time's fell hand defaced
The rich proud cost of out-worn buried age;
When sometime lofty towers I see down-razed,
And brass eternal slave to mortal rage;
When I have seen the hungry ocean gain
Advantage on the kingdom of the shore,
And the firm soil win of the watery main,
Increasing store with loss, and loss with store;
When I have seen such interchange of state,
Or state itself confounded to decay,
Ruin hath taught me thus to ruminate,
That Time will come and take my love away:
    This thought is as a death, which cannot choose
    But weep to have that which it fears to lose.

W. Shakespeare

LXV

Since brass, nor stone, nor earth, nor boundless sea,
But sad mortality o'ersways their power,
How with this rage shall beauty hold a plea,
Whose action is no stronger than a flower?
O, how shall summer's honey breath hold out
Against the wreckful siege of battering days,
When rocks impregnable are not so stout,
Nor gates of steel so strong, but Time decays?
O fearful meditation! where, alack!
Shall Time's best jewel from Time's chest lie hid?
Or what strong hand can hold his swift foot back,
Or who his spoil of beauty can forbid?
    O, none, unless this miracle have might,
    That in black ink my love may still shine bright.

W. Shakespeare

WILLIAM SHAKESPEARE

LXVI

Tired with all these, for restful death I cry,
As, to behold desert a beggar born,
And needy nothing trimm'd in jollity,
And purest faith unhappily forsworn,
And gilded honour shamefully misplaced,
And maiden virtue rudely strumpeted,
And right perfection wrongfully disgraced,
And strength by limping sway disabled,
And art made tongue-tied by authority,
And folly, doctor-like, controlling skill,
And simple truth miscall'd simplicity,
And captive good attending captain ill :
    Tired with all these, from these would I be gone,
    Save that, to die, I leave my love alone.

W. SHAKESPEARE

LXXIII

That time of year thou mayst in me behold
When yellow leaves, or none, or few do hang
Upon those boughs which shake against the cold,
Bare ruin'd choirs, where late the sweet birds sang.
In me thou see'st the twilight of such day
As after sunset fadeth in the west,
Which by and by black night doth take away,
Death's second self, that seals up all in rest.
In me thou see'st the glowing of such fire,
That on the ashes of his youth doth lie,
As the deathbed whereon it must expire,
Consumed with that which it was nourish'd by.
    This thou perceivest, which makes thy love more strong,
    To love that well which thou must leave ere long.

W. SHAKESPEARE

WILLIAM SHAKESPEARE

LXXXVI

Was it the proud full sail of his great verse,
Bound for the prize of all too precious you,
That did my ripe thoughts in my brain inhearse,
Making their tomb the womb wherein they grew?
Was it his spirit, by spirits taught to write
Above a mortal pitch, that struck me dead?
No, neither he, nor his compeers by night
Giving him aid, my verse astonished.
He, nor that affable familiar ghost
Which nightly gulls him with intelligence,
As victors of my silence cannot boast;
I was not sick of any fear from thence.
      But when your countenance fill'd up his line,
      Then lack'd I matter; that enfeebled mine.

W. SHAKESPEARE

XCIV

They that have power to hurt and will do none,
That do not do the thing they most do show,
Who, moving others, are themselves as stone,
Unmoved, cold, and to temptation slow,
They rightly do inherit heaven's graces,
And husband nature's riches from expense;
They are the lords and owners of their faces,
Others but stewards of their excellence.
The summer's flower is to the summer sweet,
Though to itself it only live and die;
But if that flower with base infection meet,
The basest weed outbraves his dignity:
      For sweetest things turn sourest by their deeds;
      Lilies that fester smell far worse than weeds.

W. SHAKESPEARE

WILLIAM SHAKESPEARE

XCVIII

From you have I been absent in the spring,
When proud-pied April dress'd in all his trim
Hath put a spirit of youth in everything,
That heavy Saturn laugh'd and leap'd with him.
Yet nor the lays of birds nor the sweet smell
Of different flowers in odour and in hue
Could make me any summer's story tell,
Or from their proud lap pluck them where they grew;
Nor did I wonder at the lily's white,
Nor praise the deep vermilion in the rose;
They were but sweet, but figures of delight,
Drawn after you, you pattern of all those.
    Yet seem'd it winter still and you away,
    As with your shadow, I with these did play.

W. SHAKESPEARE

CIV

To me, fair friend, you never can be old,
For as you were when first your eye I eyed,
Such seems your beauty still. Three winters cold
Have from the forests shook three summers' pride,
Three beauteous springs to yellow autumn turn'd
In process of the seasons have I seen,
Three April perfumes in three hot Junes burn'd,
Since first I saw you fresh which yet are green.
Ah! yet doth beauty, like a dial hand,
Steal from his figure and no pace perceived;
So your sweet hue, which methinks still doth stand,
Hath motion, and mine eye may be deceived:
    For fear of which, hear this, thou age unbred,
    Ere you were born was beauty's summer dead.

W. SHAKESPEARE

WILLIAM SHAKESPEARE

CVI

When in the chronicle of wasted time
I see descriptions of the fairest wights,
And beauty making beautiful old rhyme
In praise of ladies dead and lovely knights;
Then, in the blazon of sweet beauty's best,
Of hand, of foot, of lip, of eye, of brow,
I see their antique pen would have express'd
Even such a beauty as you master now.
So all their praises are but prophecies
Of this our time, all you prefiguring;
And, for they look'd but with divining eyes,
They had not skill enough your worth to sing:
  For we, which now behold these present days,
  Have eyes to wonder, but lack tongues to praise.

W. Shakespeare

CVII

Not mine own fears, nor the prophetic soul
Of the wide world dreaming on things to come,
Can yet the lease of my true love control,
Supposed as forfeit to a confined doom.
The mortal moon hath her eclipse endured
And the sad augurs mock their own presage;
Incertainties now crown themselves assured
And peace proclaims olives of endless age.
Now with the drops of this most balmy time
My love looks fresh, and Death to me subscribes,
Since, spite of him, I'll live in this poor rhyme,
While he insults o'er dull and speechless tribes;
  And thou in this shalt find thy monument,
  When tyrants' crests and tombs of brass are spent.

W. Shakespeare

WILLIAM SHAKESPEARE

CXVI

Let me not to the marriage of true minds
Admit impediments. Love is not love
Which alters when it alteration finds,
Or bends with the remover to remove :
O, no ! it is an ever-fixed mark
That looks on tempests and is never shaken ;
It is the star to every wandering bark,
Whose worth's unknown, although his height be taken.
Love's not Time's fool, though rosy lips and cheeks
Within his bending sickle's compass come ;
Love alters not with his brief hours and weeks,
But bears it out even to the edge of doom.
    If this be error and upon me proved,
    I never writ, nor no man ever loved.

W. SHAKESPEARE

CXXIX

The expense of spirit in a waste of shame
Is lust in action ; and till action, lust
Is perjured, murderous, bloody, full of blame,
Savage, extreme, rude, cruel, not to trust,
Enjoy'd no sooner but despised straight,
Past reason hunted, and no sooner had
Past reason hated, as a swallow'd bait
On purpose laid to make the taker mad ;
Mad in pursuit and in possession so ;
Had, having, and in quest to have, extreme ;
A bliss in proof, and proved, a very woe ;
Before, a joy proposed ; behind, a dream.
    All this the world well knows ; yet none knows well
    To shun the heaven that leads men to this hell.

W. SHAKESPEARE

WILLIAM SHAKESPEARE

CXLIV

Two loves I have of comfort and despair,
Which like two spirits do suggest me still;
The better angel is a man right fair,
The worser spirit a woman colour'd ill.
To win me soon to hell, my female evil
Tempteth my better angel from my side,
And would corrupt my saint to be a devil,
Wooing his purity with her foul pride.
And whether that my angel be turn'd fiend
Suspect I may, yet not directly tell;
But being both from me, both to each friend,
I guess one angel in another's hell:
      Yet this shall I ne'er know, but live in doubt
      Till my bad angel fire my good one out.

W. Shakespeare

CXLVI

Poor soul, the centre of my sinful earth,
[Foil'd by] these rebel powers that thee array,
Why dost thou pine within and suffer dearth,
Painting thy outward walls so costly gay?
Why so large cost, having so short a lease,
Dost thou upon thy fading mansion spend?
Shall worms, inheritors of this excess,
Eat up thy charge? is this thy body's end?
Then, soul, live thou upon thy servant's loss,
And let that pine to aggravate thy store;
Buy terms divine in selling hours of dross;
Within be fed, without be rich no more:
      So shalt thou feed on Death, that feeds on men,
      And Death once dead, there's no more dying then.

W. Shakespeare

SIR JOHN DAVIES

From Gulling Sonnets, 1595

Mine eye, mine ear, my will, my wit, my heart,
Did see, did hear, did like, discern, did love,
Her face, her speech, her fashion, judgment, art,
Which did charme, please, delight, confound and move.
Then fancy, humour, love, conceit and thought,
Did so draw, force, intice, persuade, devise,
That she was won, moved, carried, compassed, wrought,
To think me kind, true, comely, valiant, wise,
That heaven, earth, hell, my folly and her pride,
Did work, contrive, labour, conspire and swear,
To make me scorn'd, vile, cast off, base, defied,
With her my love, my light, my life, my dear.
    So that my heart, my will, my ear and eye
    Doth grieve, lament, sorrow, despair, and die.

SIR J. DAVIES

217

CLASSICAL POEMS

From Virgil's Aeneis Book II, 1557

Laocoon

Us caitiffs then a far more dreadful chance
Befell, that troubled our unarmed breasts.
Whiles Laocon, that chosen was by lot
Neptunus' priest, did sacrifice a bull
Before the holy altar, suddenly
From Tenedon, behold! in circles great
By the calm seas come fleeting adders twain,
Which plied towards the shore (I loathe to tell)
With reared breast lift up above the seas:
Whose bloody crests aloft the waves were seen;
The hinder part swam hidden in the flood;
Their grisly backs were linked manifold:
With sound of broken waves they gat the strand,
With glowing eyen tainted with blood and fire;
Whose waltring tongues did lick their hissing mouths.
We fled away; our face the blood forsook:
But they with gait direct to Lacon ran.
And first of all each serpent doth enwrap
The bodies small of his two tender sons;
Whose wretched limbs they bit and fed thereon.
Then raught they him, who had his weapon caught
To rescue them; twice winding him about,
With folded knots and circled tails, his waist:
Their scaled backs did compass twice his neck,
With reared heads aloft and stretched throats.

HENRY HOWARD EARL OF SURREY

He with his hands strave to unloose the knots,
Whose sacred fillets all-besprinkled were
With filth of gory blood and venom rank,
And to the stars such dreadful shouts he sent,
Like to the sound the roaring bull forth lows,
Which from the halter wounded doth astart,
The swerving axe when he shakes from his neck.
The serpents twine, with hasted trail they glide
To Pallas' temple, and her towers of height :
Under the feet of which the Goddess stern,
Hidden behind her target's boss they crept.
New gripes of dread then pierce our trembling breasts.
They said : Lacon's deserts had dearly bought
His heinous deed ; that pierced had with steel
The sacred bulk, and thrown the wicked lance.
The people cried with sundry greeing shouts
To bring the horse to Pallas' temple blive ;
In hope thereby the Goddess' wrath t'appease.
We cleft the walls and closures of the town ;
Whereto all help : and underset the feet
With sliding rolls, and bound his neck with ropes.
This fatal gin thus overclamb our walls,
Stuft with arm'd men : about the which there ran
Children and maids, that holy carols sang;
And well were they whose hands might touch the cords !
With threat'ning cheer thus slided through our town
The subtle tree, to Pallas' temple-ward.
O native land ! Ilion ! and of the gods
The mansion place ! O warlike walls of Troy !
Four times it stopt in th'entry of our gate ;
Four times the harness clatter'd in the womb.
But we go on, unsound of memory,
And blinded eke by rage persever still :
This fatal monster in the fane we place.

HENRY HOWARD EARL OF SURREY

SURREY *and* MARLOWE

From Virgil's Aeneis Book IV, 1557

Fame

Forthwith Fame flieth through the great Libyan towns:
A mischief Fame, there is none else so swift;
That moving grows and flitting gathers force.
First small for dread, soon after climbs the skies;
Stayeth on earth, and hides her head in clouds.
Whom our mother the earth, tempted by wrath
Of gods, begat; the last sister (they write)
To Cäeus, and to Enceladus eke:
Speedy of foot, of wing likewise as swift,
A monster huge, and dreadful to descrive.
In every plume that on her body sticks,
(A thing indeed much marvellous to hear)
As many waker eyes lurk underneath,
So many mouths to speak, and listening ears.
By night she flies amid the cloudy sky,
Shrieking, by the dark shadow of the earth,
Ne doth decline to the sweet sleep her eyes.
By day she sits to mark on the house top,
Or turrets high; and the great towns affrays;
As mindful of ill and lies, as blasing truth.

HENRY HOWARD EARL OF SURREY

From Hero and Leander, First Sestiad, 1598

' Who ever lov'd, that lov'd not at first sight?'

On this feast-day, O cursed day and hour,
Went Hero thorough Sestos, from her tower
To Venus' temple, where unhappily,
As after chanced, they did each other spy.
So fair a church as this had Venus none:
The walls were of discolour'd jasper stone,
Wherein was Proteus carved; and over head
A lovely vine of green sea-agate spread,
Where by one hand light-headed Bacchus hung,
And with the other wine from grapes out-wrung.

CHRISTOPHER MARLOWE

Of crystal shining fair the pavement was ;
The town of Sestos called it Venus' glass :
There might you see the gods in sundry shapes,
Committing heady riots, incest, rapes.
For know, that underneath this radiant floor
Was Danäe's statue in a brazen tower ;
Jove slyly stealing from his sister's bed,
To dally with Idalian Ganymed ;
And for his love Europa, bellowing loud,
And tumbling with the rainbow in a cloud ;
Blood-quaffing Mars heaving the iron net
Which limping Vulcan and his Cyclops set ;
Love kindling fire to burn such towns as Troy ;
Silvanus weeping for the lovely boy
That now is turned into a cypress tree,
Under whose shade the wood-gods love to be.
And in the midst a silver altar stood ;
There Hero sacrificing turtle's blood,
Vail'd to the ground, veiling her eyelids close ;
And modestly they opened as she rose :
Thence flew Love's arrow with the golden head ;
And thus Leander was enamoured.
Stone-still he stood, and evermore he gazed,
Till with the fire, that from his countenance blaz'd
Relenting Hero's gentle heart was shook ;
Such force and virtue hath an amorous look.
   It lies not in our power to love or hate,
For will in us is over-ruled by fate.
When two are stript long e'er the course begin,
We wish that one should lose the other win ;
And one especially do we affect
Of two gold ingots, like in each respect :
The reason no man knows ; let it suffice
What we behold is censur'd by our eyes.
Where both deliberate, the love is slight :
Who ever lov'd, that lov'd not at first sight ?
He kneel'd, but unto her devoutly pray'd :
Chaste Hero to herself thus softly said,
'Were I the saint he worships, I would hear him ' ;
And, as she spake those words, came somewhat near him.

CHRISTOPHER MARLOWE

He started up ; she blush'd as one asham'd ;
Wherewith Leander much more was inflam'd.
He touch'd her hand ; in touching it, she trembled :
Love deeply grounded, hardly is dissembled :
These lovers parled by the touch of hands :
True love is mute, and oft amazed stands.
Thus while dumb signs their yielding hearts entangled,
The air with sparks of living fire was spangled ;
And night, deep-drenched in misty Acheron,
Heav'd up her head, and half the world upon
Breath'd darkness forth, (dark night is Cupid's day) :
And now begins Leander to display
Love's holy fire with words, with sighs and tears ;
Which, like sweet music, entered Hero's ears ;
And yet at every word she turn'd aside,
And always cut him off as he replied.

*   *   *   *   *   *

'Though neither gods nor men may thee deserve,
Yet for her sake whom you have vowed to serve
Abandon fruitless cold Virginity,
The gentle queen of Love's sole enemy.
Then shall you most resemble Venus' nun,
When Venus' sweet rites are performed and done.
Flint-breasted Pallas joys in single life,
But Pallas and your mistress are at strife.
Love ! Hero then, and be not tyrannous,
But heal the heart that thou hast wounded thus,
Nor stain thy youthful years with avarice,
Fair fools delight to be accounted nice.
The richest corn dies if it be not reapt,
Beauty alone is lost, too warily kept.'
These arguments he used and many more ;
Wherewith she yielded, that was won before.
Hero's looks yielded, but her words made war :
Women are won when they begin to jar.
Thus having swallow'd Cupid's golden hook,
The more she striv'd, the deeper was she strook :
Yet evilly feigning anger strove she still,
And would be thought to grant against her will.

CHRISTOPHER MARLOWE

So having paused awhile, at last she said,
'Who taught thee rhetoric to deceive a maid?
Ay me! Such words as these should I abhor,
And yet I like them for the orator.'
With that Leander stoop'd to have embrac'd her,
But from his spreading arms away she cast her,
And thus bespake him: 'Gentle youth, forbear
To touch the sacred garments which I wear.
Upon a rock and underneath a hill,
Far from the town, (where all is whist and still,
Save that the sea, playing on yellow sand,
Sends forth a rattling murmur to the land,
Whose sound allures the golden Morpheus
In silence of the night to visit us,)
My turret stands; and there, God knows, I play
With Venus' swans and sparrows all the day.
A dwarfish beldam bears me company,
That hops about the chamber where I lie,
And spends the night, that might be better spent,
In vain discourse and apish merriment:
Come thither.' As she spake this her tongue tripp'd,
For unawares 'Come thither' from her slipp'd;
And suddenly her former colour changed,
And here and there her eyes through anger rang'd;
And, like a planet moving several ways
At one self instant, she, poor soul, assays,
Loving, not to love at all, and every part
Strove to resist the motions of her heart:
And hands so pure, so innocent, nay, such
As might have made Heaven stoop to have a touch,
Did she uphold to Venus, and again
Vow'd spotless chastity; but all in vain;
Cupid beats down her prayers with his wings;
Her vows above the empty air he flings:
All deep enrag'd, his sinewy bow he bent,
And shot a shaft that burning from him went;
Wherewith she strooken, look'd so dolefully,
As made Love sigh to see his tyranny;
And, as she wept, her tears to pearl he turn'd,
And wound them on his arm, and for her mourn'd.

C. MARLOWE

223

GEORGE CHAPMAN

From The Iliad Book IV, 1598—1611

Agamemnon and Nestor

Then held he on to other troops, and Nestor next beheld,
(The subtle Pylian orator) range up and down the field,
Embattelling his men at arms, and stirring all to blows,
Points every legion out his chief, and every chief he shows
The forms and discipline of war, yet his commanders were
All expert, and renowned men.   Great Pelagon was there,
Alastor, manly Chromius, and Hæmon worth a throne,
And Byas that could armies lead.   With these he first put on
His horse troops with their chariots; his foot (of which he choosed
Many, the best and ablest men, and which he ever used
As rampire to his general power) he in the rear disposed.
The slothful, and the least of spirit, he in the midst inclosed,
That such as wanted noble wills base need might force to stand.
His horse troops, that the vanguard had, he strictly did
    command
To ride their horses temperately, to keep their ranks, and shun
Confusion, lest their horsemanship and courage made them run
(Too much presumed on) much too far, and, charging so alone,
Engage themselves in th' enemy's strength, where many fight
    with one.
'Who his own chariot leaves to range, let him not freely go,
But straight unhorse him with a lance; for 'tis much better so.
And with this discipline,' said he, 'this form, these minds, this
    trust,
Our ancestors have walls and towns laid level with the dust.'
    Thus prompt, and long inured to arms, this old man did
        exhort;
And this Atrides likewise took in wondrous cheerful sort,
And said: 'O father, would to heaven, that as thy mind
    remains
In wonted vigour, so thy knees could undergo our pains!
But age, that all men overcomes, hath made his prise on thee;
Yet still I wish that some young man, grown old in mind,
    might be
Put in proportion with thy years, and thy mind, young in age,
Be fitly answered with his youth; that still where conflicts rage,

224

GEORGE CHAPMAN

And young men used to thrust for fame, thy brave exampling
    hand
Might double our young Grecian spirits, and grace our whole
    command.'
    The old knight answered : 'I myself could wish, O Atreus'
    son,
I were as young as when I slew brave Ereuthalion,
But Gods at all times give not all their gifts to mortal men.
If then I had the strength of youth, I missed the counsels then
That years now give me; and now years want that main
    strength of youth ;
Yet still my mind retains her strength (as you now said the sooth)
And would be where that strength is used, affording counsels sage
To stir youths' minds up ; 'tis the grace and office of our age ;
Let younger sinews, men sprung up whole ages after me,
And such as have strength use it, and as strong in honour be.'

G. CHAPMAN

From The Iliad Book XXII, 1598—1611

Priam, Hector and Achilles

                When aged Priam spied
The great Greek come, sphered round with beams, and showing
    as if the star,
Surnamed Orion's hound, that springs in autumn, and sends far
His radiance through a world of stars, of all whose beams his own
Cast greatest splendour ; the midnight that renders them most
    shown
Then being their foil, and on their points, cure-passing fevers
    then
Come shaking down into the joints of miserable men ;
As this were fall'n to earth, and shot along the field his rays
Now towards Priam, when he saw in great Æacides,
Out flew his tender voice in shrieks, and with raised hands he
    smit
His reverend head, then up to heaven he cast them, showing it
What plagues it sent him ; down again then threw them to
    his son,
To make him shun them.   He now stood without steep Ilion,

GEORGE CHAPMAN

Thirsting the combat : and to him thus miserably cried
The kind old king : 'O Hector ! fly this man, this homicide,
That straight will stroy thee.   He's too strong, and would to
heaven he were
As strong in heaven's love as in mine ! Vultures and dogs
should tear
His prostrate carcass, all my woes quenched with his bloody
spirits.
He has robbed me of many sons and worthy, and their merits
Sold to far islands.   Two of them, ay me ! I miss but now,
They are not entered, nor stay here.   Laothoe, O 'twas thou,
O queen of women, from whose womb they breathed.   O did
the tents
Detain them only, brass and gold would purchase safe events
To their sad durance ; 'tis within.   Old Altes, young in fame,
Gave plenty for his daughter's dow'r ; but if they fed the flame
Of this man's fury, woe is me, woe to my wretched Queen !
But in our state's woe their two deaths will nought at all
be seen
So thy life quit them.   Take the town, retire, dear son, and save
Troy's husbands and her wives, nor give thine own life to the
grave
For this man's glory.   Pity me, me, wretch, so long alive,
Whom in the door of age Jove keeps, that so he may deprive
My being in fortune's utmost curse, to see the blackest thread
Of this life's miseries, my sons slain, my daughters ravished,
Their resting chambers sacked, their babes, torn from them, on
their knees
Pleading for mercy, themselves dragged to Grecian slaveries,
And all this drawn through my red eyes.   Then last of all kneel I,
Alone, all helpless at my gates, before my enemy,
That ruthless gives me to the dogs, all the deformity
Of age discovered ; and all this thy death, sought wilfully,
Will pour on me.   A fair young man at all parts it beseems,
Being bravely slain, to lie all gashed, and wear the worst
extremes
Of war's most cruelty, no wound of whatsoever ruth
But is his ornament ; but I, a man so far from youth,
White head, white-bearded, wrinkled, pined, all shames must
show the eye.
Live, prevent this then, this most shame of all man's misery.'

GEORGE CHAPMAN

Thus wept the old king, and tore off his white hair; yet all
these
Retired not Hector.   Hecuba then fell upon her knees,
Stripped naked her bosom, showed her breasts, and bad him
reverence them,
And pity her ; if ever she had quieted his exclaim,
He would cease hers, and take the town, not tempting the rude
field
When all had left it : 'Think,' said she, 'I gave thee life to
yield
My life recomfort; thy rich wife shall have no rites of thee,
Nor do thee rites ; our tears shall pay thy corse no obsequy,
Being ravished from us, Grecian dogs nourished with what I
nursed.'

*   *   *   *   *   *   *

These thoughts employed his stay ; and now Achilles comes;
now near
His Mars-like presence terribly came brandishing his spear,
His right arm shook it, his bright arms like day came glittering on,
Like fire-light, or the light of heaven shot from the rising sun.
This sight outwrought discourse, cold fear shook Hector from
his stand.
No more stay now, all ports were left, he fled in fear the hand
Of that Fear-Master, who, hawk-like, air's swiftest passenger,
That holds a timorous dove in chase, and with command doth
bear
His fiery onset, the dove hastes, the hawk comes whizzing on,
This way and that he turns and winds, and cuffs the pigeon,
And, till he truss it, his great spirit lays hot charge on his wing;
So urged Achilles Hector's flight, so still fear's point did sting
His troubled spirit, his knees wrought hard, along the wall he flew,
In that fair chariot-way that runs beneath the tow'r of view
And Troy's wild fig-tree, till they reached where those two
mother springs
Of deep Scamander poured abroad their silver murmurings,
One warm and casts out fumes as fire, the other cold as snow
Or hail dissolved.   And when the sun made ardent summer glow,
There water's concrete crystal shined, near which were cisterns
made,
All paved and clear, where Trojan wives and their fair daughters
had

P 2   227

GEORGE CHAPMAN

Laundry for their fine linen weeds, in times of cleanly peace
Before the Grecians brought their siege. These captains noted
    these,
One flying, th' other in pursuit, a strong man flew before,
A stronger followed him by far and close up to him bore;
Both did their best, for neither now ran for a sacrifice,
Or for the sacrificer's hide, our runners' usual prize;
These ran for tame-horse Hector's soul. And as two running
    steeds,
Backed in some set race for a game that tries their swiftest speeds
(A tripod, or a woman, given for some man's funerals)
Such speed made these men, and on foot ran thrice about the walls.
    The Gods beheld them, all much moved; and Jove said:
      ' O ill sight!
A man I love much I see forced in most unworthy flight
About great Ilion. My heart grieves, he paid so many vows,
With thighs of sacrificed beeves, both on the lofty brows
Of Ida, and in Ilion's height. Consult we, shall we free
His life from death, or give it now t' Achilles' victory?'
    Minerva answered: ' Alter Fate? One long since marked
    for death
Now take from death? Do thou; but know, he still shall run
    beneath
Our other censures.' ' Be it then,' replied the Thunderer,
' My loved Tritonia, at thy will; in this I will prefer
Thy free intention, work it all.' Then stooped she from the sky
To this great combat. Peleus' son pursued incessantly
Still-flying Hector. As a hound that having roused a hart,
Although he tappish ne'er so oft, and every shrubby part
Attempts for strength, and trembles in, the hound doth still
    pursue
So close that not a foot he fails, but hunts it still at view;
So plied Achilles Hector's steps; as oft as he assailed
The Dardan ports and tow'rs for strength (to fetch from thence
    some aid
With winged shafts) so oft forced he amends of pace, and stept
'Twixt him and all his hopes, and still upon the field he kept
His utmost turnings to the town. And yet, as in a dream,
One thinks he gives another chase, when such a fained extreme
Possesseth both; that he in chase the chaser cannot fly,
Nor can the chaser get to hand his flying enemy;

GEORGE CHAPMAN

So nor Achilles' chase could reach the flight of Hector's pace,
Nor Hector's flight enlarge itself of swift Achilles' chase.
  But how chanced this ?   How, all this time, could Hector
    bear the knees
Of fierce Achilles with his own, and keep off destinies,
If Phœbus, for his last and best, through all that course had failed
To add his succours to his nerves, and, as his foe assailed,
Near and within him, fed his 'scape ?   Achilles yet well knew
His knees would fetch him, and gave signs to some friends,
    making show
Of shooting at him, to forbear, lest they detracted so
From his full glory in first wounds, and in the overthrow
Make his hand last.   But when they reached the fourth time
    the two founts,
Then Jove his golden scales weighed up, and took the last
    accounts
Of Fate for Hector ; putting in for him and Peleus' son
Two fates of bitter death, of which high heaven received the one,
The other hell ; so low declined the light of Hector's life.

G. Chapman

From The Odyssey Book XI, 1616

Spirits in Hades

                            I saw likewise stand,
Up to the chin, amidst a liquid lake,
Tormented Tantalus, yet could not slake
His burning thirst. Oft as his scornful cup
Th' old man would taste, so oft twas swallow'd up,
And all the black earth to his feet descried ;
Divine power (plaguing him) the lake still dried.
About his head, on high trees clustering, hung,
Pears, apples, granates, olives ever-young,
Delicious figs, and many fruit-trees more
Of other burthen ; whose alluring store
When th' old soul striv'd to pluck, the winds from sight,
In gloomy vapours, made them vanish quite.

GEORGE CHAPMAN

There saw I Sisyphus in infinite moan,
With both hands heaving up a massy stone,
And on his tip-toes racking all his height,
To wrest up to a mountain-top his freight;
When prest to rest it there (his nerves quite spent)
Down rusht the deadly quarry, the event
Of all his torture, new to raise again;
To which straight set his never-rested pain.
The sweat came gushing out from ev'ry pore,
And on his head a standing mist he wore,
Reeking from thence, as if a cloud of dust
Were rais'd about it. Down with these was thrust
The idol of the force of Hercules;
But his firm self did no such Fate oppress,
He feasting lives amongst th' immortal States,
White-ankled Hebe and himself made mates
In heavenly nuptials; Hebe, Jove's dear race,
And Juno's, whom the golden sandals grace.
About him flew the clamours of the dead
Like fowls, and still stoopt cuffing at his head.
He with his bow, like Night, stalkt up and down,
His shaft still nockt, and hurling round his frown
At those vex'd hoverers, aiming at them still,
And still, as shooting out, desire to still.
A horrid bawdrick wore he thwart his breast,
The thong all gold, in which were forms imprest,
Where art and miracle drew equal breaths,
In bears, boars, lions, battles, combats, deaths.
Who wrought that work, did never such before,
Nor so divinely will do ever more.
Soon as he saw, he knew me, and gave speech:
'Son of Laertes, high in wisdom's reach,
And yet unhappy wretch, for in this heart,
Of all exploits achiev'd by thy desert,
Thy worth but works out some sinister Fate,
As I in earth did. I was generate
By Jove himself, and yet past mean opprest
By one my far inferior, whose proud hest
Impos'd abhorred labours on my hand.
Of all which, one was, to descend this strand

GEORGE CHAPMAN

And hale the dog from thence. He could not think
An act that danger could make deeper sink.
And yet this depth I drew, and fetcht as high,
As this was low, the dog. The Deity
Of sleight and wisdom, as of downright power,
Both stoopt, and rais'd, and made me conqueror.'
This said, he made descent again as low
As Pluto's court; when I stood firm, for show
Of more Heroës of the times before;
And might perhaps have seen my wish of more,
(As Theseus and Pirithous, deriv'd
From roots of Deity) but before th' achiev'd
Rare sight of these, the rank-soul'd multitude
In infinite flocks rose, venting sounds so rude,
That pale Fear took me, lest the Gorgon's head
Rusht in amongst them, thrust up, in my dread,
By grim Persephone. I therefore sent
My men before to ship, and after went.
Where, boarded, set, and launcht, th' ocean wave
Our oars and forewinds speedy passage gave.

G. CHAPMAN

From The Odyssey Book XII, 1616
The Sirens

In mean time flew our ships, and straight we fetcht
The Sirens' Isle; a spleenless wind so stretcht
Her wings to waft us, and so urg'd our keel.
But having reacht this Isle, we could not feel
The least gasp of it, it was stricken dead,
And all the sea in prostrate slumber spread,
The Sirens' devil charm'd all. Up then flew
My friends to work, strook sail, together drew,
And under hatches stow'd them, sat, and plied
Their polisht oars, and did in curls divide
The white-head waters. My part then came on;
A mighty waxen cake I set upon,
Chopt it in fragments with my sword, and wrought
With strong hand every piece, till all were soft.

231

GEORGE CHAPMAN

The great power of the sun, in such a beam
As then flew burning from his diadem,
To liquefaction helpt us. Orderly
I stopt their ears ; and they as fair did ply
My feet and hands with cords, and to the mast
With other halsers made me soundly fast.
  Then took they seat, and forth our passage strook,
The foamy sea beneath their labour shook,
Row'd on, in reach of an erected voice.
The Sirens soon took note, without our noise,
Tun'd those sweet accents that made charms so strong,
And these learn'd numbers made the Sirens' song :
  '*Come here, thou worthy of a world of praise,*
That dost so high the Grecian glory raise,
Ulysses! stay thy ship, and that song hear
That none past ever but it bent his ear,
But left him ravish, and instructed more
By us, than any ever heard before.
For we know all things whatsoever were
In wide Troy labour'd ; whatsoever there
The Grecians and the Trojans both sustain'd,
By those high issues that the Gods ordain'd.
And whatsoever all the earth can show
T' inform a knowledge of desert, we know.'
  This they gave accent in the sweetest strain
That ever open'd an enamour'd vein.
When my constrain'd heart needs would have mine ear
Yet more delighted, force way forth, and hear.
To which end I commanded with all sign
Stern looks could make (for not a joint of mine
Had power to stir) my friends to rise, and give
My limbs free way. They freely striv'd to drive
Their ship still on. When, far from will to lose,
Eurylochus and Perimedes rose
To wrap me surer, and opprest me more
With many a halser than had use before.
When, rowing on without the reach of sound,
My friends unstopt their ears, and me unbound,
And that Isle quite we quitted.

G. CHAPMAN

HISTORICAL POEMS

From The Mirror for Magistrates, The Induction, 1559—1571

Led by Sorrow the Poet visits the place of the dead

I shall thee guide first to the grisly lake,
And thence unto the blissful place of rest,
Where thou shalt see, and hear, the plaint they make
That whilom here bare swinge among the best :
This shalt thou see : but great is the unrest
   That thou must bide, before thou canst attain
   Unto the dreadful place where these remain.

And, with these words, as I upraised stood,
And 'gan to follow her that straight forth pac'd,
Ere I was ware, into a desert wood
We now were come, where, hand in hand embrac'd,
She led the way, and through the thick so trac'd,
   As, but I had been guided by her might,
   It was no way for any mortal wight.

But lo, while thus amid the desert dark
We passed on with steps and pace unmeet,
A rumbling roar, confus'd with howl and bark
Of dogs, shook all the ground under our feet,
And struck the din within our ears so deep,
   As, half distraught, unto the ground I fell,
   Besought return, and not to visit Hell.

233

THOMAS SACKVILLE LORD BUCKHURST

But she, forthwith, uplifting me apace,
Remov'd my dread, and, with a steadfast mind,
Bade me come on ; for here was now the place,
The place where we our travail end should find :
Wherewith I rose, and to the place assign'd
   Astoin'd I stalk, when straight we approached near
   The dreadful place, that you will dread to hear.

An hideous hole all vast, withouten shape,
Of endless depth, o'erwhelmed with ragged stone,
With ugly mouth, and grisly jaws doth gape,
And to our sight confounds itself in one :
Here enter'd we, and yeding forth, anon
   An horrible loathly lake we might discern
   As black as pitch, that cleped is *Avern.*

A deadly gulf where nought but rubbish grows,
With foul black swelth in thicken'd lumps that lies,
Which up in th' air such stinking vapours throws,
That over there may fly no fowl but dies
Chok'd with the pestilent savours that arise :
   Hither we come; whence forth we still did pace,
   In dreadful fear amid the dreadful place.

And, first, within the porch and jaws of Hell,
Sat deep Remorse of conscience, all besprent
With tears ; and to herself oft would she tell
Her wretchedness, and cursing never stent
To sob and sigh ; but ever thus lament,
   With thoughtful care, as she that, all in vain
   Would wear and waste continually in pain.

Her eyes unsteadfast, rolling here and there,
Whirl'd on each place, as place that vengeance brought,
So was her mind continually in fear,
Toss'd and tormented with tedious thought
Of those detested crimes which she had wrought ;
   With dreadful cheer, and looks thrown to the sky,
   Wishing for death, and yet she could not die.

THOMAS SACKVILLE LORD BUCKHURST

Next saw we Dread, all trembling how he shook,
With foot uncertain, proffer'd here and there :
Benumb'd of speech, and, with a ghastly look,
Search'd every place, all pale and dead for fear,
His cap born up with staring of his hair,
   'Stoin'd and amaz'd at his own shade for dread,
   And fearing greater dangers than was need.

And next, within the entry of this lake,
Sat fell Revenge, gnashing her teeth for ire,
Devising means how she may vengeance take,
Never in rest, till she have her desire :
But frets within so far forth with the fire
   Of wreaking flames, that now determines she
   To die by death, or veng'd by death to be.

When fell Revenge, with bloody foul pretence
Had show'd herself as next in order set,
With trembling limbs we softly parted thence,
Till in our eyes another sight we met :
When from my heart a sigh forthwith I fet,
   Rueing, alas ! upon the woeful plight
   Of Misery, that next appear'd in sight.

His face was lean, and somedeal pin'd away,
And eke his hands consumed to the bone,
But what his body was, I cannot say,
For on his carcass raiment had he none,
Save clouts and patches, pieced one by one ;
   With staff in hand, and scrip on shoulder cast,
   His chief defence against the winter's blast.

His food, for most, was wild fruits of the tree,
Unless sometime some crumbs fell to his share,
Which in his wallet long, God wot, kept he,
As on the which full daintily would fare :
His drink, the running stream ; his cup, the bare
   Of his palm clos'd ; his bed, the hard cold ground :
   To this poor life was Misery ybound.

THOMAS SACKVILLE LORD BUCKHURST

Whose wretched state when we had well beheld
With tender ruth on him, and on his fears,
In thoughtful cares forth then our pace we held;
And, by and by, another shape appears,
Of greedy Care, still brushing up the breres,
   His knuckles knobb'd, his flesh deep dented in,
   With tawed hands, and hard ytanned skin.

The morrow gray no sooner hath begun
To spread his light, even peeping in our eyes,
When he is up, and to his work yrun:
But let the night's black misty mantles rise,
And with foul dark never so much disguise
   The fair bright day, yet ceaseth he no while,
   But hath his candles to prolong his toil.

By him lay heavy Sleep, the cousin of Death,
Flat on the ground, and still as any stone,
A very corpse, save yielding forth a breath:
Small keep took he, whom Fortune frowned on,
Or whom she lifted up into the throne
   Of high renown; but, as a living death,
   So, dead alive, of life he drew the breath.

The body's rest, the quiet of the heart,
The travail's ease, the still night's fear was he,
And of our life in earth the better part;
Reaver of sight, and yet in whom we see
Things oft that tide, and oft that never be;
   Without respect, esteeming equally
   King *Crœsus'* pomp, and *Irus'* poverty.

And next, in order sad, Old Age we found:
His beard all hoar, his eyes hollow and blind,
With drooping cheer still poring on the ground,
As on the place where Nature him assign'd
To rest, when that the sisters had untwin'd
   His vital thread, and ended with their knife
   The fleeting course of fast declining life.

THOMAS SACKVILLE LORD BUCKHURST

There heard we him with broke and hollow plaint
Rue with himself his end approaching fast,
And all for nought his wretched mind torment
With sweet remembrance of his pleasures past,
And fresh delights of lusty youth forewaste ;
　　Recounting which, how would he sob and shriek,
　　And to be young again of *Jove* beseek ?

But, and the cruel fates so fixed be,
That time forepast cannot return again,
This one request of *Jove* yet prayed he :
That in such wither'd plight, and wretched pain,
As eld, accompanied with his loathsome train,
　　Had brought on him, all were it woe and grief,
　　He might a while yet linger forth his life,

And not so soon descend into the pit,
Where Death, when he the mortal corpse hath slain,
With reckless hand in grave doth cover it,
Thereafter never to enjoy again
The gladsome light, but in the ground ylain,
　　In depth of darkness waste and wear to nought,
　　As he had never into the world been brought.

But who had seen him sobbing, how he stood
Unto himself, and how he would bemoan
His youth forepast, as though it wrought him good
To talk of youth, all were his youth foregone,
He would have mus'd, and marvell'd much, whereon
　　This wretched Age should life desire so fain,
　　And knows full well life doth but length his pain.

Crookback'd he was, tooth-shaken, and blear-eyed,
Went on three feet, and sometime crept on four,
With old lame bones that rattled by his side,
His scalp all pill'd, and he with eld forlore :
His wither'd fist still knocking at Death's door,
　　Fumbling and drivelling as he draws his breath ;
　　For brief, the shape and messenger of Death.

THOMAS SACKVILLE LORD BUCKHURST

237

SACKVILLE *and* WARNER

From The Mirror for Magistrates, The Complaint
of Buckingham, 1559—1571

Midnight

Midnight was come, when every vital thing
With sweet sound sleep their weary limbs did rest,
The beasts were still, the little birds that sing,
Now sweetly slept beside their mother's breast,
The old and all were shrouded in their nest:
   The waters calm, the cruel Seas did cease,
   The woods, the fields, and all things held their peace.

The golden stars were whirl'd amid their race,
And on the earth did laugh with twinkling light,
When each thing nestled in his resting place.
Forgot day's pain with pleasure of the night:
The hare had not the greedy hounds in sight,
   The fearful deer of death stood not in doubt,
   The partridge drept not of the falcon's foot.

The ugly bear now minded not the stake,
Nor how the cruel mastiffs do him tear,
The stag lay still unroused from the brake,
The foamy boar fear'd not the hunter's spear;
All thing was still in desert, bush, and brear:
   With quiet heart now from their travails ceas'd,
   Soundly they slept in midst of all their rest.

THOMAS SACKVILLE LORD BUCKHURST

From Albion's England, XLIX, 1586—1602

The Armada

The Spaniards' long time care and cost, invincible surnam'd,
Was now afloat, whilst Parma too from Flanders hither aim'd,
Like fleet, of eight score ships and odd, the ocean never bore,
So huge, so strong, and so complete, in every strength and store:
Carracks, galleons, argosies, and galliasses, such
That seem'd so many castles and their tops the clouds to touch.

238

WILLIAM WARNER

These on the Lizards show themselves and threaten England's
 fall ;
But there with fifty ships of ours that fleet was fought withall.
Howbeit of a greater sort our navy did consist,
But part kept diet in the port, that might of health have miss'd,
Had Spain's armada of our wants in Plymouth's haven wist.
The rest had eye on Parma, that from Flanders armour threats;
Meanwhile Lord Charles our admiral, and Drake, did worthy
 feats,
Whose fearless fifty mole-hills bode their tripled mountains
 base,
And even at first (so pleas'd it God) pursued as if in chase.
By this (for over-idle seemed to English hearts the shore)
Our gallants did embark each-where, and make our forces more.
But in such warlike order then their ships at anchor lay
That we, unless we them disperse, on bootless labour stay :
Nor lacked policy that to that purpose made us weigh.
Ours fired divers ships that down the current sent so scared,
That cables cut and anchors lost, the Spaniards badly fared.
Dispersed thus, we spare not shot, and part of them we sink,
And part we board, the rest did fly, not fast enough they think.
Well guided little axes so force tallest oaks to fall,
So numerous herds of stately harts fly beagles few and small.
Nine days together chas'd we them, not actious, save in flight,
About eight thousands perished by famine, sea, and fight.
For treasure, ships and carriages, lost honour, prisoners ta'en,
The Spaniards hardly 'scaping hence, 'scap'd not rebukes in
 Spain.
 Well might thus much (as much it did) cheer England, but
 much more
Concurrency from one to all to stop that common sore.
Even catholics (that erred name doth please the papists) were
As forward in this quarrel as the foremost arms to bear :
Recusants and suspects of note ; of others was no care.
And had not our God-guided fight on seas prevailed, yet
The Spaniards, land whereso they could, had with our armies
 met.
Our common courage wished no less, so lightly feared we foes,
Such hope in God, such hate of them, such hearts to barter
 blows.

WILLIAM WARNER

Here flam'd the Cyclops' forges, Mars his armoury was here,
Himself he sheds in us, and with our cause ourselves we cheer.
But (which had scarified our wounds, if wounded, with the balm
Of her sweet presence, so applaus'd as in sea storms a calm)
Her royal self, Elizabeth, our sovereign gracious Queen
In magnanimous majesty amidst her troops was seen.
Which made us weep for joy, nor was her kindness less to us.
Think nothing letting then that might the common cause
    discuss,
Where prince and people have in love a sympathy as thus.
    Howbeit force nor policy, but God's sole providence,
Did clear fore-boasted conquest and benighted thraldom hence.
He in Sennacherib his nose did put His hook, and brought
Him back again the way he came, without performing aught.
He fought for us, alonely we did shout and trumpets sound,
When as the walls of Jericho fell flat unto the ground.
Yea lest, (for erst did never here like strong supplies befall,
Like loyal hearts in every one, like warlike minds in all,
Less spare of purses, more foresight, and valiant guides to act,
As showed our hardy little fleet that battle never slacked)
Lest these, I say, might have been said the cause that we
    subdu'd,
Even God to glorify Himself our gained cause pursu'd,
Without our loss of man, or mast, or foe once touching shore,
Save such as wreckt, were prisoners, or but landing liv'd not
    more.
And as in public prayers we did His defence implore,
So being victors publicly, we yielded thanks therefore.
Her highness-self, good cause she had, in view of every eye,
On humble knees did give Him thanks that gave her victory.
    Remaineth, what she won, what Spain and Rome did lose
        in fame :
    Remaineth, popes use potentates but to retrieve their game.

                                            W. WARNER

GEORGE PEELE

A Farewell Entituled to the famous and fortunate Generals of our English forces, Sir John Norris and Sir Francis Drake, Knights, and all their brave and resolute followers, 1589

Have done with care, my hearts! aboard amain,
With stretching sails to plough the swelling waves.
Bid England's shore and Albion's chalky cliffs
Farewell. Bid stately Troynovant adieu,
Where pleasant Thames from Isis' silver head
Begins her quiet glide, and runs along
To that brave bridge, the bar that thwarts her course,
Near neighbour to the ancient stony Tower,
The glorious hold that Julius Cæsar built.
Change love for arms; girt-to your blades, my boys!
Your rests and muskets take, take helm and targe,
And let God Mars his consort make you mirth,
The roaring cannon, and the brazen trump,
The angry-sounding drum, the whistling fife,
The shrieks of men, the princely courser's neigh.
Now vail your bonnets to your friends at home:
Bid all the lovely British dames adieu,
That under many a standard well-advanced
Have hid the sweet alarms and braves of love;
Bid theatres and proud tragedians,
Bid Mahomet's Pow, and mighty Tamburlaine,
King Charlemaine, Tom Stukeley, and the rest,
Adieu. To arms, to arms, to glorious arms!
With noble Norris, and victorious Drake,
Under the sanguine cross, brave England's badge,
To propagate religious piety,
And hew a passage with your conquering swords
By land and sea, wherever Phœbus' eye,
Th' eternal lamp of heaven, lends us light;
By golden Tagus, or the western Inde,
Or through the spacious bay of Portugal,
The wealthy ocean-main, the Terrhene sea,
From great Alcides' pillars branching forth
Even to the gulf that leads to lofty Rome:
There to deface the pride of Antichrist,
And pull his paper walls and popery down,

GEORGE PEELE

A famous enterprise for England's strength;
To steel your swords on Avarice' triple crown,
And cleanse Augeas' stalls in Italy.
To arms, my fellow-soldiers! Sea and land
Lie open to the voyage you intend;
And sea or land, bold Britons, far or near,
Whatever course your matchless virtue shapes,
Whether to Europe's bounds, or Asian plains,
To Afric's shore, or rich America,
Down to the shades of deep Avernus' crags,
Sail on, pursue your honours to your graves.
Heaven is a sacred covering for your heads,
And every climate virtue's tabernacle.
To arms, to arms, to honourable arms!
Hoise sails, weigh anchors up, plough up the seas
With flying keels, plough up the land with swords.
In God's name venture on; and let me say
To you, my mates, as Cæsar said to his,
Striving with Neptune's hills; 'You bear,' quoth he,
'Cæsar and Cæsar's fortune in your ships.'
You follow them, whose swords successful are;
You follow Drake by sea, the scourge of Spain,
The dreadful dragon, terror to your foes,
Victorious in his return from Inde,
In all his high attempts unvanquished.
You follow noble Norris, whose renown,
Won in the fertile fields of Belgia,
Spreads by the gates of Europe to the courts
Of Christian kings and heathen potentates.
You fight for Christ, and England's peerless queen
Elizabeth, the wonder of the world,
Over whose throne the enemies of God
Have thundered erst their vain successless braves.
O, ten times treble happy men, that fight
Under the cross of Christ and England's queen,
And follow such as Drake and Norris are!
All honours do this cause accompany;
All glory on these endless honours waits:
These honours and this glory shall He send,
Whose honour and whose glory you defend.

G. PEELE

EDMUND SPENSER

From Colin Clouts Come Home Againe, 1591

The Ocean

'When thus our pipes we both had wearied well,
(Quoth he) and each an end of singing made,
He gan to cast great lyking to my lore,
And great dislyking to my lucklessse lot,
That banisht had my selfe, like wight forlore,
Into that waste, where I was quite forgot.
The which to leave, thenceforth he counseld mee,
Unmeet for man, in whom was ought regardfull,
And wend with him, his Cynthia to see;
Whose grace was great, and bounty most rewardfull.
Besides her peerlesse skill in making well,
And all the ornaments of wondrous wit,
Such as all womankynd did far excell;
Such as the world admyr'd, and praised it:
So what with hope of good, and hate of ill,
He me perswaded forth with him to fare.
Nought tooke I with me, but mine oaten quill:
Small needments else need shepheard to prepare.
So to the sea we came; the sea, that is
A world of waters heaped up on hie,
Rolling like mountaines in wide wildernesse,
Horrible, hideous, roaring with hoarse crie.'
    'And is the sea (quoth Coridon) so fearfull?'
    'Fearful much more (quoth he) then hart can fear:
Thousand wyld beasts with deep mouthes gaping direfull
Therin stil wait poore passengers to teare.
Who life doth loath, and longs death to behold,
Before he die, alreadie dead with feare,
And yet would live with heart halfe stonie cold,
Let him to sea, and he shall see it there.
And yet as ghastly dreadfull, as it seemes,
Bold men, presuming life for gaine to sell,
Dare tempt that gulf, and in those wandring stremes
Seek waies unknowne, waies leading down to hell.
For, as we stood there waiting on the strond,
Behold! an huge great vessell to us came,
Dauncing upon the waters back to lond,
As if it scornd the daunger of the same;

EDMUND SPENSER

Yet was it but a wooden frame and fraile,
Glewed togither with some subtile matter.
Yet had it armes and wings, and head and taile,
And life to move it selfe upon the water.
Strange thing! how bold and swift the monster was,
That neither car'd for wynd, nor haile, nor raine,
Nor swelling waves, but thorough them did passe
So proudly, that she made them roare againe.
The same aboord us gently did receave,
And without harme us farre away did beare,
So farre that land, our mother, us did leave,
And nought but sea and heaven to us appeare.
Then hartlesse quite, and full of inward feare,
That shepheard I besought to me to tell,
Under what skie, or in what world we were,
In which I saw no living people dwell.
Who, me recomforting all that he might,
Told me that that same was the Regiment
Of a great shepheardesse, that Cynthia hight,
His liege, his Ladie, and his lifes Regent.—
   'If then (quoth I) a shepheardesse she bee,
Where be the flockes and heards, which she doth keep?
And where may I the hills and pastures see,
On which she useth for to feed her sheepe?'
   'These be the hills (quoth he), the surges hie,
On which faire Cynthia her heards doth feed:
Her heards be thousand fishes with their frie,
Which in the bosome of the billowes breed.
Of them the shepheard which hath charge in chief,
Is Triton, blowing loud his wreathed horne:
At sound whereof, they all for their relief
Wend too and fro at evening and at morne.
And Proteus eke with him does drive his heard
Of stinking Scales and Porcpisces together,
With hoary head and deawy dropping beard,
Compelling them which way he list, and whether.
And, I among the rest, of many least,
Have in the Ocean charge to me assignd;
Where I will live or die at her beheast,
And serve and honour her with faithfull mind.
Besides an hundred Nymphs all heavenly borne,

EDMUND SPENSER *and* SAMUEL DANIEL

And of immortall race, doo still attend
To wash faire Cynthiaes sheep, when they be shorne,
And fold them up, when they have made an end.
Those be the shepheards which my Cynthia serve
At sea, beside a thousand moe at land :
For land and sea my Cynthia doth deserve
To have in her commandëment at hand.'

E. Spenser

From The Complaint of Rosamond, 1592—1623

Then write, quoth she, the ruin of my youth,
Report the downfall of my slipp'ry state ;
Of all my life reveal the simple truth,
To teach to others what I learnt too late.
Exemplify my frailty, tell how fate
   Keeps in eternal dark our fortunes hidden,
   And ere they come to know them 'tis forbidden.

For whilst the sunshine of my fortune lasted,
I joy'd the happiest warmth, the sweetest heat
That ever yet imperious beauty tasted ;
I had what glory ever flesh could get ;
But this fair morning had a shameful set.
   Disgrace dark'd honour, sin did cloud my brow,
   As note the sequel, and I'll tell thee how.

The blood I stain'd was good and of the best,
My birth had honour and my beauty fame ;
Nature and fortune join'd to make me bless'd,
Had I had grace t' have known to use the same.
My education show'd from whence I came,
   And all concurr'd to make me happy first,
   That so great hope might make me more accurs'd.

Happy liv'd I whilst parents' eye did guide
The indiscretion of my feeble ways,
And country home kept me from being eyed,
Where best unknown I spent my sweetest days :
Till that my friends mine honour sought to raise
   To higher place, which greater credit yields,
   Deeming such beauty was unfit for fields.

245

SAMUEL DANIEL

From country then to court I was prefer'd,
From calm to storms, from shore into the deeps;
There where I perish'd, where my youth first err'd,
There where I lost the flower which honour keeps,
There where the worser thrives, the better weeps;
  Ah me, poor wench, on this unhappy shelf
  I grounded me and cast away myself.

There where as frail and tender beauty stands
With all assaulting powers environed;
Having but prayers and weak feeble hands
To hold their honour's fort unvanquished;
There where to stand, and be unconquered,
  Is to b' above the nature of our kind,
  That cannot long for pity be unkind.

For thither com'd when years had arm'd my youth
With rarest proof of beauty ever seen;
When my reviving eye had learnt the truth,
That it had power to make the winter green,
And flower affections whereas none had been;
  Soon could I teach my brow to tyrannize
  And make the world do homage to mine eyes.

For age I saw, though years with cold conceit
Congeal'd their thoughts against a warm desire,
Yet sigh their want and look at such a bait.
I saw how youth was wax before the fire;
I saw by stealth, I fram'd my look a lyre;
  Yet well perceiv'd how fortune made me then
  The envy of my sex and wonder unto men.

Look how a comet at the first appearing
Draws all men's eyes with wonder to behold it;
Or as the saddest tale at sudden hearing
Makes silent list'ning unto him that told it.
So did my speech when rubies did unfold it;
  So did the blazing of my blush appear
  T' amaze the world, that holds such sights so dear.

SAMUEL DANIEL

Ah! beauty syren, fair enchanting good;
Sweet silent rhetoric of persuading eyes;
Dumb eloquence, whose power doth move the blood
More than the words or wisdom of the wise;
Still harmony, whose diapason lies
    Within a brow, the key which passions move
    To ravish sense, and play a world in love.

What might I then not do whose power was such?
What cannot women do that know their power?
What woman knows it not, I fear too much,
How bliss or bale lies in their laugh or lour?
Whilst they enjoy their happy blooming flower,
    Whilst nature decks them in their best attires
    Of youth and beauty, which the world admires.

Such one was I, my beauty was mine own,
No borrowed blush which bank-rot beauties seek;
That new-found shame, a sin to us unknown,
Th' adulterate beauty of a falsed cheek:
Vild stain to honour and to women eke,
    Seeing that time our fading must detect,
    Thus with defect to cover our defect.

Impiety of times, chastity's abator,
Falsehood wherein thyself thyself deniest:
Treason to counterfeit the seal of nature,
The stamp of heaven impressed by the highest;
Disgrace unto the world, to whom thou liest.
    Idol unto thyself, shame to the wise,
    And all that honour thee idolatrize.

Far was that sin from us whose age was pure,
When simple beauty was accounted best;
The time when women had no other lure
But modesty, pure cheeks, a virtuous breast:
This was the pomp wherewith my youth was blest;
    These were the weapons which mine honour won,
    In all the conflicts which mine eyes begun;

SAMUEL DANIEL

Which were not small, I wrought on no mean object,
A crown was at my feet, sceptres obey'd me,
Whom fortune made my king, Love made my subject,
Who did command the land most humbly pray'd me.
Henry the Second that so highly weigh'd me
    Found well by proof the privilege of beauty
    That it had power to countermand all duty.

S. Daniel

From The Civil Wars, The fourth book, 1595—1623

The Battle of Shrewsbury

46

O war! begot in pride and luxury,
The child of malice and revengeful hate;
Thou impious good, and good impiety,
That art the foul refiner of a state;
Unjust-just scourge of men's iniquity,
Sharp easer of corruptions desperate;
Is there no means but that a sin-sick land
Must be let blood with such a boisterous hand?

47

How well might'st thou have here been spar'd this day,
Had not wrong-counsell'd Percy been perverse?
Whose forward hand, inur'd to wounds, makes way
Upon the sharpest fronts of the most fierce;
Where now an equal fury thrusts, to stay
And back repel that force, and his disperse;
Then these assail, then those re-chase again,
Till stay'd with new-made hills of bodies slain.

48

There, lo! that new-appearing glorious star,
Wonder of Arms, the terror of the field,
Young Henry, labouring where the stoutest are,
And even the stoutest forceth back to yield;
There is that hand bolden'd to blood and war,
That must the sword in wondrous actions wield:
Though better he had learn'd with others' blood;
A less expense to us, to him more good.

SAMUEL DANIEL

49

Yet here had he not speedy succour lent
To his endanger'd father, near opprest,
That day had seen the full accomplishment
Of all his travails, and his final rest:
For Mars-like Douglas all his forces bent
T'encounter and to grapple with the best;
As if disdaining any other thing
To do, that day, but to subdue a king.

50

And three with fiery courage he assails,
Three, all as kings adorn'd in royal wise;
And each successive after other quails,
Still wond'ring whence so many kings should rise.
And doubting lest his hand or eyesight fails,
In these confounded, on a fourth he flies,
And him unhorses too: whom, had he sped,
He then all kings in him had vanquished.

51

For Henry had divided, as it were,
The person of himself into four parts,
To be less known, and yet known everywhere,
The more to animate his people's hearts:
Who, cheered by his presence, would not spare
To execute their best and worthiest parts.
By which two special things effected are,
His safety, and his subjects' better care.

52

And never worthy prince a day did quit
With greater hazard and with more renown,
Than thou didst, mighty Henry, in this fight;
Which only made thee owner of thine own:
Thou never prov'dst the tenure of thy right,
How thou didst hold thy easy-gotten crown,
Till now: and now, thou show'st thyself chief lord,
By that especial right of kings, the sword.

S. DANIEL

249

GEORGE CHAPMAN

Riches, and conquest, and renown I sing,
Riches with honour, conquest without blood,
Enough to seat the monarchy of earth,
Like to Jove's eagle on Eliza's hand.
Guiana, whose rich feet are mines of gold,
Whose forehead knocks against the roof of stars,
Stands on her tiptoes at fair England looking,
Kissing her hand, bowing her mighty breast,
And every sign of all submission making,
To be her sister, and the daughter both
Of our most sacred maid; whose barrenness
Is the true fruit of virtue, that may get,
Bear, and bring forth anew in all perfection,
What heretofore savage corruption held
In barbarous Chaos; and in this affair
Become her father, mother, and her heir.
Then most admired sovereign, let your breath
Go forth upon the waters, and create
A golden world in this our iron age,
And be the prosperous forewind to a fleet,
That, seconding your last, may go before it
In all success of profit and renown;
Doubt not but your election was divine,
As well by fate as your high judgment order'd,
To raise him with choice bounties that could add
Height to his height; and like a liberal vine,
Not only bear his virtuous fruit aloft
Free from the press of squint-eyed Envy's feet,
But deck his gracious prop with golden bunches,
And shroud it with broad leaves of rule o'ergrown
From all black tempests of invasion.

G. CHAPMAN

MICHAEL DRAYTON

From The Barons' Wars, The third canto, 1596—1630

Mortimer

38

Whilst Mortimer (that all this while hath lain
From our fair course) by fortune strangely crost,
In France was struggling how he might regain
That which before in England he had lost,
And all good means doth gladly entertain,
No jot dismayed in all those tempests tost ;
　　Nor his great mind could so be overthrown,
　　All men his friends, all countries were his own :

39

Then Muse (transported by thy former zeal,
Led in thy progress, where his fortune lies)
To thy sure aid I seriously appeal,
To show him fully, without feigned disguise ;
The ancient Heroes then I shall reveal,
And in their patterns I shall be precise,
　　When in my verse, transparent, neat and clear,
　　They shall in his pure character appear.

40

He was a man (then boldly dare to say)
In whose rich soul the virtues well did suit,
In whom so mixed the elements all lay,
That none to one could sov'reignty impute ;
As all did govern, yet all did obey :
He of a temper was so absolute,
　　As that it seemed, when Nature him began,
　　She meant to show all that might be in man.

41

So throughly seasoned, and so rightly set,
That in the level of the clearest eye
Time never touched him with deforming fret,
Nor had the power to warp him but awry;
Whom in his course no cross could ever let,
His elevation fixed was so high
　　That those rough storms, whose rage the world doth prove,
　　Never raught him, who sat them far above.

MICHAEL DRAYTON

42

Which the Queen saw, who had a seeing spirit,
For she had marked the largeness of his mind
And with much judgment looked into his merit,
Above the usual compass of her kind,
His grandsires' greatness rightly to inherit,
Whenas the ages in their course inclined,
    And the world, weak with time, began to bow
    To that poor baseness that it rests at now.

43

He weighs not wealth, nor yet his *Wigmore* left,
Let needless heaps, as things of nothing, stand;
That was not his that man could take by theft,
He was a lord if he had sea or land,
And thought him rich, of those who was not reft;
Man of all creatures hath an upright hand,
    And by the stars is only taught to know,
    That as they progress heaven, he earth should do.

44

Wherefore wise Nature from this face of ground
Into the deep taught man to find the way,
That in the floods her treasure might be found,
To make him search for what she there did lay;
And that her secrets he might throughly sound,
She gave him courage as her only key,
    That of all creatures as the worthiest he
    Her glory there and wondrous works should see.

45

Let wretched worldlings sweat for mud and earth,
Whose grovelling bosoms lick the recreant stones,
Such peasants cark for plenty and for dearth,
Fame never looks upon those prostrate drones;
The brave mind is allotted in the birth
To manage empires from the state of thrones,
    Frighting coy fortune, when she stern'st appears,
    Which scorneth sighs and jeereth at our tears.

46

But when report (as with a trembling wing)
Tickled the entrance of his listening ear,
With news of ships sent out the Queen to bring,
For her at Sandwich which then waiting were,

He surely thought he heard the angels sing
And the whole frame of Heaven make up the quire,
  That his full soul was smothered with excess,
  Her ample joys unable to express.

47

Quoth he, 'Slide, billows, smoothly for her sake,
Whose sight can make your aged Nereus young,
For her fair passage even alleys make,
And as the soft winds waft her sails along,
Sleek every little dimple of the lake,
Sweet Syrens, and be ready with your song;
  Though 'tis not Venus that doth pass that way,
  Yet is as fair as she borne on the sea.

48

'Ye scaly creatures, gaze upon her eye,
And never after with your kind make war;
O steal the accents from her lips that fly,
Which like the tunes of the Celestials are,
And them to your sick amorous thoughts apply,
Compared with which, Arion's did but jar:
  Wrap them in air, and when black tempests rage,
  Use them as charms the rough seas to assuage.

49

'France, send to attend her with full shoals of oars,
With which her fleet may every way be plied;
And when she landeth on thy blessed shores,
And the vast navy doth at anchor ride
For her departure, when the wild sea roars,
Ship, mount to heaven, and there be stellified:
  Next Jason's *Argo*, on the burnished throne,
  Assume thyself a constellation.'   M. DRAYTON

From Poly-olbion, The first song, 1613—1622

Albion

Of Albion's glorious isle the wonders whilst I write,
The sundry varying soils, the pleasures infinite,
(Where heat kills not the cold, nor cold expels the heat,
The calms too mildly small, nor winds too roughly great,

MICHAEL DRAYTON

Nor night doth hinder day, nor day the night doth wrong,
The summer not too short, the winter not too long)
What help shall I invoke to aid my Muse the while?
    Thou *Genius* of the place (this most renowned isle)
Which lived'st long before the all-earth-drowning flood,
Whilst yet the world did swarm with her gigantic brood,
Go thou before me still thy circling shores about,
And in this wand'ring maze help to conduct me out:
Direct my course so right, as with thy hand to show
Which way thy forests range, which way thy rivers flow,
Wise *Genius*, by thy help that so I may descry
How thy fair mountains stand, and how thy valleys lie;
From those clear pearly cleeves which see the morning's pride,
And check the surly imps of Neptune when they chide,
Unto the big-swoln waves in the Iberian stream,
Where Titan still unyokes his fiery-hoofed team,
And oft his flaming locks in luscious nectar steeps,
When from Olympus' top he plungeth in the deeps:
That from th' Armoric sands, on surging Neptune's leas,
Through the Hibernic gulf (those rough Vergivian seas)
My verse with wings of skill may fly a lofty gait,
As Amphitrite clips this island fortunate,
Till through the sleepy main to Thule I have gone,
And seen the frozen isles, the cold Deucalidon,
Amongst whose iron rocks grim Saturn yet remains,
Bound in those gloomy caves with adamantine chains.
    Ye sacred bards, that to your harps' melodious strings
Sung th' ancient heroes' deeds (the monuments of kings)
And in your dreadful verse ingrav'd the prophecies,
The aged world's descents and genealogies;
If, as those Druids taught, which kept the British rites,
And dwelt in darksome groves, there counselling with sprites,
(But their opinions fail'd, by error led awry,
As since clear truth hath shew'd to their posterity)
When these our souls by death our bodies do forsake,
They instantly again do other bodies take;
I could have wisht your spirits redoubled in my breast,
To give my verse applause to time's eternal rest.
    Thus scarcely said the Muse, but hovering while she hung
Upon the Celtic wastes, the sea-nymphs loudly sung:

254

MICHAEL DRAYTON

O ever-happy isles ! your heads so high that bear,
By nature strongly fenc'd, which never need to fear
On Neptune's wat'ry realms when Eolus raiseth wars,
And every billow bounds, as though to quench the stars :
Fair Jersey first of these here scatter'd in the deep,
Peculiarly that boast'st thy double-horned sheep :
Inferior nor to thee, thou Guernsey, bravely crown'd
With rough-embattled rocks, whose venom-hating ground
The hard'ned emeril hath, which thou abroad dost send :
Thou Ligon her belov'd, and Serk, that doth attend
Her pleasure every hour ; as Jethow, them at need,
With pheasants, fallow deer, and conies that dost feed :
Ye seven small sister isles, and Sorlings, which to see
The half-sunk seaman joys ; or whatsoe'er you be,
From fruitful Aurney, near the ancient Celtic shore,
To Ushant and the Seams, whereas those nuns of yore
Gave answers from their caves, and took what shapes they please :
Ye happy islands set within the British seas,
With shrill and jocund shouts, th' unmeasur'd deeps awake,
And let the gods of sea their secret bow'rs forsake,
Whilst our industrious Muse great Britain forth shall bring,
Crown'd with those glorious wreaths that beautify the spring ;
And whilst green Thetis' nymphs, with many an amorous lay,
Sing our invention safe unto her long-wisht bay.

M. DRAYTON

From Poly-olbion, The twentieth song, 1613—1622

The Falconer

Now of a flight at brook shall my description be,
What subject can be found, that lies not fair to me ?
Of simple shepherds now my Muse exactly sings,
And then of courtly loves, and the affairs of kings.
Then in a buskin'd strain, the warlike spear and shield,
And instantly again of the disports of field ;

255

MICHAEL DRAYTON

What can this isle produce, that lies from my report?
Industrious Muse, proceed then to thy hawking sport.
　When making for the brook, the falconer doth espy,
On river, plash, or mere, where store of fowl doth lie,
Whence forced over land, by skilful falconer's trade,
A fair convenient flight may easily be made,
He whistleth off his hawks, whose nimble pinions straight
Do work themselves by turns, into a stately height;
And if that after check, the one or both do go,
Sometimes he them the lure, sometimes doth water show;
The trembling fowl that hear the jigging hawk-bells ring,
And find it is too late to trust then to their wing,
Lie flat upon the flood, whilst the high-mounted hawks,
Then being lords alone in their ethereal walks,
Aloft so bravely stir their bells so thick that shake,
Which when the falconer sees, that scarce one plane they make,
'The gallant'st birds,' saith he, 'that ever flew on wing,'
And swears there is a flight, were worthy of a king.
　Then making to the flood to force the fowls to rise,
The fierce and eager hawks, down thrilling from the skies,
Make sundry canceleers e'er they the fowl can reach,
Which then to save their lives, their wings do lively stretch.
But when the whizzing bells the silent air do cleave,
And that their greatest speed them vainly do deceive,
And the sharp cruel hawks they at their backs do view,
Themselves for very fear they instantly ineaw.
　The hawks get up again into their former place,
And ranging here and there, in that their airy race,
Still as the fearful fowl attempt to 'scape away,
With many a stouping brave, them in again they lay.
But when the falconers take their hawking poles in hand,
And crossing of the brook, do put it over land,
The hawk gives it a souse, that makes it to rebound
Well near the height of man sometime, above the ground,
Oft takes a leg, or wing, oft takes away the head,
And oft from neck to tail the back in two doth shred.
With many a wo ho ho! and jocund lure again,
When he his quarry makes upon the grassy plain.

M. DRAYTON

256

MICHAEL DRAYTON

From England's Heroical Epistles, 1597—1605

Isabel to Richard II

Oh, how even yet I hate these wretched eyes,
And in my glass oft call them faithless spies
Prepared for Richard, that unawares did look
Upon that traitor Henry Bulingbrooke :
But that excess of joy my sense bereaved,
So much my sight had never been deceived.
Oh, how unlike to my loved lord was he,
Whom rashly I, sweet Richard, took for thee !
I might have seen the courser's self did lack
That princely rider should bestride his back ;
He that, since Nature her great work began,
She made to be the mirror of a man,
That when she meant to form some matchless limb,
Still for a pattern took some part of him,
And jealous of her cunning, brake the mould,
In his proportion done the best she could.

*   *   *   *   *   *

When thou to Ireland took'st thy last farewell,
Millions of knees upon the pavements fell,
And everywhere the applauding echoes ring
The joyful shouts that did salute a King.
Thy parting hence what pomp did not adorn ?
At thy return who laughed thee not to scorn ?
Who to my lord a look vouchsafed to lend ?
Then all too few on Herford to attend.
Princes, like suns, be evermore in sight,
All see the clouds betwixt them and their light :
Yet they which lighten all down from the skies,
See not the clouds offending others' eyes,
And deem their noontide is desired of all,
When all expect clear changes by their fall.

*   *   *   *   *   *

When I to England came, a world of eyes
Like stars attended on my fair arise,

MICHAEL DRAYTON

At my decline, like angry planets frown,
And all are set before my going down :
The smooth-faced air did on my coming smile,
But with rough storms are driven to exile :
But Bulingbrooke devised we thus should part,
Fearing two sorrows should possess one heart,
To make affliction stronger, doth deny
That one poor comfort left our misery.
He had before divorced thy crown and thee,
Which might suffice, and not to widow me ;
But that to prove the utmost of his hate,
To make our fall the greater by our state.

*   *   *   *   *   *

Then loose thy care, where first thy crown was lost,
Sell it so dearly, for it dearly cost :
And sith they did of liberty deprive thee,
Burying thy hope, let not thy care outlive thee.
But hard, God knows, with sorrow doth it go,
When woe becomes a comforter to woe :
Yet much methinks of comfort I could say,
If from my heart pale fear were rid away ;
Something there is which tells me still of woe,
But what it is, that Heaven above doth know :
Grief to itself most dreadful doth appear,
And never yet was sorrow void of fear.
But yet in death doth sorrow hope the best,
And with this farewell wish thee happy rest.

M. DRAYTON

REFLECTIVE AND MORAL POEMS

From The Faerie Queene I ix 39, 1590

Ease after War

Who travailes by the wearie wandring way,
To come unto his wished home in haste,
And meetes a flood that doth his passage stay,
Is not great grace to helpe. him over past,
Or free his feet that in the myre sticke fast?
Most envious man, that grieves at neighbours good;
And fond, that joyest in the woe thou hast!
Why wilt not let him passe, that long hath stood
Upon the bancke, yet wilt thy selfe not pas the flood?

He there does now enjoy eternall rest
And happy ease, which thou doest want and crave,
And further from it daily wanderest:
What if some little payne the passage have,
That makes frayle flesh to feare the bitter wave,
Is not short payne well borne, that bringes long ease,
And layes the soule to sleepe in quiet grave?
Sleepe after toyle, port after stormie seas,
Ease after warre, death after life, does greatly please.

E. Spenser

From An Hymne in Honour of Beautie, 1596

Soul is Form

But ah! beleeve me there is more then so,
That workes such wonders in the minds of men;
I, that have often prov'd, too well it know,
And who so list the like assayes to ken,
Shall find by tryall, and confesse it then,
That Beautie is not, as fond men misdeeme,
An outward shew of things that onely seeme.

EDMUND SPENSER

For that same goodly hew of white and red,
With which the cheekes are sprinckled, shal decay,
And those sweete rosy leaves, so fairely spred
Upon the lips, shall fade and fall away
To that they were, even to corrupted clay:
That golden wyre, those sparckling stars so bright,
Shall turne to dust, and loose their goodly light.

But that faire lampe, from whose celestiall ray
That light proceedes, which kindleth lovers fire,
Shall never be extinguisht nor decay;
But, when the vitall spirits doe expyre,
Unto her native planet shall retyre;
For it is heavenly borne and can not die,
Being a parcell of the purest skie.

For when the soule, the which derived was,
At first, out of that great immortall Spright,
By whom all live to love, whilome did pas
Downe from the top of purest heavens hight
To be embodied here, it then tooke light
And lively spirits from that fayrest starre
Which lights the world forth from his firie carre.

Which powre retayning still or more or lesse,
When she in fleshly seede is eft enraced,
Through every part she doth the same impresse,
According as the heavens have her graced,
And frames her house, in which she will be placed,
Fit for her selfe, adorning it with spoyle
Of th' heavenly riches which she robd erewhyle.

Therof it comes that these faire soules, which have
The most resemblance of that heavenly light,
Frame to themselves most beautifull and brave
Their fleshly bowre, most fit for their delight,
And the grosse matter by a soveraine might
Tempers so trim, that it may well be seene
A pallace fit for such a virgin Queene.

EDMUND SPENSER *and* SIR JOHN DAVIES

So every spirit, as it is most pure,
And hath in it the more of heavenly light,
So it the fairer bodie doth procure
To habit in, and it more fairely dight
With chearefull grace and amiable sight ;
For of the soule the bodie forme doth take ;
For soule is forme, and doth the bodie make.

E. SPENSER

From Orchestra, 1594—1622

The Dancing of the Elements

For that brave Sun, the Father of the Day,
Doth love this Earth, the Mother of the Night,
And like a reveller in rich array
Doth dance his galliard in his leman's sight ;
Both back, and forth, and sideways passing light,
His princely grace doth so the gods amaze,
That all stand still and at his beauty gaze.

But see the Earth, when she approacheth near,
How she for joy doth spring, and sweetly smile ;
But see again her sad and heavy cheer
When changing places he retires a while :
But those black clouds he shortly will exile,
And make them all before his presence fly,
As mists consum'd before his cheerful eye.

Who doth not see the measures of the Moon,
Which thirteen times she danceth ev'ry year ?
And ends her pavin, thirteen times as soon
As doth her brother, of whose golden hair
She borroweth part and proudly doth it wear :
Then doth she coyly turn her face aside,
That half her cheek is scarce sometimes descry'd.

*　　*　　*　　*　　*　　*

261

SIR JOHN DAVIES

For when you breathe, the air in order moves,
Now in, now out, in time and measure true;
And when you speak, so well she dancing loves,
That doubling oft, and oft redoubling new,
With thousand forms she doth herself endue:
    For all the words that from your lips repair
    Are naught but tricks and turnings of the air.

Hence is her prattling daughter Echo born,
That dances to all voices she can hear:
There is no sound so harsh that she doth scorn,
Nor any time wherein she will forbear
The airy pavement with her feet to wear:
    And yet her hearing sense is nothing quick,
    For after time she endeth ev'ry trick.

*   *   *   *   *   *

For lo the Sea that fleets about the Land,
And like a girdle clips her solid waist,
Music and measure both doth understand:
For his great crystal eye is always cast
Up to the moon, and on her fixed fast:
    And as she danceth in her pallid sphere,
    So danceth he about the centre here.

Sometimes his proud green waves in order set,
One after other flow unto the shore,
Which when they have with many kisses wet,
They ebb away in order as before;
And to make known his Courtly Love the more,
    He oft doth lay aside his three-fork'd Mace,
    And with his arms the tim'rous Earth embrace.

*   *   *   *   *   *

Since when all ceremonious mysteries,
All sacred orgies and religious rites,
All pomps, and triumphs, and solemnities,
All funerals, nuptials, and like public sights,
All parliaments of peace, and warlike sights,
    All learned arts, and every great affair,
    A lively shape of dancing seems to bear.

SIR J. DAVIES

SIR JOHN DAVIES

From **Nosce Teipsum, 1599—1622**

Why the soul is united to the body

This substance, and this spirit of God's own making,
  Is in the body plac'd, and planted here,
'That both of God, and of the world partaking,
  Of all that is, man might the image bear.'

God first made angels, bodiless pure minds ;
  Then other things, which mindless bodies be ;
Last, he made man, th' horizon 'twixt both kinds,
  In whom we do the world's abridgment see.

Besides, this world below did need one wight,
  Which might thereof distinguish ev'ry part ;
Make use thereof, and take therein delight ;
  And order things with industry and art :

Which also God might in his works admire,
  And here beneath yield him both pray'r and praise ;
As there, above, the holy angels' quire
  Doth spread his glory with spiritual lays.

Lastly, the brute unreasonable wights
  Did want a visible king, on them to reign :
And God himself thus to the world unites,
  That so the world might endless bliss obtain.

In what manner the soul is united to the body

But how shall we this union well express ?
  Nought ties the soul, her subtlety is such ;
She moves the body, which she doth possess ;
  Yet no part toucheth, but by virtue's touch.

Then dwells she not therein, as in a tent ;
  Nor as a pilot in his ship doth sit ;
Nor as the spider in his web is pent ;
  Nor as the wax retains the print in it ;

263

SIR JOHN DAVIES *and* SAMUEL DANIEL

Nor as a vessel water doth contain;
   Nor as one liquor in another shed;
Nor as the heat doth in the fire remain;
   Nor as a voice throughout the air is spread:

But as the fair and cheerful morning light
   Doth here and there her silver beams impart,
And in an instant doth herself unite
   To the transparent air, in all and part:

Still resting whole, when blows the air divide;
   Abiding pure, when th' air is most corrupted;
Throughout the air, her beams dispersing wide;
   And when the air is toss'd, not interrupted;

So doth the piercing soul the body fill,
   Being all in all, and all in part diffus'd;
Indivisible, incorruptible still;
   Not forc'd, encounter'd, troubled, or confus'd.

And as the sun above the light doth bring,
   Though we behold it in the air below;
So from th' eternal Light the soul doth spring,
   Though in the body she her pow'rs do show.

Sir J. Davies

From **Musophilus, 1599**

The power of verse

Pow'r above pow'rs, O heav'nly Eloquence!
That with the strong rein of commanding words
Dost manage, guide, and master th' eminence
Of men's affections, more than all their swords;
Shall we not offer to thy excellence
The richest treasure that our wit affords?

Thou that canst do much more with one poor pen,
Than all the pow'rs of princes can effect;
And draw, divert, dispose, and fashion men,
Better than force or rigour can direct!
Should we this ornament of glory then,
As th' unmaterial fruits of shades, neglect?

SAMUEL DANIEL

Or should we careless come behind the rest
In pow'r of words, that go before in worth;
When as our accent's equal to the best,
Is able greater wonders to bring forth?
When all that ever hotter spirits express'd,
Comes better'd by the patience of the north?

And who (in time) knows whither we may vent
The treasure of our tongue? To what strange shores
This gain of our best glory shall be sent,
T' enrich unknowing nations with our stores?
What worlds in th' yet unformed Occident,
May come refin'd with th' accents that are ours?

Or who can tell for what great work in hand
The greatness of our style is now ordain'd?
What pow'rs it shall bring in; what spirits command;
What thoughts let out; what humours keep restrain'd;
What mischief it may pow'rfully withstand;
And what fair ends may thereby be attain'd?

And as for Poesy, mother of this force!
That breeds, brings forth, and nourishes this might,
Teaching it in a loose, yet measur'd course,
With comely motions how to go upright;
And fost'ring it with bountiful discourse,
Adorns it thus in fashions of delight;

What should I say?—Since it is well approv'd
The speech of heav'n, with whom they have commerce,
That only seem out of themselves remov'd,
And do with more than human skills converse.
Those numbers wherewith heav'n and earth are mov'd
Show weakness speaks in prose, but pow'r in verse.

S. Daniel

265

SAMUEL DANIEL

From A Panegyric Congratulatory, 1603

To the Lady Margaret, Countess of Cumberland

He that of such a height hath built his mind,
And rear'd the dwelling of his thoughts so strong,
As neither fear nor hope can shake the frame
Of his resolved powers; nor all the wind
Of vanity or malice pierce to wrong
His settled peace, or to disturb the same:
What a fair seat hath he, from whence he may
The boundless wastes and weilds of man survey!

And with how free an eye doth he look down
Upon these lower regions of turmoil!
Where all these storms of passions mainly beat
On flesh and blood; where honour, power, renown,
Are only gay afflictions, golden toil;
Where greatness stands upon as feeble feet
As frailty doth; and only great doth seem
To little minds, who do it so esteem.

He looks upon the mightiest Monarch's wars
But only as on stately robberies;
Where evermore the fortune that prevails
Must be the right: the ill-succeeding mars
The fairest and the best-fac'd enterprise.
Great pirate Pompey lesser pirates quails:
Justice, he sees, as if seduced, still
Conspires with power, whose cause must not be ill.

He sees the face of right t' appear as manifold
As are the passions of uncertain man,
Who puts it in all colours, all attires,
To serve his ends, and make his courses hold.
He sees, that let deceit work what it can,
Plot and contrive base ways to high desires;
That the all-guiding Providence doth yet
All disappoint, and mocks this smoke of wit.

SAMUEL DANIEL

Nor is he mov'd with all the thunder-cracks
Of tyrants' threats, or with the surly brow
Of pow'r, that proudly sits on others' crimes,
Charg'd with more crying sins than those he checks.
The storms of sad confusion, that may grow
Up in the present for the coming times,
Appal not him, that hath no side at all,
But of himself, and knows the worst can fall.

Although his heart so near allied to earth
Cannot but pity the perplexed state
Of troublous and distress'd mortality,
That thus make way unto the ugly birth
Of their own sorrows, and do still beget
Affliction upon imbecility:
Yet seeing thus the course of things must run,
He looks thereon, not strange, but as fore-done.

And whilst distraught ambition compasses,
And is encompass'd; whilst as craft deceives,
And is deceiv'd: whilst man doth ransack man,
And builds on blood, and rises by distress;
And th' inheritance of desolation leaves
To great-expecting hopes: he looks thereon,
As from the shore of peace, with unwet eye,
And bears no venture in impiety.

Thus, Madam, fares the man, that hath prepar'd
A rest for his desires, and sees all things
Beneath him, and hath learn'd this book of man,
Full of the notes of frailty, and compar'd
The best of glory with her sufferings;
By whom, I see, you labour all you can
To plant your heart; and set your thoughts as near
His glorious mansion, as your pow'rs can bear.

Which, Madam, are so soundly fashioned
By that clear judgment, that hath carried you
Beyond the feeble limits of your kind,
As they can stand against the strongest head

SAMUEL DANIEL

Passion can make; inur'd to any hue
The world can cast; that cannot cast that mind
Out of her form of goodness, that doth see
Both what the best and worst of earth can be.

Which makes, that whatsoever here befalls,
You in the region of yourself remain:
Where no vain breath of th' impudent molests,
That hath secur'd within the brazen walls
Of a clear conscience, that (without all stain)
Rises in peace, in innocency rests;
Whilst all what malice from without procures,
Shows her own ugly heart, but hurts not yours.

And whereas none rejoice more in revenge,
Than women use to do, yet you well know,
That wrong is better check'd by being contemn'd,
Than being pursu'd; leaving to him t' avenge,
To whom it appertains. Wherein you show
How worthily your clearness hath condemn'd
Base malediction, living in the dark,
That at the rays of goodness still doth bark.

Knowing the heart of man is set to be
The centre of his world, about the which
These revolutions of disturbances
Still roll; where all th' aspects of misery
Predominate: whose strong effects are such,
As he must bear, being pow'rless to redress:
And that unless above himself he can
Erect himself, how poor a thing is man!

And how turmoil'd they are that level lie
With earth, and cannot lift themselves from thence;
That never are at peace with their desires,
But work beyond their years; and ev'n deny
Dotage her rest, and hardly will dispense
With death. That when ability expires,
Desire lives still. So much delight they have,
To carry toil and travail to the grave.

SAMUEL DANIEL *and* GEORGE CHAPMAN

Whose ends you see ; and what can be the best
They reach unto, when they have cast the sum
And reck'nings of their glory. And you know,
This floating life hath but this port of rest,
A heart prepar'd, that fears no ill to come.
And that man's greatness rests but in his show,
The best of all whose days consumed are,
Either in war, or peace conceiving war.

This concord, Madam, of a well-tun'd mind
Hath been so set by that all-working hand
Of heaven, that though the world hath done his worst
To put it out by discords most unkind ;
Yet doth it still in perfect union stand
With God and man ; nor ever will be forc'd
From that most sweet accord ; but still agree,
Equal in Fortune's inequality.

And this note (Madam) of your worthiness
Remains recorded in so many hearts,
As time nor malice cannot wrong your right,
In th' inheritance of Fame you must possess :
You that have built you by your great deserts
Out of small means a far more exquisite
And glorious dwelling for your honour'd name,
Than all the gold of leaden minds can frame.

S. Daniel

From The Tears of Peace, 1609

The end of knowledge

But this is Learning ; to have skill to throw
Reins on your body's powers that nothing know,
And fill the soul's powers so with act and art
That she can curb the body's angry part ;
All perturbations ; all affects that stray
From their one object, which is to obey
Her sovereign empire ; as herself should force
Their functions only to serve her discourse ;

GEORGE CHAPMAN

And that, to beat the straight path of one end,
Which is to make her substance still contend
To be God's image; in informing it
With knowledge; holy thoughts and all forms fit
For that eternity ye seek in way
Of his sole imitation; and to sway
Your life's love so that he may still be centre
To all your pleasures; and you here may enter
The next life's peace; in governing so well
Your sensual parts that you as free may dwell,
Of vulgar raptures here, as when calm death
Dissolves that learned empire with your breath.
To teach and live thus, is the only use
And end of Learning. Skill that doth produce
But terms, and tongues, and parroting of art
Without that power to rule the errant part,
Is that which some call learned ignorance;
A serious trifle, error in a trance.
And let a scholar all earth's volumes carry,
He will be but a walking dictionary,
A mere articulate clock that doth but speak
By others' arts; when wheels wear, or springs break,
Or any fault is in him, he can mend
No more than clocks; but at set hours must spend
His month as clocks do: if too fast speech go,
He cannot stay it, nor haste if too slow.
So that as travellers seek their peace through storms,
In passing many seas for many forms
Of foreign government; endure the pain
Of many faces seeing, and the gain
That strangers make of their strange-loving humours;
Learn tongues; keep note-books; all to feed the tumours
Of vain discourse at home, or serve the course
Of state-employment, never having force
T' employ themselves; but idle compliments
Must pay their pains, costs, slaveries, all their rents;
And though they many men know, get few friends.
So covetous readers, setting many ends
To their much skill to talk; studiers of phrase;
Shifters in art, to flutter in the blaze

GEORGE CHAPMAN *and* JOHN DONNE

Of ignorant countenance; to obtain degrees
And lie in learning's bottom, like the lees;
To be accounted deep by shallow men;
And carve all language in one glorious pen;
May have much fame for learning, but th' effect
Proper to perfect Learning—to direct
Reason in such an art as that it can
Turn blood to soul, and make both one calm man,
So making peace with God, doth differ far
From clerks that go with God and man to war.

G. CHAPMAN

From An Anatomy of the World, 1633

Mankind diminished

There is not now that mankind which was then,
When as the sun and man did seem to strive
—Joint-tenants of the world—who should survive;
When stag, and raven, and the long-lived tree,
Compared with man, died in minority;
When if a slow-paced star had stolen away
From the observer's marking, he might stay
Two or three hundred years to see it again,
And then make up his observation plain;
When, as the age was long, the size was great;
Man's growth confess'd, and recompensed the meat;
So spacious and large, that every soul
Did a fair kingdom and large realm control;
And when the very stature, thus erect,
Did that soul a good way towards heaven direct.
Where is this mankind now? who lives to age
Fit to be made Methusalem his page?
Alas! we scarce live long enough to try
Whether a true-made clock run right, or lie.
Old grandsires talk of yesterday with sorrow;
And for our children we reserve to-morrow.
So short is life, that every peasant strives,
In a torn house, or field, to have three lives;

271

JOHN DONNE

And as in lasting, so in length is man,
Contracted to an inch, who was a span.
For had a man at first in forests stray'd,
Or shipwreck'd in the sea, one would have laid
A wager, that an elephant or whale,
That met him, would not hastily assail
A thing so equal to him ; now, alas !
The fairies and the pigmies well may pass
As credible ; mankind decays so soon,
We're scarce our fathers' shadows cast at noon.
Only death adds to our length ; nor are we grown
In stature to be men, till we are none.
But this were light, did our less volume hold
All the old text ; or had we changed to gold
Their silver, or disposed into less glass
Spirits of virtue, which then scatter'd was.
But 'tis not so ; we're not retired, but damp'd ;
And, as our bodies, so our minds are cramp'd.
'Tis shrinking, not close weaving, that hath thus
In mind and body both bedwarfed us.
We seem ambitious God's whole work to undo ;
Of nothing He made us, and we strive too
To bring ourselves to nothing back ; and we
Do what we can to do 't so soon as He.
With new diseases on ourselves we war,
And with new physic, a worse engine far.
This man, this world's vice-emperor, in whom
All faculties, all graces are at home
—And if in other creatures they appear,
They're but man's ministers and legates there,
To work on their rebellions, and reduce
Them to civility, and to man's use—
This man, whom God did woo, and, loth to attend
Till man came up, did down to man descend ;
This man so great, that all that is, is his,
O, what a trifle, and poor thing he is !
If man were anything, he's nothing now.
Help, or at least some time to waste, allow
To his other wants, yet when he did depart
With her whom we lament, he lost his heart.

JOHN DONNE

She, of whom th' ancients seemed to prophesy,
When they called virtues by the name of *she*;
She, in whom virtue was so much refined,
That for allay unto so pure a mind
She took the weaker sex; she that could drive
The poisonous tincture, and the stain of Eve,
Out of her thoughts and deeds, and purify
All by a true religious alchemy;
She, she is dead; she's dead; when thou know'st this
Thou know'st how poor a trifling thing man is.

J. DONNE

From An Anatomy of the World, 1633

The World's disproportion

We think the heavens enjoy their spherical,
Their round proportion, embracing all;
But yet their various and perplexed course,
Observed in divers ages, doth enforce
Men to find out so many eccentric parts,
Such diverse downright lines, such overthwarts,
As disproportion that pure form; it tears
The firmament in eight-and-forty shares,
And in these constellations then arise
New stars, and old do vanish from our eyes;
As though heaven suffered earthquakes, peace or war,
When new towers rise, and old demolish'd are.
They have impaled within a zodiac
The free-born sun, and keep twelve signs awake
To watch his steps; the Goat and Crab control,
And fright him back, who else to either pole,
Did not these tropics fetter him, might run.
For his course is not round, nor can the sun
Perfect a circle, or maintain his way
One inch direct; but where he rose to-day
He comes no more, but with a cozening line,
Steals by that point, and so is serpentine;
And seeming weary with his reeling thus,
He means to sleep, being now fallen nearer us.

JOHN DONNE

So of the stars which boast that they do run
In circle still, none ends where he begun.
All their proportion's lame, it sinks, it swells;
For of meridians and parallels
Man hath weaved out a net, and this net thrown
Upon the heavens, and now they are his own.
Loth to go up the hill, or labour thus
To go to heaven, we make heaven come to us.
We spur, we rein the stars, and in their race
They're diversely content to obey our pace.
But keeps the earth her round proportion still?
Doth not a Teneriffe or higher hill
Rise so high like a rock, that one might think
The floating moon would shipwreck there and sink?
Seas are so deep that whales, being struck to-day,
Perchance to-morrow scarce at middle way
Of their wish'd journey's end, the bottom, die.
And men, to sound depths, so much line untie
As one might justly think that there would rise
At end thereof one of th' antipodes.

J. Donne

POETICAL ADDRESSES

From Epigrams, folio 1616

To John Donne

Donne, the delight of Phoebus and each Muse,
Who to thy one, all other brains refuse;
Whose every work, of thy most early wit,
Came forth example and remains so yet;
Longer a-knowing than most wits do live,
And which no affection praise enough can give.
To it, thy language, letters, arts, best life,
Which might with half mankind maintain a strife.
All which I meant to praise and yet I would,
But leave, because I cannot as I should !

BEN JONSON

From Epigrams, folio 1616

Inviting a friend to supper

To-night, grave sir, both my poor house and I
Do equally desire your company :
Not that we think us worthy such a guest,
But that your worth will dignify our feast,
With those that come ; whose grace may make that seem
Something, which else could hope for no esteem.
It is the fair acceptance, sir, creates
The entertainment perfect, not the cates.

s 2

BEN JONSON

Yet shall you have, to rectify your palate,
An olive, capers, or some better salad
Ushering the mutton : with a short-legg'd hen,
If we can get her full of eggs, and then,
Limons, and wine for sauce : to these, a coney
Is not to be despair'd of for our money ;
And though fowl now be scarce, yet there are clerks,
The sky not falling, think we may have larks.
I'll tell you of more, and lie, so you will come :
Of partridge, pheasant, woodcock, of which some
May yet be there ; and godwit if we can ;
Knat, rail, and ruff too. Howsoe'er, my man
Shall read a piece of Virgil, Tacitus,
Livy, or of some better book to us,
Of which we'll speak our minds, amidst our meat ;
And I'll profess no verses to repeat :
To this if aught appear, which I not know of,
That will the pastry, not my paper, show of.
Digestive cheese, and fruit there sure will be ;
But that which most doth take my muse and me,
Is a pure cup of rich Canary-wine,
Which is the Mermaid's now, but shall be mine :
Of which had Horace or Anacreon tasted,
Their lives, as do their lines, till now had lasted.
Tobacco, nectar, or the Thespian spring,
Are all but Luther's beer, to this I sing.
Of this we will sup free, but moderately,
And we will have no Pooly' or Parrot by ;
Nor shall our cups make any guilty men ;
But at our parting we will be as when
We innocently met. No simple word
That shall be uttered at our mirthful board,
Shall make us sad next morning ; or affright
The liberty that we'll enjoy to-night.

BEN JONSON

BEN JONSON

From Shakespeare, folio 1623

On the Portrait of Shakespeare

This figure that thou here seest put,
It was for gentle SHAKESPEARE cut,
Wherein the graver had a strife
With nature, to out-do the life :
O could he but have drawn his wit
As well in brass, as he hath hit
His face ; the print would then surpass
All that was ever writ in brass.
But since he cannot, reader, look
Not on his picture, but his book.

BEN JONSON

From Shakespeare, folio 1623

To the memory of my beloved, the Author Mr William Shakespeare : and what he hath left us

To draw no envy, SHAKESPEARE, on thy name,
Am I thus ample to thy book and fame ;
While I confess thy writings to be such,
As neither man, nor muse, can praise too much.
Tis true, and all men's suffrage. But these ways
Were not the paths I meant unto thy praise ;
For seeliest ignorance on these may light,
Which, when it sounds at best, but echoes right ;
Or blind affection, which doth ne'er advance
The truth, but gropes, and urgeth all by chance ;
Or crafty malice might pretend this praise,
And think to ruin, where it seemed to raise.
These are, as some infamous bawd, or whore,
Should praise a matron ; what could hurt her more ?
But thou art proof against them, and, indeed,
Above the ill fortune of them, or the need.
I, therefore, will begin : Soul of the age !
The applause ! delight ! the wonder of our stage !

BEN JONSON

My SHAKESPEARE rise! I will not lodge thee by
Chaucer, or Spenser, or bid Beaumont lie
A little further to make thee a room;
Thou art a monument without a tomb,
And art alive still, while thy book doth live,
And we have wits to read, and praise to give.
That I not mix thee so, my brain excuses,
I mean with great, but disproportioned Muses.
For if I thought my judgment were of years,
I should commit thee surely with thy peers;
And tell how far thou did'st our Lyly outshine,
Or sporting Kyd, or Marlowe's mighty line.
And though thou hadst small Latin and less Greek,
From thence to honour thee, I would not seek
For names: but call forth thund'ring Æschylus,
Euripides, and Sophocles to us,
Pacuvius, Accius, him of Cordoua dead,
To life again, to hear thy buskin tread,
And shake a stage: or when thy socks were on,
Leave thee alone for the comparison
Of all, that insolent Greece, or haughty Rome
Sent forth, or since did from their ashes come.
Triumph, my Britain, thou hast one to show,
To whom all scenes of Europe homage owe.
He was not of an age, but for all time!
And all the Muses still were in their prime,
When, like Apollo, he came forth to warm
Our ears, or like a Mercury to charm!
Nature herself was proud of his designs,
And joyed to wear the dressing of his lines!
Which were so richly spun, and woven so fit,
As, since, she will vouchsafe no other wit.
The merry Greek, tart Aristophanes,
Neat Terence, witty Plautus, now not please;
But antiquated and deserted lie,
As they were not of nature's family.
Yet must I not give nature all; thy art,
My gentle SHAKESPEARE, must enjoy a part.
For though the poet's matter nature be,
His art doth give the fashion: and, that he

278

BEN JONSON

Who casts to write a living line, must sweat,
(Such as thine are) and strike the second heat
Upon the Muses' anvil ; turn the same,
And himself with it, that he thinks to frame ;
Or for the laurel, he may gain a scorn ;
For a good poet's made, as well as born.
And such wert thou. Look how the father's face
Lives in his issue, even so the race
Of SHAKESPEARE's mind and manners brightly shines
In his well torned, and true-filed lines ;
In each of which he seems to shake a lance,
As brandish'd at the eyes of ignorance.
Sweet Swan of Avon ! what a sight it were
To see thee in our waters yet appear,
And make those flights upon the banks of Thames,
That so did take Eliza, and our James !
But stay, I see thee in the hemisphere
Advanced, and made a constellation there !
Shine forth, thou Star of poets, and with rage,
Or influence, chide, or cheer the drooping stage ;
Which, since thy flight from hence, hath mourn'd like night,
And despairs day, but for thy volume's light.

BEN JONSON

From **Underwoods**, folio 1640

Lord Bacon's birthday, 1621

Hail, happy Genius of this ancient pile !
How comes it all things so about thee smile?
The fire, the wine, the men ; and in the midst
Thou stand'st as if some mystery thou didst.
Pardon, I read it in thy face, the day
For whose returns, and many, all these pray;
And so do I. This is the sixtieth year,
Since BACON, and thy lord, was born, and here ;
Son to the grave wise Keeper of the Seal,
Fame and foundation of the English Weal.
What then his father was, that since is he,
Now with a title more to the degree ;

279

BEN JONSON *and* MICHAEL DRAYTON

England's high Chancellor : the destin'd heir,
In his soft cradle, to his father's chair :
Whose even thread the fates spin round and full,
Out of their choicest and their whitest wool.
  'Tis a brave cause of joy, let it be known,
For 'twere a narrow gladness, kept thine own.
Give me a deep-crowned bowl, that I may sing,
In raising him, the wisdom of my king.

BEN JONSON

From Elegies, 1627

To Henry Reynolds, Of Poets and Poesy

That noble *Chaucer* in those former times,
The first enriched our English with his rhymes,
And was the first of ours that ever brake
Into the Muses' treasure, and first spake
In weighty numbers, delving in the mine
Of perfect knowledge, which he could refine
And coin for current, and as much as then
The English language could express to men
He made it do, and by his wondrous skill
Gave us much light from his abundant quill.
  And honest *Gower*, who in respect of him
Had only sipped at Aganippe's brim,
And though in years this last was him before,
Yet fell he far short of the other's store.
  When after those, four ages very near,
They with the Muses which conversed were
That princely Surrey, early in the time
Of the Eight Henry, who was then the prime
Of England's noble youth ; with him there came
Wyat, with reverence whom we still do name ;
Amongst our poets *Brian* had a share
With the two former, which accompted are
That time's best makers and the authors were
Of those small poems which the title bear
Of songs and sonnets, wherein oft they hit
On many dainty passages of wit.

MICHAEL DRAYTON

Gascoigne and *Churchyard* after them again,
In the beginning of Eliza's reign,
Accounted were great meterers many a day,
But not inspired with brave fire; had they
Lived but a little longer, they had seen
Their works before them to have buried been.

Grave moral *Spenser* after these came on,
Than whom I am persuaded there was none,
Since the blind bard his Iliads up did make,
Fitter a task like that to undertake;
To set down boldly, bravely to invent,
In all high knowledge surely excellent.

The noble *Sidney* with this last arose,
That heroe for numbers and for prose,
That throughly paced our language, as to show
The plenteous English hand in hand might go
With Greek and Latin, and did first reduce
Our tongue from *Lyly*'s writing then in use;
Talking of stones, stars, plants, of fishes, flies,
Playing with words and idle similes;
As the English, apes and very zanies be
Of everything that they do hear and see,
So imitating his ridiculous tricks,
They spake and writ all like mere lunatics.

Then *Warner*, though his lines were not so trimmed,
Nor yet his poem so exactly limned
And neatly jointed, but the critic may
Easily reprove him, yet thus let me say
For my old friend, some passages there be
In him which I protest have taken me
With almost wonder, so fine, clear, and new,
As yet they have been equalled by few.

Next *Marlowe*, bathed in the Thespian springs,
Had in him those brave translunary things
That the first poets had; his raptures were
All air and fire, which made his verses clear;
For that fine madness still he did retain
Which rightly should possess a poet's brain.

And surely *Nashe*, though he a proser were,
A branch of laurel yet deserves to bear,

281

MICHAEL DRAYTON

Sharply satiric was he, and that way
He went, since that his being to this day
Few have attempted, and I surely think
Those words shall hardly be set down with ink
Shall scorch and blast so as his could, where he
Would inflict vengeance; and be it said of thee,
Shakespeare, thou hadst as smooth a comic vein,
Fitting the sock, and in thy natural brain
As strong conception and as clear a rage,
As any one that trafficked with the stage.
    Amongst these *Samuel Daniel*, whom if I
May speak of, but to censure do deny,
Only have heard some wise men him rehearse
To be too much historian in verse;
His rhymes were smooth, his metres well did close,
But yet his manner better fitted prose.
Next these, learn'd *Jonson* in this list I bring,
Who had drunk deep of the Pierian spring,
Whose knowledge did him worthily prefer,
And long was lord here of the theatre;
Who in opinion made our learn'dst to stick
Whether in poems rightly dramatic,
Strong Seneca or Plautus, he or they
Should bear the buskin or the sock away.
Others again here lived in my days,
That have of us deserved no less praise
For their translations, than the daintiest wit
That on Parnassus thinks he high'st doth sit,
And for a chair may 'mongst the Muses call,
As the most curious maker of them all;
As reverent *Chapman*, who hath brought to us
Musæus, Homer, and Hesiodus
Out of the Greek; and by his skill hath reared
Them to that height, and to our tongue endeared,
That were those poets at this day alive,
To see their books thus with us to survive,
They would think, having neglected them so long,
They had been written in the English tongue.

M. Drayton

SATIRE

From Tottel's Songs and Sonnets, 1557

Of the Courtier's Life

To join the mean with each extremity,
With nearest virtue aye to clothe the vice ;
And, as to purpose likewise it shall fall,
To press the virtue that it may not rise.
As drunkenness good fellowship to call ;
The friendly foe, with his fair double face,
Say he is gentle, and courteous therewithal ;
Affirm that favel hath a goodly grace
In eloquence ; and cruelty to name
Zeal of justice ; and change in time and place.
And he that suffereth offence without blame,
Call him pitiful ; and him true and plain,
That raileth rechless unto each man's shame.
Say he is rude, that cannot lie and feign ;
The lecher a lover ; and tyranny
To be the right of a prince's reign :
I cannot, I ; no, no ! it will not be.
This is the cause that I could never yet
Hang on their sleeves that weigh, as thou mayst see,
A chip of chance more than a pound of wit.
This maketh me at home to hunt and hawk,
And in foul weather at my book to sit ;
In frost and snow, then with my bow to stalk ;
No man doth mark whereso I ride or go ;
In lusty leas at liberty I walk.

SIR T. WYATT

GEORGE GASCOIGNE

From The Steel Glass, 1576—1587

A Catalogue of Abuses

I tell thee, priest, when shoemakers make shoes
That are well sewed, with never a stitch amiss,
And use no craft in uttering of the same;
When tailors steal no stuff from gentlemen,
When tanners are with curriers well agreed,
And both so dress their hides that we go dry;
When cutlers leave to sell old rusty blades,
And hide no cracks with solder nor deceit;
When tinkers make no more holes than they found,
When thatchers think their wages worth their work,
When colliers put no dust into their sacks,
When maltmen make us drink no firmentie,
When Davy Diker digs and dallies not,
When smiths shoe horses as they would be shod,
When millers toll not with a golden thumb,
When bakers make not barm bear price of wheat,
When brewers put no baggage in their beer,
When butchers blow not over all their flesh,
When horse-coursers beguile no friends with jades,
When weavers' weight is found in housewives' web;
(But why dwell I so long among these louts?)

When mercers make no bones to swear and lie,
When vintners mix no water with their wine,
When printers pass none errors in their books,
When hatters use to buy none old cast robes,
When goldsmiths get no gains by solder'd crowns,
When upholsters sell feathers without dust,
When pewterers infect no tin with lead,
When drapers draw no gains by giving day,
When parchmentiers put in no ferret silk,
When surgeons heal all wounds without delay:
(Tush, these are toys, but yet my glass showeth all.)

GEORGE GASCOIGNE *and* EDMUND SPENSER

When purveyors provide not for themselves,
When takers take no bribes nor use no brags,
When customers conceal no covine used,
When searchers see all corners in a ship,
(And spy no pence by any sight they see).
When shrives do serve all process as they ought,
When bailiffs strain none other thing but strays,
When auditors their counters cannot change,
When proud surveyors take no parting pence,
When silver sticks not on the teller's fingers,
And when receivers pay as they receive :
When all these folk have quite forgotten fraud.

(Again my priests, a little by your leave.)
When sycophantes can find no place in court,
But are espied for echoes, as they are ;
When roisters ruffle not above their rule,
Nor colour craft by swearing 'precious coles';
When fencers' fees are like to apes' rewards,
A piece of bread and therewithall a bob ;
When Lais lives not like a lady's peer,
Nor useth art in dyeing of her hair ;
When all these things are ordered as they ought,
And see themselves within my glass of steel :
Even then (my priests) may you make holiday,
And pray no more but ordinary prayers.

G. GASCOIGNE

From Mother Hubberds Tale, 1591

The Suitor at Court

So pitifull a thing is Suters state !
Most miserable man, whom wicked fate
Hath brought to Court, to sue for had ywist,
That few have found, and manie one hath mist !
Full little knowest thou, that hast not tride,
What hell it is in suing long to bide :
To loose good dayes, that might be better spent ;
To wast long nights in pensive discontent ;

285

EDMUND SPENSER *and* JOSEPH HALL

To speed to day, to be put back to morrow;
To feed on hope, to pine with feare and sorrow;
To have thy Princes grace, yet want her Peeres;
To have thy asking, yet waite manie yeeres;
To fret thy soule with crosses and with cares;
To eate thy heart through comfortlesse dispaires;
To fawne, to crowche, to waite, to ride, to ronne,
To spend, to give, to want, to be undonne.
Unhappie wight, borne to desastrous end,
That doth his life in so long tendance spend!
  Who ever leaves sweete home, where meane estate
In safe assurance, without strife or hate,
Findes all things needfull for contentment meeke,
And will to Court for shadowes vaine to seeke,
Or hope to gaine, himselfe will a daw trie:
That curse God send unto mine enemie!

E. SPENSER

From Virgidemiarum II vi, 1597

The humble tutor

A gentle squire would gladly entertain
Into his house some trencher-chapelain;
Some willing man that might instruct his sons,
And that would stand to good conditions.
First, that he lie upon the truckle-bed,
While his young master lieth o'er his head.
Secondly, that he do, on no default,
Ever presume to sit above the salt.
Third, that he never change his trencher twice.
Fourth, that he use all comely courtesies;
Sit bare at meals, and one half rise and wait.
Last, that he never his young master beat,
But he must ask his mother to define
How many jerks she would his breech should line.
All these observed, he could contented be
To give five marks and winter livery.

J. HALL

JOHN DONNE

From Satires IV, 1633

An oddity of the town

Towards me did run
A thing more strange, than on Nile's slime the sun
E'er bred, or all which into Noah's ark came;
A thing which would have posed Adam to name;
Stranger than seven antiquaries' studies,
Than Afric's monsters, Guiana's rarities;
Stranger than strangers; but, who for a Dane,
In the Danes' massacre had sure been slain,
If he had lived then; and without help dies,
When next the 'prentices 'gainst strangers rise;
One, whom the watch, at noon, lets scarce go by;
One to whom th' examining justice sure would cry,
'Sir, by your priesthood tell me what you are.'
His clothes were strange, though coarse, and black,
    though bare;
Sleeveless his jerkin was, and it had been
Velvet, but 'twas now—so much ground was seen—
Become tufftaffaty; and our children shall
See it plain rash awhile, then nought at all.
The things hath travell'd, and faith, speaks all tongues,
And only knoweth what to all states belongs.
Made of th' accents and best phrase of all these,
He speaks one language.
   *   *   *   *   *   *
           He knows; he knows
When the Queen frown'd or smiled, and he knows what
A subtle statesman may gather of that;
He knows who loves whom; and who by poison
Hastes to an office's reversion;
He knows who hath sold his land, and now doth beg
A licence, old iron, boots, shoes, and egg-
Shells to transport; shortly boys shall not play
At span-counter or blow-point but shall pay
Toll to some courtier; and wiser than all of us,
He knows what lady is not painted.

J. DONNE

JOHN MARSTON

The Critic

For tell me, critic, is not fiction
The soul of poesy's invention?
Is't not the form the spirit and the essence,
The life and the essential difference,
Which *omni, semper, soli*, doth agree
To heavenly descended poesy?
Thy wit God comfort, mad chirurgion.
What, make so dangerous an incision?
At first dash whip away the instrument
Of poet's procreation? Fie, ignorant!
When as the soul and vital blood doth rest,
And hath in fiction only interest.
What, Satire! suck the soul from poesy
And leave him spriteless! O, impiety!
Would ever any erudite pedant
Seem in his artless lines so insolent?
But this it is when petty Priscians
Will needs step up to be censorians.
When once they can in true scann'd verses frame
A brave encomium of good Virtue's name;
Why thus it is when mimic apes will strive
With iron wedge the trunks of oaks to rive.
But see his spirit of detraction
Must nibble at a glorious action.
Euge! some gallant spirit, some resolved blood,
Will hazard all to work his country's good;
And to enrich his soul and raise his name,
Will boldly sail unto the rich Guiane.
What then? Must straight some shameless satirist,
With odious and opprobrious terms insist
To blast so high resolv'd intention
With a malignant vile detraction?

*　　*　　*　　*　　*　　*

JOHN MARSTON *and* BEN JONSON

So have I seen the March wind strive to fade
The fairest hue that art or nature made:
So envy still doth bark at clearest shine
And strives to stain heroic acts divine.

J. MARSTON

From **The New Inn, 1631**

The just indignation the author took at the vulgar censure of his play

Come leave the loathed stage,
And the more loathsome age,
Where pride and impudence, in faction knit,
    Usurp the chair of wit;
Indicting and arraigning every day
    Something they call a play.
Let their fastidious vain
Commission of the brain
Run on and rage, sweat, censure, and condemn;
They were not made for thee, less thou for them.

Say that thou pour'st them wheat,
And they will acorns eat;
'Twere simple fury still thyself to waste
    On such as have no taste!
To offer them a surfeit of pure bread,
    Whose appetites are dead!
No, give them grains their fill,
Husks, draff to drink and swill:
If they love lees, and leave the lusty wine,
Envy them not, their palate's with the swine.

No doubt some mouldy tale,
Like *Pericles*, and stale
As the shrieve's crusts, and nasty as his fish-
    Scraps, out of every dish
Thrown forth, and raked into the common tub,
    May keep up the *Play-club*;

There, sweepings do as well
    As the best-order'd meal ;
For who the relish of these guests will fit,
Needs set them but the alms-basket of wit.

    And much good do't you then :
    Brave *plush* and *velvet*-men,
Can feed on orts ; and, safe in your stage-clothes,
       Dare quit, upon your oaths,
The stagers and the stage-wrights too, your peers,
       Of larding your large ears
    With their foul *comic* socks,
    Wrought upon twenty blocks ;
Which, if they are torn, and turn'd, and patch'd enough,
The gamesters share your guilt, and you their stuff.—

    Leave things so prostitute
    And take the *Alcaic* lute ;
Or thine own *Horace*, or *Anacreon's* lyre ;
       Warm thee by *Pindar's* fire :
And though thy nerves be shrunk, and blood be cold
       Ere years have made thee old,
    Strike that disdainful heat
    Throughout, to their defeat,
As curious fools, and envious of thy strain,
May, blushing, swear no palsy's in thy brain.

    But when they hear thee sing
    The glories of thy *king*,
His zeal to *God*, and his just awe o'er men :
       They may, blood-shaken then,
Feel such a flesh-quake to possess their powers
       As they shall cry, Like ours,
    In sound of peace or wars,
    No harp e'er hit the stars,
In tuning forth the acts of his sweet reign ;
And raising *Charles* his chariot 'bove his *Wain*.

BEN JONSON

GLOSSARY

Amearst, punished
Astoined, astonished

Bank-rot, bankrupt
Bellibone, a beauty
Bilbows, swords from Bilboa
Bisse, an odoriferous substance
Blasing, proclaiming
Blive, immediately
Bourds, jests

Canceleer, to fly across
Check, a false swoop
Cleeves, steep hill-sides
Coles (Precious Coals!), an obsolete oath
Consort, concert
Cordiwin, Spanish leather
Covine, deceit
Cremosin, crimson
Croud, fiddle
Cutted, curt

Daw trie, to prove a fool
Day (give), to give credit
Deucalidon, the sea north of Scotland
Dewle, lamentation
Dore, deer
Drept, lost courage

Empight, fixed

Favel, flattery
Fere, companion
Ferret silk, floss silk

Galliasses, heavy low-built war-vessels
Godwit, a marsh-bird, a table delicacy
Grame, sorrow
Greeing, concordant

Halsers, hawsers
Helice, the Great Bear
Hent, to grasp

Ineaw, to plunge in the water

Lifull, life-full
Lin, to cease

Make, mate
Meet, measure
Mithridates, antidotes
Morion, helmet
Murrie-scyndal, purple-red silk
Muset, gap

Parchmentiers, makers of trimmings
Pavin, a stately dance
Paunce, pansy

Quoif, cap

Rails, nightgowns

Say, a kind of silk
Sendal, a light silk stuff
Shright, shrieked
Sousing, swooping
Specular stone, reflecting glass, mica
Stal'd, stolen
Stare, starling
Stoures, battles
Swelth, bubbling
Swinge, sway

Tappish, to lurk in covert
Tawdry, bought at St Audrey's fair
Tawed, hardened
Tead, torch
Trentals, thirty daily masses

Vild, vile

Waker, watchful
Waltring, rolling
Weene, think

Yeding, going
Y-fere, together
Y-wist (had y-wist), vain after-regret

INDEX OF AUTHORS

INDEX OF AUTHORS

293

INDEX OF AUTHORS

INDEX OF AUTHORS

INDEX OF AUTHORS

296

INDEX OF AUTHORS

T 5

INDEX OF AUTHORS

INDEX OF AUTHORS

INDEX OF AUTHORS

INDEX OF FIRST LINES

After long stormes and tempests sad assay. *Spenser,* 204
A gentle squire would gladly entertain. *Hall,* 286
Ah I remember well—and how can I. *Daniel,* 80
Alas, so all things now do hold their peace. *Earl of Surrey,* 185
All the flowers of the spring. *Webster,* 154
All ye that lovely lovers be. *Peele,* 65
All ye woods, and trees, and bowers. *J. Fletcher,* 141
And now at length the joyful time drew on. *Drayton,* 170
And when thou hast on foot the purblind hare. *Shakespeare,* 169
And wilt thou leave me thus. *Wyatt,* 5
A paradise on earth is found. *Drayton,* 179
Are they shadows that we see? *Daniel,* 80
Are women fair? aye wondrous fair to see to. *Anon.,* 74
Arm, arm, arm, arm, the scouts are all come in. *J. Fletcher,* 146
Art thou poor, yet hast thou golden slumbers. *Dekker,* 133
As I in hoary winter's night. *Southwell,* 81
Autumn hath all the summer's fruitful treasure. *Nashe,* 101

Beauty, clear and fair. *J. Fletcher,* 150
Beauty arise! show forth thy glorious shining. *Dekker,* 134
Because I breathe not love to every one. *Sidney,* 187
Begs Love, which whilom was a deity? *Barnes,* 194
Be your words made, good sir, of Indian ware. *Sidney,* 189
Blame not my lute, for he must sound. *Wyatt,* 4
Blow, blow, thou winter wind. *Shakespeare,* 169
Bright star of beauty, on whose eyelids sit. *Drayton,* 199
But ah! beleeve me there is more then so. *Spenser,* 259
But this is Learning; to have skill to throw. *Chapman,* 269
By our first strange and fatal interview. *Donne,* 125

Call for the robin-redbreast and the wren. *Webster,* 153
Care-charmer Sleep, son of the sable Night. *Daniel,* 198
Care charming sleep, thou easer of all woes. *J. Fletcher,* 144
Cast away care, he that loves sorrow. *Dekker,* 136
Charon, O, Charon. *J. Fletcher,* 145
Clear Ankor on whose silver sanded shore. *Drayton,* 200
Come all the world, submit yourselves to care. *Breton,* 18
Come away, come away, death. *Shakespeare,* 97
Come, come, dear Night, Love's mart of kisses. *Chapman,* 75
Come hither, Shepherd swain. *Earl of Oxford,* 20

INDEX OF FIRST LINES

INDEX OF FIRST LINES

INDEX OF FIRST LINES

INDEX OF FIRST LINES

INDEX OF FIRST LINES

INDEX OF FIRST LINES